TOWARD A CONTEMPORARY UNDERSTANDING OF PURE LAND BUDDHISM

SUNY series in
Buddhist Studies

Matthew Kapstein, editor

Toward a Contemporary Understanding of Pure Land Buddhism

Creating a Shin
Buddhist Theology in a
Religiously Plural World

EDITED BY

Dennis Hirota

STATE UNIVERSITY OF NEW YORK PRESS

Cover illustration: The Buddha in profound samadhi, from which he emerges to preach the dharma, as depicted in the gesture of his hands. This Heian-period wood statue of Rushana (Vairochana) Buddha is enshrined at Kaidan-in temple in Dazaifu, northern Kyushu, one of three ancient ordination platforms established in the eighth century. By permission of Kaidan-in temple. Photograph courtesy of the Dazaifu City Historical Society (Dazaifushi-shi Henshuiinkai).

Published by
State University of New York Press, Albany

For information, address the State University of New York Press
State University Plaza, Albany, NY 12246

Production by Kristin Milavec
Marketing by Patrick Durocher

Library of Congress Cataloging-in-Publication Data

Toward a contemporary understanding of Pure Land Buddhism : creating a
  Shin Buddhist theology in a religiously plural world / edited by
  Dennis Hirota.
      p.   cm. — (SUNY series in Buddhist studies)
    Includes bibliographical references and index.
      ISBN 0-7914-4529-1 (h.c.:   alk. paper) — ISBN 0-7914-4530-5 (pbk.:
  alk. paper)
      1. Shin (Sect)—Doctrines.   2. Pure Land Buddhism—Doctrines.
  I. Hirota, Dennis.   II. Series.
  BQ8718.6.T68   2000
  294.3'926—dc21   99-040513
                                                                CIP

10   9   8   7   6   5   4   3   2   1

Contents

A Note on the Format

The essays in this volume—by three Buddhists and two Christians—all have their source in two shared convictions. First, the Pure Land Buddhist tradition that survives in Japan today as one of the largest Buddhist movements in the world has a significant contribution to make to religious thought in the contemporary world. Second, despite a distinctive understanding of Mahayana Buddhist practice that brings religious realization within reach of all in everyday life, the Pure Land Buddhist message, in the form it is commonly promulgated, appears alien and muffled to the contemporary listener both East and West. Although in emphasis and detail there are considerable differences among the views of the authors, this book as a whole has been composed as an attempt to address the problem of the rift between the promise and the actuality of the Pure Land tradition.

According to the plan of the book, the three Buddhist authors first offer distinct approaches by which the Pure Land Buddhist tradition may be understood by practitioners reflecting forthrightly on their intellectual and social circumstances in the contemporary world (chapters 1 to 3). To provide some unity in their efforts, the three authors take as their starting point a series of questions presented to Shin Buddhist and religious scholars in Japan by Professor Gordon D. Kaufman in an address in 1989. These questions are given in the introduction to this volume.

Next, two Western philosophers of religion, including Kaufman, review these efforts (chapters 4 and 5). The intention is not to pursue Buddhist-Christian dialogue or explicitly comparative concerns. Rather, the religious thinkers are asked to comment on the Pure Land Buddhist proposals from the perspective of their experience in grappling in their own traditions with issues of the intelligibility of traditional religious symbols and concepts, religious response to the pressing issues of contemporary life, and religious pluralism. In this way, they allow the Buddhists to draw on resources developed in the West, in a cultural matrix that is exerting increasing influence on the entire globe. It may be said that, despite strong Western influence, Japanese Buddhists have in general failed to engage urgent problems in the world today in a systematic and persuasive fashion.

Taking into account both the responses from Western religious perspectives and discussions of their proposals among themselves, the three Buddhist authors seek to refine and develop their positions further in a second round of essays (chapters 6 to 8). These are intended to define their stances through considerations of each others proposals, and to build on the ongoing conversations among all five contributors by articulating further their general approaches to the Pure Land Buddhist path. Thus, *Toward a Contemporary Understanding of Pure Land Buddhism* comprises three main sections:

Part One: Proposals by three Buddhists (Dennis Hirota, John S. Yokota, and Musashi Tachikawa) for treating fundamental questions regarding the Pure Land teaching. (Hirota's essay has been placed first because it presents information about Pure Land Buddhism assumed in the other two essays.)

Part Two: Comment on the proposals by two Western philosophers of religion (Gordon D. Kaufman and John B. Cobb, Jr.).

Part Three: Reconsiderations of their own proposals by the three Buddhists. It should be noted that the three authors are responding to the other chapters in this section as well as to the earlier chapters, and that Part Three reflects discussions of the entire volume among all five participants.

An introduction provides historical perspective on the handling of central doctrinal issues within the Pure Land, and particularly Shin Buddhist, tradition in Japan, and in an afterword, an overview of the interrelationships among the three Buddhist proposals is given.

In September 1996 this entire group of essays formed the focus of discussion at a symposium planned by Dennis Hirota, sponsored by the Institute of Buddhist Studies, and held in Berkeley, California, on campuses affiliated with the Graduate Theological Union. During the symposium the authors of this volume were joined by a number of colleagues for three days of discussion. The authors of the Buddhist chapters wish to acknowledge the additional comments and criticisms of Professors Gordon D. Kaufman and John B. Cobb, Jr., and those of the other symposium participants, particularly Professors John B. Carman, John Ross Carter, Thomas P. Kasulis, Masatomi Nagatomi, Ann T. Rogers, and Taitetsu Unno.

DENNIS HIROTA

Introduction

Dennis Hirota

1

Toward a Contemporary Understanding of Pure Land Buddhism explores a field of inquiry that might be called the "theological" or "dharmological" construal of the Buddhist path: the articulation of a reflective self-understanding of a living Buddhist tradition that is intelligible within, and illuminating of, our contemporary life. In this volume, three Buddhists present proposals for creatively reinterpreting a Buddhist tradition in order to elucidate its enduring transformative power and to overcome critical inadequacies in the established formulations—failures to interpret traditional narratives and concepts in a manner now cogent and healing, or to treat significant issues arising from our present understanding of the world and human existence within it. These proposals, developed with recognition of the plurality of religious traditions and worldviews in interaction today, also inherently seek to provide frameworks for comparative considerations.

This book focuses on the Pure Land tradition, which radically developed the Mahayana Buddhist ideal of the bodhisattva, the being of wisdom-compassion who aspires to ferry all living things floundering in painful existence to the other shore of awakening before departing from the ocean of birth-and-death him or herself. According to the *Larger Sutra of Immeasurable Life*, the bodhisattva Dharmakara (Dharmākara) vowed to bring all beings to liberation by enabling them to be born in a realm pervaded by the virtues of his own enlightenment.[1] To fulfill those Vows, he performed practices for countless aeons, finally attaining enlightenment as Amida Buddha and establishing a Buddha realm known as the Pure Land or the Land of Bliss. Although Pure Land Buddhism grew out of contemplative practices focusing on the features of the Buddha and the Buddha land, among the primal or originary Vows of Amida is one to bring to birth in the Pure Land all beings who say Amida Buddha's Name, "Namu-amida-butsu," with sincere trust. This Vow gradually came to be viewed as the core of the Pure Land path, and Buddhist schools advocating single practice of nembutsu, or verbal utterance of the Name of Amida Buddha, reached full and independent development in Japan.

This volume treats in particular the Shin Buddhist tradition established by the medieval Japanese religious leader Shinran (1173–1263). Shin Buddhism (Jōdo Shinshū) is the preeminent model of a Buddhist path that, while grounding itself in basic Mahayana conceptions of wisdom, does not uphold a monastic ideal, but instead teaches a fully reasoned and articulated way to awakening that is accomplished while carrying on life in society. It has elaborated its position in a long scholastic tradition and evolved into a formidable ecclesiastical organization. Since the fifteenth century Shin has been one of the most influential Buddhist schools in Japan. At present its two major branches, the Nishi (West) and Higashi (East) Honganji temple systems, together constitute the largest Buddhist congregation in Japan and, in size and wealth, one of the foremost Buddhist movements in the world.

Despite its significant doctrinal and institutional evolution, Shin Buddhism has attracted disproportionately little interest in the West, but the reasons for this neglect may be precisely those that might animate our present "theological" concern. From a Western perspective, a number of elements of the Shin path—the focus on a single, universal Buddha, the centrality of a conception of "faith," the deep self-reflection and self-awareness of evil—have often seemed closer to strains of Western religious thought than to monastic Buddhism. Thus, the Shin Buddhist tradition has commonly been perceived in the West as a kind of debased religious practice, branching off from Mahayana Buddhist teachings of rigorous psychological cultivation but evolving an incongruously monotheistic or salvation-oriented outlook. Its institutional strength has been viewed as the result of a "popularization" as a "lay Buddhism" that has severed it from its Buddhist roots. By the same token, its doctrinal elaboration has seemed to researchers an "elitist" enterprise, far removed from the actuality of the simple piety of the ordinary lay faithful. Perhaps it is chiefly for such reasons that treatments of Shin thought by Western scholars have been scarce, and have tended to regard it, whether negatively or positively, as a marginal form of Buddhism.

Viewed without the preconceptions of Buddhism as essentially monastic and meditative, however, Shin may be seen as a remarkable achievement in the history of Buddhist tradition: the transformative path of Mahayana Buddhism transposed, on the basis of fundamental Mahayana insights, from a monastic setting into the context of ordinary life in society. Here, similarities in conceptual structure offer an opportunity for the close comparison of Mahayana Buddhist tradition with other world religions, and for highlighting the potential resources for contemporary religious thought offered by Japanese Pure Land Buddhism.

Regarding the specific aims of this book, however, it may be asked why there should be need to develop a new branch of Buddhist study under the non traditional term *Buddhist theology or dharmology*. Further, why should Shin Buddhism be in need of such development—particularly in the partially comparative form taken in this book—when it already possesses a highly sophisticated tradition of scholastic study that has been maintained for nearly eight centuries, and that is itself based on lineages of texts and commentaries extending back to India at the beginning of the common era. The authors of this volume amplify their own individual views on these questions. Here, I will offer some general observations by way of introduction.

The Need for a Buddhist "Theology"

The call for theological approaches in the study of Buddhism may be viewed both as an issue of Buddhist studies as an academic discipline and as a problem within particular traditions such as Shin. The general problem has been tersely stated over twenty years ago in an address to Japanese scholars by Yoshifumi Ueda, at the time one of the world's leading Buddhologists:

> Buddhist tradition is taken as an object of study in a number of academic fields, including history, anthropology, psychology, philosophy,

art, sociology, religion, and literature, but surely these cannot all be viewed as disciplines directed to probing its essential nature. If there is indeed a discipline that may be called Buddhist studies in this sense—not merely because it takes Buddhist tradition as an object— then there must be a methodology that distinguishes it from other fields treating Buddhism.[2]

Ueda was particularly concerned that rationalist philological research would overstep its methodological limitations and impose inappropriate standards of logic in establishing and interpreting texts. He called, therefore, for approaches that would treat the often paradoxical statements regarding practice and realization in Mahayana texts.

Notable differences exist in the conditions and histories of Buddhist studies in Japan and the West, and significant developments have been achieved since the time of Ueda's address. His apprehension about the dominance of philological study now seems less urgent, and his own textually based philosophical research has also come to appear partial. In addition, the presupposition of a Buddhist "essence" invites questions. Nevertheless, the central issue Ueda raises remains pertinent. If, in addition to existing disciplines that also treat Buddhist tradition, it is useful and appropriate to have a branch of learning termed "Buddhist studies," what are the questions it must ask and the methods by which it illuminates them? One approach that, drawing on textual and historical research in Buddhist studies, may provide means for formulating and treating issues of the kind indicated by Ueda is the "theological." It is the attempt to articulate the intellectual self-understanding of persons as Buddhist, and while standing within Buddhist tradition, seeks the development of the tradition through efforts to respond to contemporary concerns and to critically utilize contemporary thought.

Further, viewing various forms of sectarian Buddhism in Japan at present, it may be said that despite long and continuous scholastic traditions of scriptural and doctrinal study, formulations of religious life in the contemporary context have not been adequately developed. There are diverse reasons—historical, doctrinal, and institutional—for the general failure of the traditional temples to respond effectively to issues of modern life, but for the most part expressions of the teachings remain couched in terms and phrases codified in the Tokugawa period. Although needs and life patterns have changed, it is the exception rather than the rule to find religious engagement conceived of as

personal and individual rather than familial and communal, as elucidating concerns of the present rather than promises of the future, and
as providing orientation in practical life rather than in mortuary rituals for the repose of ancestors. While social custom may sustain ritual
or communal forms of participation in temple functions, there is a
widely felt and little answered demand for a fuller, intellectual understanding of one's daily existence as possessing a religious dimension.

Another pressing issue is the role of Buddhism in society and the
moral conduct of persons as Buddhists. Since almost all forms of
Buddhist tradition have been centered in monastic life, with the prac-
ticing monk as the religious ideal, rules governing the communal life
of monks and nuns have been elaborated as a cardinal component of
the teaching, but life in society as itself an arena of Buddhist cultivation has in general not been developed. Partly for this reason, Buddhism has been highly accommodating of native traditions of cultures
into which it was introduced, such as Confucianism and Shinto, which
provided ritual cohesiveness in social life and fulfilled popular needs
in ways deemed supportive of the Buddhist path.

To provide some historical context for the discussions in this volume, and to indicate perceptions of significant concerns within the
tradition, I will touch on the handling of these two basic issues—the
character of religious existence and the relation of religion to social
life—in premodern and modern Shin scholastics. As preliminary background, I will first mention two basic questions that have traditionally
arisen for practicers within the Shin Buddhist path.

Basic Questions of the Shin Buddhist Path

There are two broad, fundamental questions that emerge in Buddhist
practice and that Buddhists have traditionally brought to the teachings in the process of their engagement: What is the nature of the goal
in the Buddhist path, whether it be termed "enlightenment," "nirvana," "Buddha," or "true reality"? How is the goal to be attained?
Buddhist commentators have in general taken these questions as the
motive force of their writings. Underlying them, of course, is the analysis of the ordinary, unenlightened human condition as painful, impermanent, afflicted by delusional self-attachment, and in need of
transformation.

In the Pure Land path prior to Shinran, the answers were, in general, that the eventual and inexpressibly sublime goal was enlightenment and Buddhahood, but that it was attained through an intermediary goal of birth into the Pure Land of Amida Buddha, an ideal environment immeasurably more conducive to successful practice as a bodhisattva than our corrupt world of blind passions. Descriptions of the bliss and beauty of the Pure Land and its residents were found in various sutras. The means for attaining birth in the Pure Land after death in this world were variously understood, but they centered on reciting Amida's Name, Namu-amida-butsu, also known as the nembutsu, with trust that one would thereby be in accord with Amida Buddha's Vow and gain birth into the Pure Land. With Shinran's teacher Honen (Hōnen, 1133–1212), also, these answers in general hold.

When the questions regarding the nature of and the means to attainment are transposed into the Shin Buddhist tradition, however, matters grow complex. This is because of fundamental changes in thinking brought about by Shinran. Briefly stated, these may be understood as a telescoping of the linear parameters of the path, so that the intermediary terms lose their traditional status and significance. Regarding attainment, Shinran asserts that birth in the Pure Land itself signifies immediate realization of Buddhahood. Hence, the Pure Land, which had represented a medial stage leading to eventual Buddhahood and provided concrete imagery of an afterlife of bliss in the popular imagination, dissolved into the inconceivability of wisdom or enlightenment.

Moreover, regarding means, it had been taught that the practice of reciting the nembutsu was devised by Amida Buddha in order to bring to emancipation even those beings incapable of the normal Buddhist practices of precepts, good works, and meditation. It had been common, therefore, for Pure Land Buddhists to devote themselves to recitation, uttering the Name as often as possible. Shinran, however, delved into the question of why saying the nembutsu should hold the power to bring about birth in the Pure Land, especially for beings who did not bring to it any special concentration of mind and who fulfilled no other practice. His answer was that although the Name might seem merely one kind of practice among the others taught in various Buddhist texts, it was effective because it was not essentially an act of an unenlightened and delusional human being seeking

Buddhahood, but rather the act of Amida Buddha. The nembutsu spoken by a person is practice given by the Buddha, and therefore holds the virtues of the Buddha's enlightenment. For this reason, a person's own endeavor to utter the nembutsu repeatedly as a way of accumulating merit is meaningless.

The vehicle by which practice is given is *shinjin* or true entrusting. Shinran states that shinjin is itself Amida's wisdom-compassion, so that the Pure Land practicer acquires or realizes the Buddha-mind in the form of shinjin or the entrusting of oneself to Amida's Vow. Saying the nembutsu is a concretization of this mind, and thus embodies the Buddha's virtues. While persons who realize shinjin remain beings of ignorance and delusional attachments, because they have attained the Buddha's mind—their existence been transformed—they will realize Buddhahood when their present lives end. At that time, shinjin is said to unfold into the full realization of wisdom-compassion, so that they immediately return to this world with the capacity to guide beings in painful existence to emancipation. In Shinran's path, persons say the nembutsu out of the realization of shinjin, and since this is Amida Buddha's practice and mind given to them, they attain perfect enlightenment without any self-generated effort or calculation when the karmic bonds working their consequences in this life are severed upon death.

While Shinran's teaching is clear, it raises difficult questions for practicers, questions for which no concrete answers are given in his writings. As we have seen, he collapses the conception of the path as framed by the goal of birth into the Pure Land and by the means as recitation of the nembutsu. While in other forms of Buddhism clear prescriptions and guidance are given regarding the manner and content of what must be done to advance along the path, in Shinran's teaching, practice is accomplished and given by the Buddha, and the practicer is free of instrumental thinking. The fundamental questions of the path come to focus on the concept of shinjin. The practical questions become: If the immediate goal is attainment of shinjin, what is it to realize shinjin? How does it manifest itself in ordinary life, and how is it to be attained?

These questions, however, receive no answer in Shinran's writings, for Amida's Vow works precisely where one is free of contrivance and calculation. Nevertheless, problems in the understanding of the nature of religious life have been recurrent in the history of Shin tradition, beginning with serious antinomian trends that erupted during Shinran's own lifetime.[3] Below, I will sketch ways in which the concrete issues of shinjin have arisen and been dealt with in traditional Shin thought.

Honganji Orthodoxy and the Character of Realization

During the premodern period, the Tokugawa shogunate developed a variety of policies to turn Buddhist temples into active forces for stability and conservatism in the society. The populace was assigned membership by family in local temples, and the temples came to serve the authorities by keeping records of changes in the membership, including registers of births and deaths, and issuing certificates of affiliation that were necessary for travel, changes of residence, and marriage. The association of local temples in a hierarchical national temple system of branch and headquarter temples was also fixed, and these temple systems were designated as specific denominations.

Doctrinally, the temple systems were charged with codifying their teachings and ensuring the orthodoxy of the teaching as disseminated in the branch temples. Within the temple systems, learned scholar-monks devoted great creative energies to scholastic debate, scriptural study, and expanding the commentarial tradition. Within the sectarian universities today, the influence of this system remains. Study of Buddhism in Japan for most of this century has been divided into "academic" and "sectarian" fields, the former influenced by Western philological and historical scholarship and methods and focusing on Indian and Tibetan studies, the latter rooted in the tradition of Tokugawa-period scholarship circumscribed by the issues and solutions set forth in voluminous commentaries and polemical writings of the period. The dominant treatment of concrete issues in religious life developed amid the conservative pressures generated by the premodern systematization of doctrine.

Perhaps the decisive event in setting the tone and orientation of Shin scholastics over the past two centuries, particularly within the Nishi Honganji, was the incident known as the "turmoil over three kinds of religious acts" *(sangō wakuran)*. This term refers to a period of "confusion and controversy" surrounding the notion that entrusting oneself to Amida Buddha necessarily involves the expression of aspiration for the Pure Land in all of a person's "three modes of action"—physical, verbal, and mental.

In the atmosphere of concern on the part of state and temple authorities for social order and orthodoxy in doctrine and practices during the Tokugawa period, religious teachings tended to crystallize around traditional formulations of belief and formal aspects of proper ritual conduct. Shin parishioners paid close attention to meeting the precise conditions or requirements of entrusting oneself to Amida Buddha's Vows and thereby gaining birth in the Pure Land. The underlying issue was the nature of religious life, focusing on the realization of shinjin, and as mentioned before, this has been a difficult and recurring theme in Shin tradition. Two fundamentally opposing attitudes developed in the seventeenth and eighteenth centuries regarding the nature of shinjin as it is attained by Shin Buddhists.

One stream of thought was based on Shinran's sweeping rejection of all forms of self-power, or religious endeavor ultimately rooted in self-attachment. This was interpreted to mean that faith arose in a posture of complete passivity on the part of the practicer. Thus, the relationship between the person and the teaching came to be understood in terms of simple assent to beliefs about Amida Buddha and the Vows. In particular, it was taught that embracing a fervent aspiration for the Pure Land was not necessary, and even misguided; hence, this position came to be described as teaching "the settled mind [of shinjin] with no taking of refuge" (mu-kimyō no anjin). According to this view, the cause of beings' birth in the Pure Land was fulfilled by Amida Buddha aeons ago, so it makes little sense for persons to entreat the Buddha for salvation. Since one's birth in the Pure Land has already been determined, actively expressing aspiration is nothing other than a manifestation of doubting the Buddha and of self-power, as though one in fact brought about birth oneself through one's convictions or actions. It is sufficient simply to realize without doubt that Amida's Primal Vow has already saved us. This highly conceptualized notion of shinjin as belief in doctrinal assertions probably reflected the influence of other branches of Pure Land tradition.[4]

According to the opposing view of the period, the realization of shinjin was a decisive and transformative experience, and not mere acquiescence; hence, a fervent religious aspiration was the mark of authentic entrusting to Amida's Vow. This position, known as "the settled mind [manifested in] taking refuge through the three modes of action" (sangō kimyō no anjin), asserted that clearly and consciously relying on Amida, aspiring for birth in the Pure Land, and asking the Buddha for salvation were major components of shinjin. It was through the working of Amida and Shakyamuni (Śākyamuni) that aspiration arose in one's heart, but this thought of aspiration naturally manifested itself physically, as one faced the Buddha in worship, and also verbally, in the utterance of the nembutsu. Thus, this ardent aspiration for birth was enacted in all three modes of action: mental, bodily, and verbal.

In this view, aspiration for birth took on a pivotal significance not seen in Shinran's concept of shinjin, which, as the mind of Amida Buddha given to beings, was largely expounded in symbolic and abstract terms divorced from the practical life of the practicer. In other words, this position evolved out of an intensely felt need for a definition of concrete action on the part of the practicer, without which utterance of the nembutsu seemed little more than a mechanical mouthing unrelated to a person's actual experience. This understanding of active aspiration was gradually developed from the mid-seventeenth century in the official academy of scholars (Gakurin) in the Honganji and came to be propagated by the head (nōke shoku) of the Gakurin, who held responsibility in doctrinal and educational matters and served as advisor to the abbot (shūshu) of the Nishi Honganji.

The "turmoil over religious acts" grew out of a confrontation between these two positions. During the mid-eighteenth century, the notion of shinjin as simple acceptance with no requirements of affirmatively "taking refuge" spread among Shin practicers in Echizen province (present Fukui prefecture). The Honganji judged this teaching to be heterodox and ordered the head of the Gakurin academy, Kozon (Kōzon, 1720–1796), to correct the mistaken views. In 1762, Kozon journeyed to Echizen, where he was successful in clarifying the matter for leaders of the heterodoxy. He then gave a series of sermons in the province in which he strongly asserted the importance of "taking refuge" in Amida's Vows through acts of one's whole existence: mental (aspiration), bodily (worship), and verbal (nembutsu).

These sermons were recorded and published, and gradually became a target of criticism by scholar-priests outside of the official academy and active in various parts of the country. These critics did not argue from the position that shinjin was simple assent that one's birth was already settled, but nevertheless took issue with the opposing position that Kozon's had developed. They argued that in overemphasizing concrete acts of religious ferver, Kozon had diverged from Shinran's teaching of Other Power, or the working of Amida's compassionate Vow. The controversy reached its peak during a period of nearly ten years, beginning with the accession of Kozon's successor Chido (Chidō, 1736–1805), who became head of the Gakurin in 1797. Amid published scholastic criticisms of the teaching of "aspiration in the three modes of action," Chido strongly asserted this position from his office, including on formal occasions in which he spoke in place of the Honganji abbot. The debate flared, and although some priests called for academic discussion and the development of a compromise stance, factions solidified. Amid pressure to determine clearly the correct understanding, the Honganji administration, traditionally run by the lay Shimotsuna family, supported Chido's position as the authentic teaching and in 1801 began actively suppressing criticism. Accusations of obstructing the temple were brought against more than twenty critics who had journeyed to Kyoto from various areas in the country, and some of them were arrested and taken into custody or jailed. The Honganji also had local authorities forbid the sale of publications critical of Chido.

As a result of these repressive actions, incidents of public disorder involving several thousand people broke out in Mino province, and the local authorities were forced to step in. In response to stern warnings from the government to quell the turmoil, the Honganji administration shifted its standpoint to that of Chido's critics, only to find itself invaded by several hundred spear-bearing supporters of the Gakurin. Finally, the shogunate intervened, and during a four-month period in 1803, an investigation was conducted in Kyoto. It was determined that Chido and his followers had incited lay people to protest against the Honganji, and more than forty people were taken into custody. In 1804, representatives of both sides in the controversy were summoned to Edo; Chido was transported caged and under guard as a criminal. In a process lasting more than a year, detailed doctrinal arguments were heard from various representatives, and finally opposing written expositions were presented to the Honganji with a demand for adjudication. In 1805, the teaching of "aspiration in the three modes of action" was declared heterodox and punishments were meted out to participants on both sides of the controversy. Chido issued a formal statement of recantation, and died of sickness while in custody, before final sentencing of banishment could be carried out. The Honganji temple itself was put under quarantine for one hundred days during which its gates remained closed. When the quarantine was lifted, the abbot prohibited the publication of any doctrinal writings without his approval. Thereafter, the academic bureau within the temple was reformed, so that a group of scholars rather than a single person possessed final responsibility.

The significance of the "turmoil over religious acts" for our concerns here is twofold. First, while it reveals the high level of Shin scholarship and serious religious debate conducted in various parts of the country, not solely at the Kyoto headquarters, it also shows the overriding concern with social stability and orthodoxy exercised by both the state and temple authorities during the Tokugawa period and the willingness of the temple to employ its bureaucratic apparatus to determine and suppress dissent. Moreover, particularly because the temple's own academic arm was found to be in error, a cautious, backward-looking scholasticism became embedded in the succeeding Shin scholarship. The issues surrounding the understanding of shinjin that took shape during the controversy were defined and the authoritative resolutions codified on the basis of evidence chiefly from the writings of Shinran and Rennyo (1415–1499), the eighth-generation Honganji abbot. These became the one hundred "topics regarding the settled mind" (anjin rondai) that were long the mainstay of Shin theological studies and that continue to be used today as the standard of Shin scholarship within the Nishi Honganji.

More importantly, we see that the standard of orthodoxy masked the genuine underlying issue of the interpretation of religious life. The debate over the status of aspiration revolved around the problem of understanding, amid Shinran's assertion of shinjin given by Other Power, what it is concretely to realize shinjin. It may be said that both positions, though they take opposing tacks, share a common root: the need felt by Shin practicers to have a specific image of how they should conduct their lives, and how the religious dimension of their existence might be apprehended. The question of whether they should cultivate active aspiration or whether they should simply accept the teaching is, on a more abstract level, the question of whether there is something a person should do, or whether any prescription of action would invariably involve self-power.

As a result of the social and political turmoil growing out of the doctrinal debate, subsequent Shin study, particularly with regard to questions surrounding attempts to explore concretely the subjectivity or awareness of the Shin practicer, came to be characterized by a reluctance to move beyond earlier formulations and expressions supported by traditional scriptures.

The Shin Buddhist in Society

A second major issue in the attempt to treat the life of the Shin Buddhist in concrete terms is the relationship between religion and society; or, how a person, as a Shin Buddhist, should consider conduct of daily life with its moral dilemmas and ethical problems. Once again, the fundamental difficulty for Shin Buddhists has its roots in Shinran's thought, and in particular his penetrating analysis of the residue of self-power in ostensibly religious life. The focal point of Shinran's concern in his teaching is the obdurate adherence to one's own goodness, even while embracing the Pure Land path of Other Power. This attachment leads to efforts to accomplish good deeds for the sake of achieving salvation, instead of trusting in the working of Amida Buddha.

Moreover, Honen and Shinran further taught that no evil deed excludes one from Amida's compassion. This teaching led to some confusion in the community, for there were those who utilized it abusively, asserting even that to seek to curb one's nature as a "foolish being possessed of blind passions" was to exhibit distrust of Amida's Vow. Shinran denounces such understanding as self-serving, pointing out that self-awareness of wrongdoing leads not to indulgence or complacency, but to a natural eschewing of evil and of the three poisons of greed, anger, and egocentric attachments. Nevertheless, the difficulty is clear. While the value of general moral principles is assumed, Shinran's teaching asserts no specific moral or ethical precepts as means to salvation, and declares instead that no good act one can perform will move one closer to birth in the Pure Land, no evil act will obstruct one's attainment. How, then, should one conduct one's life? What standards of moral life have religious force?

The Shin temple institution has traditionally availed itself of a conceptual cleavage between the religious and secular spheres of life. By relinquishing questions of conduct in society to regulation by customary social norms and the political authorities, this device allowed for a treatment of the relationship of the temple and the congregation to society and the state that avoided conflict, whether from an affirmation of the early antinomian misunderstanding or from an affirmation of religious values that might clash with those of the state.

Two parallel pairs of terms have been used in Shin tradition, particularly from the fifteenth century through World War II, to express the distinction, and also suggest the ideal of mutual support, between the religious and secular spheres. Both sets of terms occur widely in Buddhist texts, but came to hold special meaning in Japan. The central terms are the "two truths"—the "supramundane truth" (*shintai*, literally, "genuine" or "supreme truth") and the "mundane" or "conventional truth" (*zokutai*, literally, "secular truth"). In Buddhist thought stemming from Nagarjuna (Nāgārjuna, c. 150–250), these terms normally apply to ineffable reality or wisdom, on the one hand, and the expression of this reality in the world, particularly by verbal means, for the transmission of religious awakening. In Shin tradition, however, based on usage adopted in Japan during the Heian period, the "two truths" came to signify Buddhist institutions, on the one hand, and the secular authorities, on the other. The former was also termed the "Buddhist law" or dharma (*buppō*) and the latter, the "Sovereign's law" (*ōbō*).

While the terms *Buddhist law* and *Sovereign's law* occur in Chinese Buddhist texts, their use as a complementary and inseparable pair of concepts evolved in Japan from about the eleventh century. It was emphasized that the "supramundane truth" and the "mundane truth," or the "Buddhist law" and the "sovereign's law," were like two wheels of a cart, or two horns of an ox. Behind this usage lay the desire of the Buddhist temples to solidify their status in the social system ideologically. Under the Ritsuryo (*ritsuryō*) legal system in Japan, which developed during the seventh century, temples were constructed and monks and nuns trained and supported in order that rites for the protection of the state be performed. The economic foundation for the temples was provided by the contribution of arable estates. It became increasingly necessary, however, for the temples to protect their holdings from incursion by secular powers. Thus, to justify their administration of estates and assert temple ownership and control, Buddhists propounded the ideal of the mutual support and protection of the two authorities, Buddhist and secular.

Lamp for the Last Dharma-Age, a work traditionally attributed to Saicho (Saichō, 767–822), the founder of the Tendai school in Japan, and quoted at length by Shinran in his major work, *The True Teaching, Practice, and Realization of the Pure Land Way*, is prefaced with the statement: "The benevolent king and the dharma-king, in mutual correspondence, give guidance to beings. The supramundane truth and the mundane truth, depending on each other, cause the teaching to spread."[5] We see here the idea that the Buddhist teachings and the secular rule work together for the good of the people. The sovereign and his administrators are responsible for the well-being of his subjects and, by ensuring the peace and stability of benevolent rule, make possible the spread of the dharma. The Buddhist temples function to elicit divine protection for the state and cultivate the people in the true teaching.

We must note, however, that Shinran does not himself directly advocate this understanding of the "two truths" and that he employs the extended quotation to assert not the mutual support of temple and state, but rather the integrity and autonomy of the religious sphere. This is in fact the central point of *Lamp for the Last Dharma-Age* as a whole. In 798, many monks and nuns who broke precepts were banished under enforcement of Ritsuryo codes governing temple life and personnel. *Lamp for the Last Dharma-Age* argues that, while the precepts were meant to be followed during the period of Shakyamuni's lifetime and some centuries thereafter, in the present, with the devolution of conditions in the world and growing temporal distance from the historical Buddha, the precepts could no longer be considered applicable. Thus, the punishment of monks and nuns by the state for breaking precepts was a transgression against the authority of the Buddha's teaching.

Shinran accepts this argument, but probably foremost in his mind was the persecution of the nembutsu by the imperial authorities, at the behest of established temples, leading in 1207 to the exile of Honen and a number of his followers, including Shinran himself. The cause of the persecution was the menace the older schools perceived in the nembutsu movement that was growing in the capital, but the formal charges included the failure of ordained monks to uphold their precepts. In *Teaching, Practice, and Realization*, Shinran strongly condemns the injustice of the persecution, and throughout his life we see an insistence that Buddhists are not to be mere instruments of political authority, but possess an independent foundation. Hence, even though they keep no precepts, monks "in name only" manifest dharma in the world just as did Shakyamuni's direct disciples.

Shinran did revere Prince Shotoku (Shōtoku, 573–621), who vigorously adopted Buddhism into Japan, as an incarnation of Kannon

Bodhisattva. Hence, he did not deny that compassionate bodhisattvas might manifest themselves in history as ideal rulers to spread dharma. He also states that people who have realized shinjin should say the nembutsu with the wish for peace in the world and the spread of Buddhism in their hearts.[6] Nevertheless, at a time when Buddhist monks, including Zen monks from China and even the wandering holy man Ippen, journeyed to Kamakura in hope of support from the shogun, Shinran admonished his followers not to seek the involvement even of local secular authorities in the spread of the nembutsu. His eyes were on dharma, and because of the oppression he experienced against Honen's movement and his own, he shunned political involvements.

For Shin Buddhists today seeking a fuller interpretation of the social implications of religious life, the problem is twofold. On the one hand, as outlined above, Shinran's own writings, by challenging the religious significance of our ordinary moral judgments, provide little concrete guidance for reflection on life in a pluralistic society and world, either on a personal or an institutional level. On the other hand, the treatment of these issues in Shin scholastic tradition, employing the notion of "two truths," evolved in a context of strong authoritarian and bureaucratic rule, and though this framework of the mutual support of the two spheres of life was formally abandoned after World War II, a new perspective has yet to be developed. Let us turn briefly to this latter problem.

The last major attempt by the Nishi Honganji temple to define its own role and that of its members in society occurred in the late nineteenth century, during the transition from the feudalistic state of the Tokugawa shogunate to the emperor system under Emperor Meiji. During this period, Buddhist institutions came under severe public attack as the new regime sought to drastically reduce the power and prestige of Buddhist temples, and to supplant Buddhism as a state religion with forms of Shinto that focused on the divinity of the emperor.

The Nishi and Higashi Honganji temples spearheaded efforts to mitigate the initial harsh policies enacted by the new authorities. It was in this climate that the conceptual scheme of the two truths came to be espoused as the framework for defining the relationship between Shin Buddhism and society. In the fourth year of Meiji, 1871, a formal pastoral letter by Konyo (Kōnyo, 1789–1871), the twentieth abbot of the Nishi Honganji, was posthumously issued.[7] In it, the cardinal tenets of the concept of the two truths are promulgated. That is, the Buddhist law and the sovereign's law function in conjunction, so that the spread of the dharma is dependent on the emperor's benevolent rule. Further, loyal Shin Buddhists should conduct their lives according to the two truths, obedient to the emperor in this life and mindful of their birth in the Pure Land in the next.

In 1886, in accordance with new edicts regarding temple bodies, the Nishi Honganji adopted rules and regulations that became the basis for the administration of the temple system until after World War II. Article 2 of these regulations defines the purport of the Shin teaching as the two truths: the supramundane truth as hearing and entrusting oneself to Amida Buddha's Name, which embodies great compassion, and the mundane truth as ethical conduct in accordance with human norms and reverence for imperial rule. The Buddha's dharma and the sovereign rule of the state are mutually supportive, and one should respond with gratitude for the former and act to protect the latter. The implications of this attitude in a nationalist military state were quickly drawn as the country went to war from the final decade of the nineteenth century. Repaying one's indebtedness to the emperor and the country would take the form of self sacrifice, and one would face death on the battlefield with equanimity, in the knowledge of one's certain birth in the Pure Land. In 1940, on the eve of World War II, the Higashi Honganji issued a formal pastoral letter that addressed the continuing "sacred war" in Asia to which soldiers were embarking and reminded Shin Buddhists of the mutual dependence of the two truths. In this context, the Buddhist principle of "noself" was interpreted as the annihilation of oneself for the sake of the country. Inwardly, one embraced shinjin that assured one of salvation, and outwardly, one gratefully acknowledged the benefit one had received from society, serving the emperor and the nation without attachment to body or life.[8]

Even this usage of the concept of the two truths came under the critical scrutiny of the military censors, however, and the following year, Shin Buddhists were admonished not to refer to the sacred imperial constitution as the "mundane" truth.[9] Finally, immediately following World War II, a new constitution and regulations were drafted by the Nishi Honganji. These remain in use today, and in them the two truths that had previously functioned as the overall framework of the teaching receive no mention.

Since the Meiji period, many Japanese social thinkers and intellectuals, including a number of Marxists, have found in Shinran's thought and life the native resources for building an egalitarian society. As we have seen, however, Shinran's teaching harbors at its roots the persistent issue of the relationship between moral life in society and religious engagement with the Shin path. On the one hand, no religious significance is recognized in moral conduct per se, and the observance of precepts or performance of good acts *as a form of religious practice* is rejected as tainted with self-attachment. On the other hand, Shinran emphasizes that no evil act in itself need obstruct the realization of shinjin and attainment of birth in the Pure Land. It is difficult, therefore, to delineate concretely the nature of life in society of the Shin Buddhist or the person who has realized shinjin.

Needless to say, the long usage of the two truths as a means of accommodation by which shinjin is regarded as belonging to the inner life, while in social and political life one accords with the prevailing ethic, has been detrimental to the tradition. Nevertheless, merely discrediting the wartime usage of the two truths has only driven deeper the wedge between religious and social life. The Western notion of the separation of church and state was utilized by the government during the Meiji period to reduce the power of Buddhist temples, even while promoting state Shinto as transcending the category of religion. In Japan at present, the widespread conviction that church and state must be separate derives its strength in large part from memories both of the use of Shinto in wartime indoctrination and of the complicity of Buddhist institutions in the war effort of the imperial state. Hence, religion tends to be relegated strictly to private life, and religious enthusiasm that seeks to exert public influence is viewed askance.

There have been efforts to interpret the concept of the two truths on a personal level. It has been asserted that endeavor in ethical life is a preliminary stage in religious engagement, that the two are correlative, and that the realization of shinjin, with its dimension of deep self-reflection, naturally manifests moral characteristics. It is clear, however, that in a world of shifting values, complex moral questions, and global perspectives, the simple dichotomy of religion and society is no longer tenable. As yet, however, no new conceptual framework for considering the concrete social or ethical implications of engagement with the Shin Buddhist path has gained currency. This remains a crucial topic for reflection.

Temple System as Guild

Above, I have sketched traditional treatments of two broad areas of concern regarding life as a Shin Buddhist and have indicated sources of difficulty in considering them within the traditional scholastic frameworks. A third source of difficulty regarding such reflection is found in the indirect influence of the Shin institutional structure. There are two interrelated and exceedingly distinctive facets of the Shin Buddhist temple system that contribute to its institutional cohesion and also to an inherent conservatism in doctrine and practice. Remarkably, despite their distinctiveness, Western researchers have little noted the significance of these instutional characteristics, and they are little studied in Japan. One is the practice of hereditary succession to the office of head abbot. The present abbots of both the Nishi Honganji and Higashi Honganji temple systems stand in unbroken lineages of blood descent, spanning more than twenty generations, from the founder Shinran. This hereditary succession reflects social practices deeply ingrained in Japanese culture, and analogies may be seen, in both the mechanism of succession and the sentiments of allegiance felt among the membership, in the emperor system and, to a lesser extent, the *iemoto* or head master system in schools of traditional arts.

It is not that the abbots are necessarily personally conservative in outlook. Today, their roles are largely ceremonial, although they possess significant charisma through their offices. The *office* of abbot, however, functions to undergird and legitimize the hierarchical and hereditary dimensions of the temple structure. This is the second and more consequential conservative force inherent in the temple system. The Nishi and Higashi Honganji temple organizations each consist of approximately ten thousand local temples that serve members in their neighborhoods. The office of resident minister in these temples is, like the office of Honganji abbot, commonly passed on by hereditary succession from father to son. Since ministers marry and raise their families in the temples, the temples become ancestral homes, frequently occupied by three generations of a family that has been associated with the temple for hundreds of years and many generations.

The hereditary succession to temple priesthood is not only startling to non-Japanese Buddhists, but highly unusual from the perspective of practices among the world religions. It is not simply a matter of sons of ministers often themselves following in their fathers' footsteps, for it involves in essence family ownership of temples and proprietary control of local religious life. Thus, it is not unheard of for bitter family disputes to arise over matters of succession, for many temples provide not only residences, social status in the local community, lucrative incomes, and lifetime security, but may also be maintained while holding other regular employment, including academic positions.

The adoption of the general social practice of hereditary succession into the Shin temple institution was made possible by Shinran's assumption, revolutionary at the time, of married life. By abandoning his priestly precepts, including those of celibacy, and formally marrying, he drew the natural conclusion of Honen's nembutsu teaching that persons were saved solely through the practice of the nembutsu and not any other practice, including observance of monk's precepts. This was a step that Honen himself did not take, and a radical departure from the monastic ideal officially upheld throughout the entire preceding history of Buddhism. Although at present it is common for monks of almost all schools of Buddhism in Japan to marry, apart from the Shin tradition, this practice of public recognition of the marriage of priests goes back only to the Meiji period.

It must be noted, however, that hereditary succession of the leadership of the Shin movement was not instituted by Shinran himself, but developed by his descendents after his death. In fact, the Honganji temple was not established by Shinran, but grew out of a mausoleum built for him by his daughter. Shinran spent most of his years of active propagation in the Kanto area in eastern Japan, but left the followings that had gathered in the different areas in the hands of close disciples and returned to Kyoto in his early sixties. He devoted the remaining three decades of his long life to his writings, and the domination of his movement by his blood descendents and the Honganji temple developed slowly over several generations.

At present, in addition to hereditary succession, the temple system is sustained by practices of intermarriage among temple families within the system. Thus, not only are relationships with parishioners maintained over generations, sustained by the need for funeral services, memorial services for past generations of ancestors, and care of the ancestral graves that are sometimes located in temple graveyards, but relationships within the temple system are also close-knit, supported by intermarriage and other associations within the temple administrative, educational, and propagational infrastructures. Our concern here is not a sociological analysis of this temple system, but the consequences it has regarding doctrinal issues in the two areas sketched above; namely, the nature of religious realization and its social implications.

Concerning the former, we may note that within the temple system there is what might be called a highly democratic or egalitarian attitude regarding the qualifications for temple ministry for those born within the system. In other words, minimal levels of study, much of it focused on rituals, are regarded as adequate for temple ministry, and it is not uncommon for temple offspring without strong religious motivation to succeed to the office of resident minister out of family expectation and social custom. Within such a system, it is perhaps not surprising that interpretations of what Shinran terms "realization of shinjin" should tend toward doctrinally abstract and nonexperiential formulations, and that, particularly on an academic level, resistance should arise concerning any understanding of the core of the religious path as entailing qualities of awareness or realization regarded as apart from the ordinary.

A similar inclination toward the affirmation of existing conditions is seen in considerations of moral conduct or values that might spawn a critical or disruptive attitude toward the prevailing social practices into which the temple system is interwoven. The close interconnections of academic Shin studies and temple bureaucracy, both rooted in the hereditary temple system, make it difficult to develop critical thought on a corporate level within a theological framework. This may be appreciated when it is recognized that relations of persons within the temple system extend not only back through the generations of a person's own ancestors, but also forward to the next generations of children and grandchildren. Further, they also branch out "horizontally" through extensive intermarriage within the system.

The Tokugawa-period heritage of the hierarchical temple system controlled by bureaucracies responsible for maintaining orthodoxy both in teachings and in practices, coupled with hereditary succession of the office of abbot of the Honganji and of resident priest in the local temples, has made for great stability in the institution, which may otherwise have fragmented. At the same time, it has nurtured a deeply entrenched doctrinal traditionalism. It is not that the institution itself has failed to take conscientious stands, for example with regard to widespread social discrimination and to such abusive practices common in other Buddhist temples as exorbitant fees for mortuary services. Nevertheless, an institutional authoritarianism is prevalent. In view of the revolutionary nature of Shinran's reinterpretation of the Buddhist tradition, his extraordinary personal break with the customary socio-religious practices of his times, and his astringent criticism of the wrongdoing of both the established temples and the imperial court, it appears that a revitalization of the Shin tradition may necessarily entail far-reaching efforts to envision anew the character of both personal and corporate religious life.

2

Above, I have outlined general issues surrounding the understanding of religious life that arise for Shin Buddhists, and also noted treatments in Shin scholastic study that continue to influence present formulations of doctrine within the tradition. In considering the need for new theological reflection, I have suggested that the traditional approaches fail to provide for cogent understandings in the contemporary situation. In addition to issues emerging from personal engagement with the teachings, however, there are more general questions that arise upon encounter with Shin Buddhism from outside the tradition, and that equally demand attention.

For Westerners approaching Shin in English, it is perhaps difficult to sense the peculiarity of the language in which it is commonly cast, with numerous terms and expressions drawn from texts in Chinese, often in abbreviated form, and leaps of logic based on scholastic concepts and scriptural allusion. The distance of this language from ordinary speech is illuminated by a comment of the widely respected historical novelist Shiba Ryōtarō (d. 1996). Shiba had a longstanding interest in Shinran and was known to have held *Tannisho (Tannishō)*, a record of the words of Shinran, in high esteem. Asked to contribute to a book planned by the Nishi Honganji, his response was to comment on his experience in discussing Shin Buddhist teachings with temple priests and scholars. He noted that at first the conversation would go well and he was quite able to understand their comments, but there would inevitably come a critical point in the discussion at which they seemed to switch over into a special language, a kind of technical jargon that reminded him of the signals exchanged in the bidding and bargaining at the wholesale market. For the uninitiated, such talk was complete gibberish, and he was utterly at a loss to continue the discussion. His appraisal was, "The jargon of the central market just won't do."[10] It is fair to say that Shiba has aptly expressed the impression of many Japanese today when they hear Shin Buddhist doctrine discussed by professionals. In English, this aspect of arcane terminology and cryptic debate may not be immediately apparent, but even D. T. Suzuki liked to comment on how Shin scholars tend to engage in heated arguments over one of Amida's forty-eight Vows versus another.

From a perspective outside Japan, the basic intellectual questions raised by the Pure Land teaching come sharply into focus, and it is here that the conversation represented in this volume has its roots. Partly to treat the problems of adherence to a technical terminology and highly internalist formulations of issues and solutions, I planned and drafted, under the editorial aegis of Yoshifumi Ueda, the book *Shinran: An Introduction to His Thought* (Kyoto: Hongwanji International Center, 1989). While incorporating portions of Ueda's distinctive work on Indian Mahayana thought and on Shinran, this book sought to trace anew the historical evolution of important strains of Pure Land thought from their origins in seminal concepts of the Mahayana tradition, and further to illuminate Shinran's teaching by disclosing the broad patterns of Mahayana thinking at its heart.

In 1989, a symposium was held in observance of the 350th anniversary of the founding of Ryukoku University, which has developed as one of the oldest modern institutions of higher education in Japan out of the Nishi Honganji Gakurin academy mentioned before. To the assembled Shin and religious scholars, Gordon D. Kaufman, a theologian and philosopher of religion with extensive experience in Buddhist-Christian dialogue, presented four sets of questions regarding the Pure Land teaching based largely on his reading of *Shinran: An Introduction to His Thought*. These questions have seemed to many Pure Land Buddhists searchingly focused formulations of crucial issues in need of address, and they form the impetus for the format of the present volume. To give an abbreviated version of those questions:

1. How is this Pure Land to be understood? The symbol itself suggests that it is a place of some sort, a kind of paradise of utmost beauty and purity. . . . How now are we today to understand this Pure Land? Is there really some special place other

than this world to which we may go after death? ... Perhaps sophisticated Buddhists, following the lead of Shinran, understand that the Pure Land is not a real place at all, but basically a symbol for a different state of mind; but would such a notion be attractive and acceptable to ordinary practicers? ...

2. One wonders who—or what—is Amida Buddha? Is Amida some sort of "cosmic person," a kind of god? ... If Amida is not a person of some sort, how should we think of the "vows" which he is supposed to have made? Vows are made by personal beings, beings who can carry out purposes they have set for themselves: were Amida's vows made at some particular time and place (like ordinary vows), and then carried out later through his personal activity? How are we to understand the claim that Amida's vows bring about effects in *this world*? ... Amida is said to be "the primordial Buddha who embodies the essence of all Buddhas" (Ueda and Hirota, p. 121); and this ultimate reality is taken to be utterly "formless," characterizable by such various terms as "suchness, dharma-body, thusness, oneness" (p. 176). If such characterizations are really appropriate, is it not quite misleading to put such emphasis on the importance of a particular personal name ("Amida") and to suggest that this reality makes "vows"? ...

3. My third set of questions focuses on the radical dualism suggested by the symbols of the Pure Land and Amida's Vow, a dualism that runs through all Shin Buddhist thinking. The entire understanding of human existence and its problems appears to rest on sharp contrasts like that between the Pure Land and this present world, Other Power and self-power: everything right and good and true is concentrated in the one side of this contrast; everything evil and false and wrong is to be found on the other. ...

4. [I]n what respects, and why, should we regard any or all of these Shin Buddhist claims as true? As nearly as I can see, for Shin Buddhists themselves this judgment is made on the basis of three criteria of truth: First and foremost, virtually unquestioned authority is given to certain scriptural texts (particularly those dealing with Amida's Vow), and to a specific line of interpreters of those texts—the Pure Land line culminating in Shinran. Second, cogency of argumentation on specific points

or positions in these texts is valued highly. Third, there appears to be a claim that the positions taken and points made make sense of our everyday experience of life and its problems, in a way that is ultimately totally convincing.

It is not difficult to understand why these three criteria might well appear adequate to persons living and thinking within the circle of Shin Buddhism, where the authority—that is, the ultimate truth—of these scriptural texts and this line of Pure Land interpretation is taken for granted; and where, therefore, human life, and the problems of life, are experienced, defined, and interpreted largely in Shin Buddhist terms. But it is not difficult, either, to see that arguments which invoke only these three criteria are completely *internalist* in character.[11]

Toward a Contemporary Understanding of Pure Land Buddhism seeks to carry on the conversation that has been joined and developed by Kaufman, and this volume has itself been composed in a conversational process, as outlined in the prefatory note. Taking the questions put forward by Kaufman as a springboard, the three Buddhist authors present proposals for understanding Pure Land Buddhism. Further, we have solicited comment from Kaufman and from John B. Cobb, Jr., who, in his landmark book *Beyond Dialogue* (Fortress Press, 1982), presented proposals for the "mutual transformation" of Christian and Buddhist traditions. (His most striking proposal—that Shin Buddhists recognize that Amida is Christ—is repeated in his chapter in this volume.) These two religious thinkers have been engaged in efforts to reform their own Christian traditions, and their probing comments on these essays have provided a test of the proposals, analyzing them within the framework of issues they feel challenging for Christian tradition, and indeed any religious tradition, in the contemporary world.

This project itself may require awareness of its own historical context. Since the Meiji period in Japan, with the displacement of Buddhism as a state religion, Buddhist temples have sought to enhance their own authority *within Japanese society* by incorporating Western philosophical and religious concepts and suggesting that their teachings, because they sustain comparison with Western ideas or the interest of Westerners, continue to deserve status in the rapidly changing Japanese culture. The attitude, still seen today, with which academics of the different Buddhist schools prefer to converse with

Western scholars and religious thinkers rather than with each other, suggests that the regard for the esteem conferred by Western recognition continues on institutional and personal levels. This is in part because, within the sharply graded hierarchy of prestige in the world of academic institutions in Japan today, sectarian Buddhist studies continue to be relegated to the very bottom rung. The present volume, however, has been edited neither as a presentation of Pure Land Buddhism in Western terms nor as an exercise in interreligious dialogue, but rather as an attempt to suggest, through the use of whatever conceptual tools are appropriate, directions in which the tradition might be reoriented and transformed so that the life it has harbored become manifest in the present.

The approaches of the three Buddhist authors seeking to delineate possibilities for Buddhist self-understanding are diverse, indicating differences in their views not simply of the Pure Land tradition, but also of the nature and role of the Buddhist path and the needs of contemporary life. To summarize their approaches following the order in Part One:

Dennis Hirota, who has worked to produce a translation of all Shinran's doctrinal writings, seeks to extract the Shin Buddhist tradition from the framework of religious "truth-claims" and "belief" in which it has been commonly understood both in modern Japan and the West. He delineates instead an interaction between two models of understanding the teaching, an interpersonal model based on a relationship with Amida Buddha and a teleological model based on aspiration for the Pure Land. Hirota asserts that the dialogical interaction between these two models is inherent in the Pure Land path as articulated by Shinran, and that it leads the practicer to a transformative shift in understanding. This new understanding is characterized both by self-awareness of the falsely reifying character of ordinary thought and speech and by a reorientation in which Pure Land symbols function to temper the impulses of self-attachment and enable a broadening vision of the self and the world. Hirota's approach may be described as hermeneutical, drawing on recent thinking regarding the nature of language and the dialogical construction of "self," and his assertion is that such an approach reflects Shinran's own concerns in developing a radically new conception of religious engagement.

John Yokota, a former student of Cobb, seeks to bring the issues and methods of Whiteheadian process theology to bear on the Pure Land concepts of Amida Buddha and Pure Land, thereby developing these concepts in ways comprehensible in present-day life. He finds, for example, that the understanding of Amida Buddha as compassionate presents the same difficulties for Pure Land Buddhists as the conception of God as personal and active upon the world in the contemporary West. He also seeks to probe the concept of birth in the Pure Land upon death in this world. He argues that the categories and solutions to similar difficulties formulated in process theology can be usefully adopted by Pure Land Buddhists. In doing so, Yokota develops the traditional conception of Amida in startling new ways, for example, by asserting that the Buddha is changed by how human beings act in the world, and that all acts that take place in the world are preserved in the mind of Amida.

Musashi Tachikawa is a Buddhologist who has done extensive research in Indian philosophy and Tibetan studies. His concern is to develop a systematic approach to Pure Land practice by first establishing a general basis for religious action. Thus, he seeks a broad framework for viewing the Pure Land tradition within a general Mahayana Buddhist pattern of practice, and further grounds this pattern in a broader analysis of human action, which he contrasts with natural biological processes. Employing the dichotomy of the sacred and the profane, he finds that Buddhist practice follows a basic pattern of ascent from the profane toward the sacred (emptiness), manifestation of the sacred, and return to the profane. As a form of Buddhist practice that may illuminate the Pure Land path, Tachikawa offers a detailed outline of the process of mandala practice in esoteric traditions. While following a pattern similar to mandala practice, in which the wisdom of emptiness is attained and the oneness of the self with the cosmos as mandala is achieved, Pure Land practice differs in being characterized by an abandonment of the self to emptiness that is conceived as a personal being (Amida). By drawing this comparison, Tachikawa suggests that Pure Land tradition must develop a systematic view of the world that might correspond to the sacralized world that becomes manifest in mandala practice. (Some comparative comments on the three approaches may be found in the afterword to this volume.)

In Part Two, Kaufman and Cobb discuss the three Buddhist presentations. Kaufman looks closely at the assumptions underlying the three approaches, pointing out their adoption both of scholarly methods and of concepts of Western religious studies: Hirota's use of modern methods of interpretation; Yokota's effort to "demythologize" through reference to concepts of process theology; and Tachikawa's use of procedures of historical reconstruction and of the distinction of the sacred and the profane developed in modern history of religions. He calls for greater methodological self-awareness, and for clarification of the criteria and principles that undergird the different approaches, in order that the issues and their treatment be brought into sharper focus. Cobb, taking an explicitly Christian perspective, raises several concrete issues, including historical grounding for the narrative of the Primal Vow and a foundation for action in the world for corporate, and not merely personal, good. He finds that, historically, Buddhism in general has not focused on these concerns, and asks whether Shin Buddhists today should not develop their tradition with attention to them.

The development of a Buddhist theology is undertaken in the face of two distinct and constant hazards. On the one hand, in seeking to be true to the central concerns of the tradition, one may assume too easily presuppositions in need of investigation and reinterpretation within the contemporary intellectual landscape. On the other hand, in an eagerness to reformulate and augment the tradition in order to address contemporary intellectual and social issues, one may fail to give adequate recognition to critical elements of the tradition. In Part Three, the three Buddhist authors seek to refine and articulate their methodological assumptions and to address issues raised in the conversation among themselves and with Kaufman and Cobb. The chapters of Part Three were shared and discussed at various stages of composition among all five participants, and are intended to reflect that discussion. Although it has been impossible within the compass of this book to detail treatments of the various concrete issues Pure Land Buddhists must consider, it is hoped that, by presenting outlines of general approaches, this volume might provide suggestions for the future development of Buddhist theological reflection.

Notes

1. The Japanese Pure Land tradition is based on three sutras. Two (the "Larger" and "Smaller" sutras on the Land of Bliss) may be found in Luis O. Gómez, trans., *Land of Bliss: The Paradise of the Buddha of Measureless Light* (University of Hawaii Press and Higashi Honganji Shinshū Ōtani-ha, 1996). The third is translated in Meiji Yamada, ed., *The Sūtra of Contemplation on the Buddha of Immeasurable Life as Expounded by Śākyamuni Buddha* (Kyoto: Ryukoku University, 1984).

2. Ueda Yoshifumi, "Reflections on the Study of Buddhism: Notes on the Approaches of Ui Hakuju and D. T. Suzuki," trans. Dennis Hirota, *Eastern Buddhist* 18: 2 (Autumn 1985): 114. This adapted and augmented translation is a composite of several articles.

3. Among followers of both Honen and Shinran, there were some who, in the teaching that no wrongdoing obstructed Amida's compassion, found an excuse to engage in conduct that brought criticism on the movement from the larger society. It appears that there was even advocacy of the notion that self-restraint manifested doubt in the salvific power of Amida's Vow.

4. See the discussion of the Seizan branch of the Pure Land school in Dennis Hirota, *No Abode: The Record of Ippen* (University of Hawaii Press, 1997), xlvii–li. For attitudes reflecting the mainstream Pure Land school, see *idem, Plain Words on the Pure Land Way: Sayings of the Wandering Monks of Medieval Japan* (Kyoto: Ryukoku University, 1989).

5. *Lamp for the Last Dharma-Age (Mappōtōmyōki)*, quoted in *The True Teaching, Practice, and Realization of the Pure Land Way* (hereafter *Teaching, Practice, and Realization*), in Dennis Hirota et al., trans., *The Collected Works of Shinran* (Kyoto: Jōdo Shinshū Hongwanji-ha, 1997), 1: 244.

6. *A Collection of Letters*, letter 2, in *The Collected Works of Shinran*, 1: 560.

7. For a translation, see Minor L. Rogers and Ann T. Rogers, *Rennyo: The Second Founder of Shin Buddhism* (Berkeley: Asian Humanities Press, 1991), pp. 320–22.

8. *Shinshū Shōgyō Zensho* (Kyoto: Ōyagi Kōbundō, 1941), 5: 812–13. It should be noted that in 1987, the Higashi Honganji, as a religious body, was the first of only a handful of Japanese Buddhist temples to formally repudiate their institutional complicity in the war. It was followed after several years by the Nishi Honganji.

9. Regarding censorship of Shinran's own writings, including the passage in *Teaching, Practice, and Realization* in which he criticizes the imperial court for its persecution of Honen and his teaching of the nembutsu, see Rogers and Rogers, pp. 329–31.

10. "Chūō ichiba no fuchō wa dame," Nonomura Chiken, *Chūgai Nippō*, February 22, 1996, p. 1.

11. "Religious Diversity and Religious Truth," in *Shinran and the Contemporary World: Internationalization and the Encounter with World Religions* (Kyoto: Ryukoku University, 1989), pp. 43–48.

PART ONE

Contemporary Interpretations of Pure Land Buddhist Tradition

1. Images of Reality in the Shin Buddhist Path

A Hermeneutical Approach

Dennis Hirota

Conceptions of Truth and Religious Engagement

In an address to Japanese religious scholars in 1989, Gordon Kaufman raised four sets of questions concerning the teachings of the Shin Buddhist tradition. The first three deal with essentially doctrinal issues: how are we to understand the Pure Land, Amida Buddha, and the dualism of good and evil that characterizes much of Shin thought? These central symbols and concepts appear in need of clarification, particularly from a contemporary perspective broader then the tightly "internalist" stance of the tradition. There is, however, a larger issue underlying these inquiries into specific Shin teachings, and it is stated directly in the fourth question: "In what respects, and why, should we regard any or all of these Shin Buddhist claims as *true*?" Kaufman's general aim is to point out the need to develop, among people of different religious traditions, a "pluralistic conception of truth, or a conception of pluralistic truth," arrived at through a model in which traditional claims to the sole possession of saving truth give way to the free play of the conversation. It is in the spirit of such conversation that he raises his questions concerning central Shin symbols.

Although Kaufman advocates that "we reconsider our conception of what religious truth is," the focus of his concern lies in recognizing and coming to terms with the fact that many religious traditions co-exist in the world and that they advance various and conflicting truth-claims. He puts his fundamental question—In what respect and why should certain claims be regarded as true?—to both Christian and Buddhist traditions, and thereby seeks a larger arena in which conversation can flourish as participants come to speak not only from within their particular traditions but also from the newly discovered and shared field of conversation.

If our concern is with our very conception of religious truth, however, there is a prior question that must be dealt with, one that has to do not only with ceasing to assess the validity of the assertions of other traditions in terms of conformity with our own, but also with the conceptual makeup of the larger arena. That is, even with highly scriptural traditions, if we begin by grasping the teachings in terms of "truth-claims," are we not already assuming features of religious traditions that limit too narrowly the kind of conversation that can develop? Rather, in attempting to move beyond the horizons of a merely internalist stance, we must pursue not only the reasons certain assertions should be regarded as true, or the broader, common frames of reference in which to interpret and evaluate traditional truth-claims, but what it means within a tradition to say that a statement is true, and the very nature of our engagement with the teachings and our quest for what is true and meaningful.

These questions concerning the meaning of "truth" itself are particularly significant if Shin Buddhists are to enter into such conversation, for similarities with Christian teachings have often led to fundamental difficulties in expressing and understanding Shin thought in the context of dialogue with other traditions. Because Shin Buddhist statements about reality and human engagement with it have seemed so similar in certain respects to some Christian doctrines, it has been assumed that the conceptions of truth are the same, and therefore such problems as the nature of religious engagement or the ontological status of a supreme being are the same. Even where similarities have been noted, however, perceptive observers have also discerned fundamental differences, and for demarcating larger spheres for conversation, the differences sometimes offer more significant hints than the similarities. I will consider briefly the discussion of Pure Land Buddhist thought by Karl Barth.

Barth on Pure Land Buddhism

Barth's comparative comments on Pure Land thought and Reformed Christianity in *Church Dogmatics* are particularly relevant because his basic concern is religious truth. There he declares Shin Buddhism to be "the most adequate and comprehensive and illuminating heathen parallel to Christianity." Further, he comments that "it is a wholly providential disposition" that this parallel should be "not to Roman or Greek Catholicism, but to Reformed Christianity." In other words, the parallels between Shin and Barth's Reformed Christianity are quite specific and deep, and precisely because of this it becomes apparent that

> [the truth of the Christian religion] is not enclosed . . . in its more or less explicit structure as the religion of grace, nor in the Reformation doctrines of original sin, representative satisfaction, justification by faith alone, the gift of the Holy Ghost and thankfulness. All this, . . . the heathen, too, can in their own way teach and even live and represent as a church.[1]

In the closely similar contours charted by a number of parallel concepts, Barth finds reason to conclude that, with regard to truth, finally "only one thing is decisive. That one thing is the name of Jesus Christ."

Barth's list of specific parallels is insightful: centrality of grace (in the Pure Land path, Amida's all-embracing compassion), original sin (the "karmic evil" of "foolish beings possessed of blind passions transmigrating since the beginningless past"), representative satisfaction (the Primal Vow to liberate beings incapable of performing good, fulfilled through aeons of practice by Bodhisattva Dharmakara), justification by faith alone ("the true cause of attaining nirvana is *shinjin*[2] alone"), gift of the Holy Ghost (Amida[3] directs his-her own true mind to beings, who attain it as the realization of shinjin), and thankfulness (those who realize shinjin "respond in gratitude to the Buddha's benevolence"). Just as good works without faith are of no avail, or even sinful, so recitation of the nembutsu without shinjin is a futile exertion of the egocentric self, however much it may appear to be an act of religious aspiration. Barth singles out for comparative attention a phrase of Shinran—"If the righteous enter into life, how much more in the case of sinners."[4] The paradoxical self-awareness of being both "justified and a sinner" might be said to be present in the attainment of faith or shinjin in the respective traditions. As we have seen, however, Barth's conclusion is that precisely because of these resemblances, what we may call truth must ultimately lie elsewhere.

If I understand Barth correctly here, truth depends finally on God's self-revelation in Jesus Christ and cannot be adjudicated by imposing the standard of conformity with any particular formulation of doctrine or conceptual structure, which may after all be no more than the work of the human intellect. The Pure Land Buddhist thought of Honen and Shinran provides Barth with precisely the full-blown example of religion that, possessing Christianlike doctrines yet lacking the name of Jesus Christ, buttresses his rejection of any framework or foundation in merely human ideas. Barth's stance precludes conversation, but despite his polemical use of Pure Land thought, his comparative comments are illuminating for two reasons. First, they cast light on the dominant understanding of Pure Land tradition in the West, which has commonly been articulated in terms of the parallel concepts he points out. Second, the basic differences that he also enumerates, though less often noted, suggest lines of inquiry by which to pursue our basic concern with religious truth. They are especially significant because, coming after prominent patterns in doctrinal thought have been recognized as strikingly similar, they suggest other, broader dimensions in which fundamental differences occur, differences that may afford a basis for the kind of conversation Kaufman suggests.

To take up this second point first, in his note Barth provides two distinct lists: one of similarities between Pure Land thought and Christianity, and one of differences. The similarities concern the psychology and dynamics of attainment of Christian faith or shinjin in the Pure Land path—their sources and manifestations; the contrastive side concerns the conceptual contexts in which faith and shinjin have their significance. Regarding the differences, he points out that

> the starting-point of the Jodo-movement is obviously the popular demand for an easier and simpler road to salvation; but no one can say of either Luther or Calvin that they begin at that point . . . among the Jodoistic ideas parallel to the Reformed, we miss any doctrine of the law and also of the holiness, or wrath of Amida. . . . In the Jodo religion it is *not Amida or faith in him, but this human goal* of desire [for nirvana] which is the really controlling and determinative power.[5]

We see that even after cataloging an arresting series of parallel concepts, Barth recognizes radical differences regarding the place of faith and shinjin in the larger frameworks of the traditions. On the one hand, he notes that the "doctrine of the law" and any "holiness, or wrath of Amida" are not to be found in the Pure Land tradition; perhaps we may view these as elements of a juridical framework in which an interpersonal relationship between God and human beings is emphasized. On the other hand, Barth discerns that, despite the remarkable similarities in conceptions of faith and shinjin, it is not "Amida or faith in him" that is central and ultimate in Pure Land Buddhism, but the "goal of desire [for nirvana]." That is, rather than the juridical imagery of an interpersonal framework, it is the image of the path—the "road to salvation"—in terms of which the significance of shinjin is understood. Below, I will speak of this dimension as a teleological mode of apprehending reality.

To return to the first point regarding the importance of Barth's comparison for our concerns here, as noted above, it has been the perceived resemblance with a Christian understanding of the dynamics of faith that has shaped understanding of the Japanese Pure Land tradition in the West, and the differences Barth notes have tended to be ignored. One recent example of the often unconscious attempt to force Shin Buddhist thought into a Western mold is a study by James Dobbins, *Jōdo Shinshū: Shin Buddhism in Medieval Japan*, the best historical survey in English of the first four centuries of the Shin tradition. Dobbins asserts his Western perspective at the beginning of his work, "Shinshū derives its strength from the great number of ordinary people drawn to its *simple doctrine of salvation through faith*,"[6] and expands it in his conclusion by identifying Shin tradition as a highly developed example of what he terms "lay Buddhism," which can be found all across Asia. He explains: "If Shin is demythologized—that is, if its specific aspects are stripped away—then the religious sensibilities and practices remaining are not significantly different from those found in lay Buddhism throughout Asia."[7] The list of what Dobbins considers "specific aspects" of Shin tradition capable of being "stripped away" to disclose its essence is revealing: "its [particular] Buddha, Amida; its path to enlightenment, via Pure Land; its sacred story of how Amida established that path; and its practices, the nembutsu and otherwise." In short, Dobbins finds that he can peel away the concrete elements of path and of the practices undertaken to traverse it in order to find the core of the tradition. It may be said that he chooses to obliterate precisely that dimension that Barth notes as a difference between Pure Land and Christian traditions—the fact that "in the Jodo religion it is not Amida or faith in him . . . which is the really controlling and determinative power"—in order to discover his conception of "lay religiosity" that "consists primarily of reverence for the Buddha." Whereas Barth moves from similarities in notions concerning faith to larger "controlling and determinative" dissimilarities, Dobbins seeks to understand Shin tradition by "stripping away" the very differences Barth notes and reducing it to an interpersonal relationship easily accommodated in Western conceptions.

We must note here that both approaches are partial and unsatisfactory, though Barth's is useful in that, at the same time that it seeks to impose a Christian framework on Shin, it perceptively gives hints of what is required to go beyond. If in our present context conversation is to be pursued rather than terminated, then new and broader frames of reference must be developed that can accommodate not only the similarities Barth notes but also the differences. This may be seen, for example, by comparing not the mechanics of faith and shinjin, but their significance for the lives of persons who have attained them. Luther, drawing on imagery of spiritual struggle, speaks of faith as a lifelong endeavor and of the need to increase faith day by day. Further, he gives detailed advice for preparation for death, for it is necessary to resist the temptations to fall into despair and unbelief at the very end. It might be asked why, if faith is the gift of God's grace, it is so vulnerable once a person has attained it? This question does not seem to have arisen as an issue for Luther, perhaps because the final concern remained justification or righteousness, which must take into account one's entire lifetime.

Shinran, working within another framework—that of religious practice—articulates a very different sense of transformed existence occurring with attainment of shinjin. He states that since shinjin is not simply given by Amida, but is itself the Buddha's mind, the utterance of the nembutsu that is the concrete manifestation of this mind in one is perfect practice, full of the Buddha's virtues; hence, with realization of shinjin one's attainment of enlightenment becomes settled immediately. This will occur at the time of death, when the karmic bonds of this life are broken. Because the Buddha's mind is attained and practice fulfilled in the present, the circumstances of one's final moments are of no consequence. Shinran explicitly rejects the need for anxiety or concern about one's state in one's last moments. In this point, the thought of Luther and of Shinran are quite distinct.

Shinran, in fact, departed from the Pure Land tradition that preceded him, which taught that the practicer who said the nembutsu at the point of death went to the Pure Land and there, in the ideal environment presided over by Amida, performed practices and eventually attained enlightenment. Based on his conception of shinjin as the Buddha's mind given to beings, he teaches that practice resulting in enlightenment is accomplished in the present, in ordinary, ongoing life, so that to be born in the Pure Land is to attain enlightenment. No further practice for Buddhahood is necessary. Interestingly, Dobbins misrepresents Shinran's thinking on this point, stating only that one is born in the Pure Land, where after a time "enlightenment will occur swiftly and effortlessly." This is closer to the understanding prior to Shinran, but even if speaking of the earlier tradition, the necessity for practice would have to be mentioned. The source of this confusion may be precisely the imposition of Christian modes of thought on Shinran that we have considered before. That is, the failure to recognize the significance of shinjin in terms of the finality of practice in the immediate present is perfectly consistent with the view of Shin Buddhism as a developed form of lay Buddhism based on faith in and reverence for the Buddha—a Buddhism in essence without practice, but rather focusing on a personal relationship.

Thus, although there are close structural parallels between faith in some Christian traditions and shinjin in the Shin tradition, the implications are not necessarily identical. If, for example, one seeks to fit Shinran's thought into the model of the interpersonal relationship that is implied in the juridical imagery surrounding the idea of "salvation through faith" in Luther, one runs the risk of being led to a reductive understanding, where the concepts of path and of practice dissolve and vanish altogether. It is important to keep this in mind when considering the conversation Kaufman speaks of, for there may be an inclination to employ a framework of doctrinal teachings ("truth-claims") and belief ("regarding those claims to be true") and to direct the discussion toward exploring the criteria for acceptance. A conversation concerning religious truth between Shin and traditions dominant in the West requires, rather, a step back from the verbal formulations understood as presenting the object or the content of faith, and a further step back from the apparent similarities in the elements of faith in Western and shinjin in Shin traditions, to reflect on the emergence, functioning, and significance of that engagement with the teaching referred to as faith or shinjin.

As one response to Kaufman's call for conversation and Cobb's earlier call for a move "beyond dialogue" to efforts toward the transformation of the tradition,[8] I will seek here to develop certain implications of Shinran's thought so as to disclose aspects of truth in the Shin path and possible avenues for understanding the practicer's religious awareness in the contemporary world. This will be accomplished by distinguishing two modes of engagement with the Pure Land teaching and by delineating the Shin path as a movement from one mode of engagement to the other.

Modes of Engagement in the Shin Buddhist Path

At the heart of the Shin Buddhist path lies an integrative dynamic. Shinran speaks of it when he states that Amida's Vow "breaks through the darkness and ignorance of all foolish beings and gives rise in them to shinjin (true entrusting to the Vow)," or that it itself "causes beings to flow into the ocean of the Vow."[9] The Vow does not merely draw beings to itself, but actively moves toward them. It becomes the source of beings' aspiration for and movement toward the transcendent, and further is identified with the inconceivable goal itself. This dynamic circularity—inherent in a conception of true reality as love or wisdom-compassion—is experienced by the person entering the Shin path as an interaction between basic elements of the teaching, one that we sense immediately when we ask such rudimentary questions as why the path requires both Amida Buddha and the Pure Land if they are, as Shinran teaches, identical in their essence (as light or wisdom),[10] or why the Vow requires the Name also— from the practicer's perspective, why practice of the nembutsu is necessary as well as shinjin.[11]

A coherent formulation of this dynamic as characterizing the nature of reality and underlying the expressions of the path distinguishes Shinran's interpretation of the Pure Land teaching from those that preceded, and a grasp of it is helpful both in understanding a variety of difficulties in Shinran's thought and in seeing it in broader perspectives of other Buddhist and non-Buddhist traditions. Here, I will sketch its general contours in terms of the practicer's perception of the path in two distinct phases along it. The major points are:

1. The person entering the Pure Land path may find that it harbors an interior dialectic. This dialectic may be experienced as an interaction—

a shifting of frames of reference—between two fundamental modes or models of apprehending true reality, which transcends the direct experience of unenlightened beings. In order to view them in a broad context, we may label these modes the "teleological" and the "interpersonal."[12]

The teleological mode—based on the aspiration and will of beings to accord with the good and true that, exceeding their present state, can heal and fulfill their existence by transforming them into itself—develops in the teaching in terms of a dualism between this world and the Pure Land. The interpersonal mode—based on the revelation of the transcendent to us in human terms, making possible both relation to it and movement toward it—develops in terms of a dualism of self and Buddha.

(2) In the Pure Land teaching, both modes of apprehension are established, but inevitably come into a tension that brings the practicer to self-reflection and at times to a growing sense of distance from the teaching. At some point along the path, however, this tension may be resolved and the dualisms implied (this world/Pure Land, self/Buddha) in some sense overcome, though not eliminated. The overcoming of the dualities (manifestations of nonduality) occurs with the attainment of shinjin, and leads both to a negation of the earlier conceptual structures of the teaching and further to their reemergence, this time transformed and integrated.

Since the attainment of shinjin typically occurs after a period of engagement with the teaching, two distinct phases or modalities of engagement with the Pure Land path—initial and fulfilled or mature—may be distinguished, with entrance into the mature phase marked by the attainment of shinjin.

(3.) The structure of the basic modes of apprehension in the second, mature phase of engagement—integrated in a polarity in which their dualisms are both negated and affirmed—constitutes the precise articulation of religious existence that is Shinran's major contribution to Buddhist tradition and religious thought. On the one hand, in teaching that birth in the Pure Land is completely settled with one's realization of shinjin, Shinran delineates an attainment of the transcendent in the present in which teleological will and the temporal dimension in which it works toward its goal are effectively dissolved. In this way, he comes to stand beyond the absoluteness of the initial teleological duality of this world/Pure Land; he thus avoids an ultimately monistic understanding of reality and its attendant dichotomy of appearance (illusion)/reality or time/eternity. Further, in teaching that shinjin is itself the mind of Amida realized by beings, he also stands beyond the interpersonal duality of self/Buddha; he thus avoids a voluntaristic or theistic view of reality, with such concomitant problems as predestination, the need for a theodicy, and a substantialist understanding of reality or of self. In place of human will directed toward accord with a transcendent goal or theistic will, Shinran develops a perception of present life as the locus of ongoing transformation (presencing of reality in the midst of samsaric existence) that occurs "of itself" *(jinen)* and that eventually unfolds in full awakening to true reality (which is itself termed *"jinen"*). It may be said that *jinen* is Shinran's characterization of truth or reality as creative, in that it is itself the collapse of habitual understandings based on self-attachment, and disclosive, in that it enables a broadened and renewed seeing of the self and the world.

Thus, on the other hand, by framing the narrative of Dharmakara-Amida and the Vow with a conception of them as forms emerging from formless, transcendent reality in order to awaken each being, Shinran reaffirms the power and validity of Amida and the Pure Land—not as objects of will, but as manifestations of reality as wisdom-compassion perceiving beings and moving toward and within them. Here, genuine aspiration for the Pure Land emerges for the first time as itself an expression of the Buddha's mind.

In this way, Shinran forges a grasp of reality as compassion that, being based on an immediate apprehension of the transcendent that is nondual with existence, is consonant with reality or nondichotomous wisdom as it is understood in Mahayana tradition. The absolutizing of doctrinal concepts and reifying of images as objects of will is discouraged; at the same time, both personal and teleological images are affirmed as expressive of the natural dynamic of the transcendent, and they direct the practicer to a new awareness of the self in the world, and to a full and positive involvement in everyday life.

I will take up these points in a consideration of the two phases of engagement.

Initial Engagement

Teleological Conception of the Transcendent. The Pure Land path leads to the attainment of birth in Amida Buddha's Pure Land through the nembutsu. In the later Japanese tradition, this was understood to mean that if one says the Name of Amida Buddha—Namu-amida-butsu—

entrusting oneself to his/her Vow to save all sentient beings, one will be born in the Pure Land over which s/he presides. We find even in this rough outline the two basic, intertwined dualities mentioned above.

For Pure Land practicers, the duality of this world/Pure Land may resemble mythologically elaborated views of the universe as two tiered: this world of ignorance, temporality, and pain versus the other world of wisdom, eternity, and bliss. The name of Amida's land is "Bliss" or "Delight" (*sukhāvatī*), and in the sutras it is described as a kind of paradise of golden splendor. As a religious goal, however, it does not represent an ideal place of pleasure and succor conceived in mundane terms. Rather, aspiration for the Pure Land is understood to mean turning or redirecting (*ekō*) the desire for a better life in this world toward the Buddha's land instead; thus, the Pure Land is conceived as transcending the realm of worldly desires and all human contingency.

Further, the duality of this world/Pure Land corresponds, in general Buddhist terms, to that between samsaric existence and the realm of nirvana. The cyclic repetition of temporal existence characterized by anxious clinging and aversion arising from ignorance is sundered by a vector breaking through from this world of samsara to the Pure Land. Since entrance into the Pure Land occurs at death in this world, this duality may also be seen as that between present life and the afterlife. Moreover, the sutras teach that in the Pure Land, one attains enlightenment or Buddhahood; thus, it represents the place of the full unfolding of one's highest and genuine destiny. With birth in the Pure Land, one overcomes the ignorance that characterizes mundane existence and achieves awakening. The Pure Land may be characterized as a teleological goal, then, for it is that to which one turns ultimately with aspiration and will, and that which is seen as holding the authentic fulfillment of one's existence—one's desires for wholeness and happiness—and indeed, that of all beings.

I use the term *teleological*, then, to suggest the involvement of desire for and effort toward self-fulfillment represented as attainment of a goal that transcends our present experience. In traditional Buddhist terms, such a concept may be seen in the bodhisattva path, which is characterized by aspiration or vow (*gan*) and practice (*gyō*). Awakening aspiration for enlightenment, the bodhisattva makes vows resolving to persevere in practice until attainment. This path leads from the defiled world to a pure land, for enlightenment always unfolds in the purification of a sphere of activity not so much created as transformed by the influence of the enlightened one's wisdom-compassion.

In the Pure Land path, however, the consequences of such a teleological mode of apprehending reality differ from those found in some Western, particularly Platonic, instances. According to Kaufman, teleological transcendence is based on the striving of the self toward that which is assumed to be appropriate to it—an "Infinite Source and Goal" that, being itself perfect, exhibits no such motion. Thus, he states, a teleological perspective inevitably leads to a theology of being. Ultimate reality is understood as good "which moves all other things but is itself unmoved," and all finite reality is viewed as necessarily grounded in this ultimate reality toward which all things inherently strive. Here, the transcendent is not personal or anthropomorphic; it does not act toward beings.[13]

The Pure Land is indeed a nonanthropomorphic goal and is viewed as the transcendent objective to be aspired to by all beings. It is the "city of nirvana" to which we are urged to "return," a sphere or realm into which we enter to realize the true reality of ourselves and all things. Nevertheless, it differs from the model described by Kaufman in that it shares with general Buddhist thought the rejection of a notion of the ultimate as substantial. This is reflected in various aspects of the Pure Land.

First, while the Pure Land stands as the supreme goal for human beings in this world, it is not in itself the final end of the Buddhist path. In figures prior to Shinran, it is understood to represent an ideal environment in which one will be able to accomplish the bodhisattva practices that will lead to perfect awakening, but even when (as in Shinran) attainment of enlightenment or Buddhahood is considered to be simultaneous with birth into the Pure Land, the Pure Land itself is not regarded as a final abode or a place of ultimate repose. Thus, it is the highest aspiration of this lifetime, to be sure, but birth there is also conceived as either a step to final attainment of Buddhahood (e.g., in Honen), or as attainment itself, in which case one at the same time returns to this world to work compassionately to save other beings (Shinran). Ultimate reality transcends all conceptualizing, and further is inseparable from contingent, defiled existence in this world and the dynamic activity of wisdom-compassion. As Shinran states, "Reaching the ultimate end of the One Vehicle (the way by which all beings are liberated) is without bound and without cessation."[14] Thus, the

Mahayana admonition against attachment to a limited conception of nirvana wholly separate from samsara applies also to the Pure Land viewed as a resting place of peace and bliss.

At the same time, in the tradition of Honen and Shinran, a strict dichotomy divides this world and the Pure Land. From the perspective of beings, this is an absolute gulf, and there is nothing in human beings or existence in this world that can be the cause for bridging it and attaining the Pure Land. Thus both teachers modify the basic teaching, stressed in the Tendai tradition out of which they emerged, that all being possess Buddha-nature. Attainment of the Pure Land cannot be understood as the simple development or unfolding of the inherent nature of sentient beings or as union with that which is immanent in them. Even the aspiration for enlightenment—for that which genuinely transcends samsaric existence—is not intrinsic; hence, the natural presence of a teleological desire for the Pure Land is denied.

The concept of the Pure Land does not develop directly from beings' longing for the real, but exists precisely to enable them to overcome their attachment to their own self-existence, their "ontological thirst." How then can beings relate themselves to the Pure Land? Here we find that the Pure Land implies an interpersonal dimension. It was established by Amida Buddha in order to provide a genuine and effective means of transcendence accessible to ignorant minds and to draw beings toward attainment of enlightenment. The land is, therefore, a manifestation of the Buddha's compassionate activity toward living things. It is the crystallization of the Buddha's work to guide beings to enlightenment and not the source of their being.

Interpersonal Conception of the Transcendent.   In the Pure Land teachings, the concept of a field of bliss attainable after leaving this world is encompassed in a larger framework that gives rise to a concept of reality as personal. According to Kaufman, the transcendent conceived as personal develops from a model that corresponds to our knowledge of other persons.[15] A personal center apart from us always transcends our direct experience; we can know other persons only through acts in which they reveal themselves to us. Likewise, according to this model, God is known only through the acts of self-revelation that have developed in human history. The transcendent conceived in interpersonal terms, then, is known above all through the aspect of will; without the will of the transcendent to reveal itself to beings, there can be no revelatory activity in the world.

In the Pure Land context, Amida vows not to attain Buddhahood unless he liberates beings by revealing himself to them as his Name, Namu-amida-butsu, and taking all who say it into his Pure Land. What is, above all, necessary for beings is trust in Amida. Here, however, the basic teleological perspective is not simply replaced by an interpersonal model; the interpersonal develops from within a teleological framework, for the Buddha's activity of self-revelation is encompassed within his own movement to highest enlightenment. As a consequence, a theistic conception of the transcendent characterized by will is always tempered by being held within a broader framework; the Buddha's liberation of beings is incorporated within his self-fulfillment.

Encapsulating the path of the practicer within that of the Buddha does, however, lead to the second basic duality in the Pure Land tradition: self/Buddha, or, in terms of the dynamic of the path, self-power/other-power. These latter terms first enter the Pure Land tradition in China. As concepts, however, they are implicit in basic Pure Land teachings, and the history of the tradition may be viewed as the history of their reinterpretation and refinement. Basically, self-power refers to a person's own exertion of effort and will to attain the world of enlightenment (the Pure Land) and other-power denotes the power and working of Amida's Vow, which was undertaken to establish the Pure Land and enable all beings to enter it (I use the term *other-power* in lower case to indicate the understanding of the Vow's working as relative to self-power, and *Other Power* to indicate it as apprehended where self-power has been abandoned in the mature phase of engagement).

Dynamics of Engagement in the Initial Phase. In the initial phase, interaction between the teleological and interpersonal modes of apprehension results in a tension between the concepts of self-power and other-power as relative. On the one hand, the teleological aspiration calls for an active orientation of one's life toward attainment of the Pure Land (affirmation not only of capacity for religious cultivation but also of a basis in oneself for apprehending the goal and determining and adopting a method of attainment). On the other hand, the interpersonal relation with Amida calls for orientation of one's life toward reception of the Buddha's aid (trust in other-power/negation of self-power). For the practicer, this may be viewed as a tension between horizontal and vertical vectors (see figure 1.1).

It may be said that the path of Mahayana Buddhists is "twofold always," consisting of both teleological and interpersonal dimensions. The bodhisattva, whose path is the model for that of Dharmakara-Amida, integrates the two vectors of activity toward attainment of Buddhahood and activity toward the enlightenment of other beings—in traditional terms, self-benefit and benefit of others *(jiri-rita)*—on the basis of nondiscriminative wisdom. Through the practice of nondiscrimination (emptiness contemplation), bodhisattvas eradicate the dichotomous thinking that distinguishes self and other, subject and object (here, "form is emptiness"); at the same time, through the wisdom that unfolds from such practice, they perceive beings in samsaric existence and work to save them ("emptiness is form").

Pure Land practicers, however, find themselves incapable of stilling discriminative thought and accomplishing emptiness contemplation; for them, the path is informed by the conceptual modes of apprehending reality that we have considered, and not the eradication of conceptual thought. These modes lead the practicer along two vectors that form a mirror image of the general bodhisattva path, but they cannot achieve a resolution through their own powers.

It is possible for either mode of apprehension to serve as the basis for attempts at resolution, but with distinct consequences. If the teleological mode is stressed, other-power is drawn into the dimension of personal effort toward birth, so that self-power and other-power are seen as complementary. Even when the goal is reception of other-power, self-power is viewed as a means of attaining it. In the early

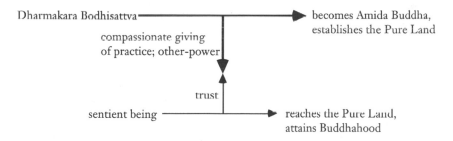

FIGURE 1.1 Teleological and Interpersonal Vectors in Initial Engagement

Pure Land commentarial tradition, no clear qualitative distinction was drawn between self-power and other-power: they both represented the virtue or power dedicated to or derived from practice that moved one toward the realm of enlightenment. Their fundamental difference was conceived as quantitative; other-power, as the power of the Buddha's Vow, was vastly greater. Originally, then, these terms were used to suggest that in the Pure Land way one could also avail oneself of the Buddha's power instead of depending solely on one's own merits. To the follower of the Pure Land path who performed worship and contemplation of Amida Buddha and the Pure Land, the Buddha would give the virtues of his own aeons of practice. Even in the developed tradition in Japan, recitation of the nembutsu was often pursued as a means by which to maintain mindfulness of Amida or accumulate merit, thus turning oneself into a worthy recipient of the Buddha's compassion or coming to share in his virtues.

If the interpersonal mode of apprehension is emphasized, the inherent opposition in the dualism of self-power/other-power emerges clearly; this developed in the later Chinese tradition and in Japan. The need for the Pure Land path turns, to begin with, on the inability of at least some—for Shinran, all—beings to fulfill the bodhisattva path on their own. Thus, the concept of self-power holds within itself the sense of its own inadequacy. Moreover, as long as one adheres to the worth of one's own practice, by that measure one fails to depend on Amida. The dualism of self-power/other-power arising from the interpersonal model, then, includes a motion from reliance on self-power toward reliance on other-power. This integrated pair of motive forces— reflection on the ineffectiveness of one's own efforts and trust in true reality as compassionately working towards one from beyond the confines of egocentric experience—is what moves one along the path. Some may find affirmation of this movement in confrontations with human limitation and in common experiences of self-forgetfulness or self-transcendence.[16] Nishida Kitarō sketches a broad vision of the advance of human knowledge as an overcoming of "subjective delusions" and a move toward true knowledge that is also love, employing the dichotomy of self-power and other-power.[17]

This double impetus of negation of self-power and affirmation of other-power, which exerted itself with increasing strength in theological reflection in the history of the Pure Land tradition in China and Japan, leads to two general trends of thought. First, the shift from the horizontal vector (teleological) to the vertical (trust in the Other) comes to be conceived in terms of a subordination of self-will and an alignment of it with the encompassing will of Amida. Thus, saying the nembutsu is said to lead to birth precisely because it is the act prescribed in the Vow (accords with the Buddha's will). The practicer's will and aspiration remain central, just as in the teleological model, but come to be directed toward establishment of a relationship with the Buddha rather than directly toward attainment of the Pure Land. Persons seek peace of mind in a wholehearted trust in Amida's Vow.

Second, in this shift of orientation—a kind of postponement of the teleological vector until after death—even the interpersonal relation with the Buddha, since it comes to bear teleological significance, tends to be located in the future. Thus, on the one hand, other-power comes to be associated with the world beyond; that is, entry into Amida's compassionate activity is regarded as occurring at the time of death. This outlook is expressed in the teaching of Amida's coming for one at the moment of death. On the other hand, the negative appraisal of self-power is broadly associated with existence in this world and its delusions and ills, for the self is inextricably involved in the world as long as life continues. Thus, such traditional conceptions of this world as "the world of the five defilements" and "the last dharma-age" are emphasized.

Even with the development of these conceptions—wholehearted interpersonal trust and postponed teleology—the engagement with the teaching in the initial stage that I have been describing holds, at its core, a self-contradiction. One must bring one's powers of reflection to bear on experience in order to grasp the significance of self-power and other-power, but this dualism itself implies the rejection of reliance on such self-examination. Similarly, one must direct one's will toward achieving the goal of the Pure Land through saying the Name in trust, but at the same time, that will cannot be the cause of attainment. As long as one seeks to bring one's will into accord with Amida's, the duality of self-power/other-power remains as an unresolved contradiction of self-power working to negate itself, and heightens awareness of one's own distance from the teaching.

This is not simply a dilemma inherent in any concept of "salvation through faith alone," where faith, if employed as a means, becomes self-contradictory; rather, it develops directly from the basic dialectical structure of the teaching. That is, while the Mahayana bodhisattva path inevitably involves both teleological and interpersonal (compassionate) aspects for the bodhisattva, it is in Amida's Vow that these aspects are apprehended as seamlessly fused from the stance of recipient beings. Hence, the conception of the path is shifted so that the interpersonal aspect is not first subsumed within the teleological goal (emptiness, in which perception of ignorant beings and self dissolves) and then reinstated; rather, both interpersonal (compassionate working upon oneself) and teleological (Amida's Buddhahood, one's own Buddhahood) are conceivable only conjointly.

Thus, in the initial stage, practicers tend to conceive the real either in terms of a theistic being (Amida) who works for their salvation (interpersonal model) or as the power of the Vow that functions as a universal law to effect the birth of beings who accord with it (teleological model). Neither model can be wholly satisfactory. This is because in the former case, the interpersonal mode of apprehension is rooted in a broader, shared teleological context, and because of this, Amida cannot be conceived as an omnipotent being who judges beings and who can determine their fate. The power that brings beings to attainment of birth is the power of his own movement to enlightenment according to dharma.

Further, in the latter case, though we seek to experience the power of the Vow to effect our own attainment directly, this teleological aspect ultimately depends on the Buddha who acts to bring us to awakening precisely because of our own complete incapacity to move toward it ourselves. Apprehension is only possible, therefore, through an interpersonal relationship in which we entrust our fate entirely to Amida. The Buddha is spoken of as one's own parent, oneself as an only child. Shinran states that the Vow was made for himself alone, and also that he does not know whether the nembutsu will lead to birth into the Pure Land.[18] Without Amida's personal call to oneself, there can be no relationship with the dynamic of the Vow.

Fulfilled Engagement

Distinguishing Two Phases of Engagement. In traditional Shin dogmatics, the idea of distinct phases or stages in a process leading to realization of shinjin is generally avoided. Shinran teaches no method by which one can attain shinjin—any method would fail to lead beyond the sphere of self-power—and excessive concern over whether one has or has not attained it complicates and obscures the path. Nevertheless, there are several reasons for distinguishing two general modes of engagement.

Although the core of Shinran's teaching is the nature of shinjin and the condition of the person who has attained it, the admonition against adherence to self-power even while following the Pure Land path is also a highly elaborated theme. He cautions Pure Land practicers against "imperfect realization of shinjin" and "imperfect realization of hearing" of the dharma.[19] Further, he distinguishes "true and real practice and shinjin" from "practice and shinjin that are provisional means,"[20] and the true and real Buddha and Land—Amida and the Pure Land—from "transformed Buddha-bodies and lands."[21] "Transformed lands," described as performing a purgatorial function, are provided by the Buddha to guide those who cannot enter the true teaching directly and are characterized by concrete images and numerical measurements corresponding to the conceptualized projections of practicers entangled in self-attachment. Forms of adherence to self-power within the Pure Land path belong to the initial stage of engagement outlined above, while realization of shinjin is represented by a second stage.

Further, Shinran himself speaks of different stages in the process by which he personally reached the attainment of shinjin, although he does not present this as a model for others.[22] Biographies of people who have been considered exemplary practicers of shinjin (myōkōnin) also often include a lengthy period of engagement with the teaching before attainment of shinjin.

Concerning the two phases outlined above, the following points should be noted. (1) According to Shinran, a person either has realized shinjin or has not—in terms of this paper, has entered the second phase or has not—and never regresses. (2) While theoretically it is not impossible to pass immediately, on encountering the teaching, into the mature phase, it appears that a period of involvement with the teaching would normally be required before attainment of shinjin occurs. (3) In Shinran's writings, "shinjin" refers, with only few exceptions, to the second mode of engagement and not the first. It is here that we see the ambiguity of employing the translation "faith" for shinjin: "faith" as commonly understood would be applicable to the mode of engagement in the first phase also, while in Shinran's writings, shinjin does not refer to such initial engagement except when qualified, for example as "shinjin of self-power" or "shinjin that is a provisional means."

The mature phase of engagement holds both a superficial continuity with and a fundamental transcendence of the attitudes and outlook of the initial phase. The chief point of continuity is the impetus underlying the entire path—informing the mode of existence of the Pure Land practicer at all points along it—toward an ever-broader perspective; this is a movement against the centripetal forces of self-attachment, so that one is propelled toward a stance beyond the boundaries and perceptions of the egocentric self. In the initial phase, this is the movement from self-power toward other-power; it is not yet true Other Power, but what Shinran calls "self-power within Other Power,"[23] which can lead only to a "provisional" attainment. In the mature phase, it is a deepening awareness and reflection within Other Power.

Further, since the dialectical interaction between the teleological and interpersonal modes of apprehension does not lead to elimination of one side or the other, basic attitudes of the initial phase are also found in the mature phase. On the teleological side, one continues to look toward attainment of the Pure Land, which lies in one's future. We find that in his letters, for example, Shinran expresses his happiness for people who have finally achieved—with death—their lifelong aspiration for birth, and also speaks of reunion with others in the Pure Land. Such feelings of longing for one's spiritual home—return to the city of nirvana—continue throughout one's life on the path. On the interpersonal side, one continues to worship Amida, to feel gratitude for his compassion, and to say the Name out of mindfulness and reverence.

At the same time, between the initial and mature phases there is a distinct break. The second phase does not occur along a direct and continuous line of progression from the first. It may be said that the second phase is entered when a person has broken through and gone beyond the frames of reference of the first. This occurs as a transformation, and by undergoing such a transformation, the attitudes of aspiration and gratitude become genuine for the first time.

A number of crucial, interrelated issues arise here: the nature of the transformation termed the "realization of shinjin," how it comes about, and the way it manifests itself in the ongoing life of practicers. Although Shinran develops upon the tradition decisively by describing the transformation as Amida giving his mind to beings, in his expression of it he remains largely within the mythic-narrative terms of the tradition, choosing to formulate his new insight through shifts in the interpretation of scriptural texts. It remains, therefore, to explore the various dimensions of this transformation using more general frames of reference. One such possible field of investigation, for example, is that of language, and elsewhere I have attempted to delineate an understanding of the view of language implied in Shinran's thought and to sketch understandings of the issues mentioned above in terms of it.[24]

With regard to our concern here with the nature of religious truth, some clarification is possible by viewing it in terms of the movement from a provisional mode of apprehending reality to the fulfilled mode, and the nature of the fulfilled or mature mode and its expression.

The Integrated Structure of Reality. In the initial phase, a person's movement toward the transcendent as goal (Pure Land) is understood to be embraced within a larger teleology (Dharmakara becoming Amida), giving rise to a conception of an interpersonal relationship. Both the teleological and interpersonal images of the transcendent tend to be framed in terms of will and the temporal dimension of its unfolding: self-will to reach the Pure Land through placing oneself in accord with Amida (by reliance, awareness, religious acts, or moral conduct) and Amida's will to save all sentient beings by bringing them to his Pure Land. In this case, the narrative of Dharmakara-Amida functions as a myth that, as an account of events that take place in primordial time prior to all history, presents the origins of salvific features of the cosmos. The myth of Amida provides for an understanding of the Buddha and the Pure Land and the effectiveness of the nembutsu as the means for attaining it. At the same time, there is an implied continuity or contiguity with the history of this world. Again, as typical of such myths, the problem for the practicer is to relate that time in the infinite past with the time of present existence. In this view, Amida's Vow is objectified and accepted as the ongoing working of Amida's will or as a kind of natural law that has been set in motion and whose operation one seeks to appropriate from the stance of the self, through an alignment or subordination of will.

Further, the negative view of self-power in this initial or provisional phase tends to result, as we have seen, in a futuristic outlook or a postponed teleology: as the scope of the negation of self-power as doctrinally understood broadens to include all personal efforts toward good in this world, actual entrance into the working of Other Power comes to be envisioned as occurring only at the time of death (Amida's

coming to welcome one, the Pure Land as environment for practice).
Here, the significance of a person's life in this world—one's actions
within one's own particular circumstances—is not recognized; only
the link binding one to the action of the Vow is relevant. Salvation is
predicated on the strength of the vertical will, and the temporal dimension of actual existence holds no meaning. For this reason, the
final moments of life tend to be considered decisive in determining
one's future.

Mature or fulfilled engagement, which harbors a fusion of temporal existence and true reality (as shinjin), is marked by an integration
of the teleological and interpersonal modes of apprehension. Such
integration is requisite for a coherent understanding of reality as itself
wisdom-compassion. Here, the narrative of the Primal Vow ceases to
be grasped as an account of the primordial past as an anterior extension of this world, and comes to inform present existence with the
disclosive quality by which the practicer lives in self-awareness of
delusional attachment as awareness of truth. Shinran's understanding
of the integrated structure of the apprehension of reality may be considered in terms of his statements regarding two sources—or perhaps
a twofold character—of shinjin. These correspond to two dimensions
of reality (dharma-body) or Buddha.

Borrowing from the thought of T'an-luan, Shinran distinguishes
two aspects of dharma-body: dharma-body as suchness (formless, true
reality) and dharma-body as compassionate means (Buddha possessing form; Shinran identifies it with Amida). With regard to shinjin, he
states on the one hand that it is Buddha-nature, which is dharma-body
as suchness that pervades all beings, and on the other, that it is the
sincere mind of Amida that Amida gives to beings.

Concerning shinjin as Buddha-nature, Shinran states:

> Tathagata (dharma-body as suchness) pervades the countless worlds; it
> fills the hearts and minds of the ocean of all beings. . . . Since it is with
> this heart and mind of all sentient beings (pervaded by Tathagata) that
> they entrust themselves to the Vow of the dharma-body as compassion-
> ate means (Amida), this shinjin is none other than Buddha-nature.[25]

Here, shinjin—the mind with which one entrusts oneself to the Vow—
is identified with true reality that fills the minds of all beings, including "plants, trees, and land." This idea shares structural features similar

to those of teleological perspectives in which the ultimate good is also the source of beings, and its presence in beings is the basis for their natural inclination toward it or its power to draw them to itself.

There is a fundamental difference, however. In the realization of shinjin, the direction of movement is not from the practicer toward Buddha (aspiration arising from Buddha-nature) but from Buddha toward the practicer. Although Tathagata, or true reality, is said to pervade all beings, since it completely transcends the conceptualization of human intellect, ordinarily it lies beyond our awareness; its presence therefore holds no significance for our existence. As long as we remain ignorant of it, our delusional attachments bind us solely to samsaric life. Thus, the idea of immanence in the teleological structure is balanced by a movement toward beings, which is formulated as an interpersonal element of self-revelation:

> Dharma-body as suchness has neither color nor form; thus, the mind cannot grasp it nor words describe it. From this oneness was manifested form, called dharma-body as compassionate means. Taking this form, the Buddha announced the name Bhiksu Dharmakara and established the Forty-eight great Vows that surpass conceptual understanding.[26]

Here, form emerges in self-revelatory activity directed to ignorant beings. It is through Amida's arising from formless reality and the self-revelation of Amida to beings that Buddha-nature can manifest itself in them as the entrusting of themselves to the Vow. Formless reality cannot simply unfold itself in beings; its emergence takes place only through provision for an apprehension of itself as personal. Beings' attainment of shinjin, then, represents a movement of reality toward beings. Further, while it is not beings' will to reach the transcendent, this attainment of shinjin harbors their natural and necessary movement toward awakening to reality.

The personal model also, however, is maintained only together with a balancing perspective. What is soteriologically significant in the nature of shinjin is not a person's own reliance on Amida's power. One is not saved simply because of a relationship with Amida (one's trust in him, his will to save one), but because the realization of shinjin is Amida's giving his pure mind to beings, and therefore is itself the emergence of Buddha-nature in them.

On the one hand, an absolute gulf lies between unenlightened existence and true reality—between human intellect and will, which are dominated by discriminative thought and egocentric attachment, and wisdom-compassion. Having long been conditioned by ignorance, our feelings and perceptions arise with only distorted images of actuality as their objects. On the other hand, true reality that transcends such discrimination is nondichotomous, and does not stand apart from unenlightened existence. It gives rise to compassionate activity that reaches toward beings by manifesting form, and this movement is at the same time for that which transcends form to pervade beings. In beings, then, there is the delusional self of samsaric existence, and this self is pervaded by and interfused with the mind of Buddha in the form of shinjin, which is the sincere mind with which one entrusts oneself to the Vow, and which is also suchness or true reality. In this sense, the source of shinjin may be understood in both interpersonal and teleological frameworks.

The Integrated Apprehension of Reality.   The perception of the entire Vow as encompassed within the framework of form emerging from formless reality is unique to Shinran.[27] It functions to remove Amida and the Vow from a merely conceptual grasp within our ordinary frames of reference and to delineate an existential apprehension in the realization of shinjin. We find Shinran's description of realization of shinjin and its consequences from the practicer's perspective in his interpretation of the following passage of the *Larger Sutra:*

> All sentient beings, as they hear the Name, realize even one thought-moment of shinjin and joy, which is directed to them from Amida's sincere mind, and aspiring to be born in that land, they then attain birth and dwell in the stage of nonretrogression.[28]

Shinran explains that to "hear" in this passage "indicates shinjin."[29] More specifically, "sentient beings, having heard how the Buddha's Vow arose—its origin and fulfillment—are altogether free of doubt."[30] To "hear" the Name is to apprehend the central moments of the Vow that it embodies—its "origin and fulfillment." From the viewpoint of our concerns here, it may be said that this apprehension embraces two poles: a negative one, in which the dualisms of the two modes of apprehension as they had been construed in the initial phase are dissolved, and a positive one, in which they are newly established.

NEITHER TELEOLOGICAL NOR INTERPERSONAL:
NEGATION OF CONCEPTUAL FRAMEWORKS OF TIME AND WILL

In the initial phase, one steps beyond the dimension of one's own teleological activity by finding that one's desire for the Pure Land is encompassed by the aspiration of Dharmakara-Amida to save all beings. To
hear the "origin and fulfillment of the Vow," however—"the most difficult
among difficulties"—implies stepping beyond all exertion of will toward
the Vow's fulfillment. Such motion lies between the moments of origin
and fulfillment in our ordinary conception, but to hear the Vow is to
grasp these two moments together, so that the temporal dimension of the
Vow is collapsed. This does not mean that the Vow is relegated to "that
time" in the mythological past, for it inherently involves the movement
toward the Pure Land of beings presently existing in the world.[31] Rather,
the Vow's being already fulfilled expresses its stance beyond the imposition of the temporal framework of this world and access by the will of
beings. In the same way, since realization of shinjin is not the result of any
process initiated by the practicer—it is "shinjin that has no root in one's
own heart"[32]—it is attained in "one thought-moment," the briefest instant
of time. There is room neither for objectification of the Vow in time nor
any effort to make oneself its object.

The fulfilled Vow, no longer conceived as volition, calls not for an
accordance of wills but rather for the relinquishment of self-will.
Shinran states:

> Through the fulfillment of the Eighteenth Primal Vow, Bodhisattva
> Dharmakara has become Amida Tathagata, and the benefit that sur-
> passes conceptual understanding has come to transcend all bounds. . . .
> Know, therefore, that without any differentiation between good and
> bad people, and regardless of one's having a heart of blind passion,
> all beings are certain to attain birth.[33]

The fulfillment of the Vow implies movement to all beings without
differentiation. For beings, no effort or designing to bring oneself into
its scope is necessary. This is the meaning of Shinran's repeated insistence that one be "free of calculation."

Further, shinjin is not only given by Amida, but is itself the
Buddha's sincere mind. This means, as we have seen, that the realization of shinjin is the unfolding in one of Buddha-nature, or the pervading of one's mind by what is true and real. As a consequence,

when one attains shinjin, one enters the stage of nonretrogression; one's attainment, at death in this world, of birth in the Pure Land and perfect enlightenment has become completely settled, being the natural culmination of the unfolding of Buddha-nature that has already begun in one. Shinran uses the metaphor of "seed," stating that shinjin (or nembutsu) is the "seed of enlightenment, the seed for realizing the supreme nirvana,"[34] stressing the "naturalness" (freedom from will and design) of movement to Buddhahood. Thus, although one remains a being of delusional passions, Shinran interprets the *Larger Sutra* as teaching entrance into the working of the Primal Vow and emergence of Buddha-nature in the present as "immediate attainment of birth," stressing the sense of "immediate" as "without any time elapsing."[35] The temporal framework of teleological movement is broken through; one already has "attained what one shall attain."[36]

Thus, where the Vow is heard, the linear vector toward transcendence of samsaric existence is intersected and severed: "Already the causes leading to the six courses and the four modes of birth have died away and their results become null. Therefore we immediately and swiftly cut off birth-and-death."[37] The transcendence expressed by the fulfilled Vow is a transcendence of teleological will itself that temporally divorces reality from present existence. In Buddhist teachings, such will is ultimately viewed as a kind of craving.

In the thought-moment of the realization of shinjin, persons stand grasped by the Vow-mind and thus isolated from temporal acts and conditions of both the past and future, none of which either result in or affect their stance in the Vow. To have been grasped is to have attained the transcendent, and is expressed as "immediately attaining birth." Thus, shinjin or the mind of Amida not only emerges isolated from the horizontal motion of existence, but further severs the person from such existence. This is the significance of its arising where the teleological will (the impulse toward self-fulfillment included in what Shinran calls "doubt")—as it weighed the past and anticipated the future—has vanished. On the one hand, the Pure Land has already been attained (entrance in the future at the time of death is completely settled in the present); on the other, it has lost its significance as a goal ("I have no idea whether the nembutsu is truly the seed for my being born in the Pure Land or whether it is the karmic act for which I must fall into hell").[38]

The conception of willed movement toward transcendence in the initial phase is replaced by a conception of "transformation" that comes about by *jinen* ("spontaneous" working of the Vow, without one's calculation) and that therefore cannot be framed by the elements of volition or time. In moral terms, "all one's past, present, and future evil karma is transformed into good" upon realization of shinjin; "we are made to acquire Amida's virtues through entrusting ourselves to his Vow-power."[39] The conception of will that had animated the teleological mode of apprehension as progress toward the Pure Land through accomplishing worthy acts is dissolved; neither worship nor good thoughts or deeds hold any significance for teleological ascent, and acts of evil no longer obstruct future enlightenment.

Similarly, the conception of will—whether Amida's or beings'— that had formed the core of the interpersonal apprehension of the transcendent in the initial phase, leading to effort to accord with the Vow, is dissolved as our minds of ignorance and blind passions "are immediately transformed into the (Buddha's) mind of great compassion"[40] upon realization of shinjin. This occurs "spontaneously" or "naturally" *(jinen)*, not by any determination of the Buddha's judgment of us. Thus, there is no room for an idea of trust or faith as an alignment of one's will with the will of Amida; shinjin is itself the mind of the Buddha realized by the practicer. Rather than relationship, then, there is an aspect of nonduality. Because of this, Shinran states, "The person who rejoices in shinjin is equal to all the Tathagatas."[41]

Since it cannot be framed in terms of time or will, Shinran states that the Vow is "inconceivable," and frequently employs the image of "ocean" to characterize its nature. To enter the ocean of the Vow is to be transformed in the immediate present so that, "without seeking it, we are made to receive the supreme virtues, and without knowing it, we acquire the great and vast benefit [of definitely attaining Buddhahood]."[42] Within the ocean of the Vow, the Pure Land loses its character as the transcendent goal divided from this world ("The heart of the person of shinjin already and always resides in the Pure Land")[43] and Amida loses his character as active subject separate from ourselves (he gives us his sincere mind as a transformation of self).

The elimination of the dualisms of the teleological and interpersonal perspectives as they function in the initial phase does not mean that these modes of apprehension are discarded and vanish. The Vow as fulfilled is also the matrix from which Amida and the Pure Land arise as embodiments or expressions. Rather than these modes of apprehending the transcendent falling away, they are transmuted within the polarity in which they remain present to validate and orient lives of practicers.

BOTH TELEOLOGICAL AND INTERPERSONAL:
TEMPORAL AND SPACIAL UNFOLDING OF TRUE REALITY

In the one thought-moment of the realization of shinjin, the "origin and fulfillment" of the Vow unfolds in the practicer in an isolate moment of the path and utterly dissolves need for action to reach the Pure Land or bring oneself into relation with Amida. The realization of shinjin removes persons from the context of their existence in history and the world by actualizing the transcendent in them (in the form of realizing the mind of the Buddha); this is the significance of shinjin as suchness or as arising from the Vow.

At the same time, however, the undercutting of the initial teleological and interpersonal conceptions that occurs through the collapse of temporal and volitional frameworks represents only one aspect or pole of the realization of shinjin, for such realization must also be an actual occurrence in the life of the practicer, and further must have the character of integrity with the practicer's temporal existence. The negative pole is balanced by a positive pole in which teleological and interpersonal perceptions are affirmed within the frameworks of time and the world, though freed now of the impositions of egocentric will. In this perspective, Amida and the Pure Land are grasped not as means toward transcendence—as agent or object of will—as in the initial phase, but as images of the way in which wisdom-compassion has moved toward one, continues to grasp one, and becomes authentic aspiration for enlightenment in one.

Interpersonal Perspective: Light and Name

With regard to conceptions of Amida and the Pure Land in the mature phase, we can only note several aspects pertinent to our concerns here, drawing on Shinran's writings. First, dharma-body as true reality does not simply emerge as Amida and require acknowledgment by revealing, through Shakyamuni, the Name or the practice of the nembutsu. Amida's call or summons through his Name is one aspect, but is embraced in a larger context, for it is the entire Vow story—the awakening of aspiration, establishment of the Vow, fulfillment of practice, and realization of Buddhahood—that is said to be manifested. In each of these moments as expressed in Shinran's writings, the Vow may be said to embody above all the act of awareness or perception of beings in samsaric existence. This is the nature of reality as wisdom-compassion.

In determining his Vow, Dharmakara viewed all the worlds throughout the cosmos and the beings in them, perceiving their qualities and moral nature. He then contemplated what he saw for five kalpas. Based on the Vow arising out of his perception of and reflection on each being throughout the history of existence, Dharmakara next performed practices for aeons to bring every one of them to enlightenment. This is not, however, the usual conception of practice as religious cultivation undertaken to purify the mind and attain enlightenment. Rather, from the beginning, his mind was completely pure. His practice for "countless, incalculable, unequaled . . . kalpas," during which "he always embraced a heart of compassion and patience for all sentient beings,"[44] unfolded naturally from his vision.

The bodhisattva finally completed his practices, fulfilled his Vows, and attained Buddhahood. This attainment as Buddha of immeasurable life and light further emphasizes Dharmakara-Amida's quality of embracing each being throughout time and space. He is "Amida" ("boundless," "infinite") precisely because of this:

> Seeing the sentient beings of the nembutsu
> Throughout the worlds, countless as particles, in the ten quarters,
> The Buddha grasps and never abandons them,
> And therefore is named "Amida."[45]

Amida's essential nature is that he sees all beings in existence; he touches and pervades them as light.

This seeing is reality as inherently personal, acting toward and embracing beings, yet without judgment or discrimination. The Pure Land teachings specify that Amida grasps those who say his Name. This is not a requirement, but rather a consequence of the fact that light, while it manifests the nature of Amida as wisdom-compassion, is "formless form"; it is expressive of the Buddha's working, but cannot be directly apprehended by beings, and they therefore cannot be directly transformed by it. Just as formless dharma-body lies beyond the awareness of beings except through Dharmakara-Amida, so the light cannot by itself lead beings from ignorance. Thus Shinran states, in analyzing the causes of birth in the Pure Land: "Without the virtuous Name, our compassionate father, we would lack the direct cause of birth. Without the light, our compassionate mother, we would stand apart from the indirect cause of birth."[46] If beings who cannot eradicate discriminative thought through contemplative practice are to be reached, light must be accompanied by the aspect of the Name. Here the concept of "design" is reintroduced. The movement of beings to enlightenment must be free of their self-will and calculation; the movement of form arising from suchness, however, culminates in Amida's "design" to awaken beings, thus fulfilling the nature of reality as wisdom-compassion.

Although the realization of shinjin is characterized as "spontaneous," being essentially divided from the will of beings and any process of attainment we might initiate, it is not merely accidental or mechanical, nor is it predetermined. Since it is a being's attainment of shinjin, it must possess an aspect or dimension of a particular person's act in the course of life. It cannot, however, be an act arising from the egocentric perspective of our ordinary existence or the aims and devices of our will, based on the delusional separation of self from others and the objectification of all beings in the world. The human act that manifests the emergence of the Buddha's mind in beings and that further is an act of one's own, free of teleological or calculative will, is to say the Name of the Other in response to the Buddha's self-revelation, thereby entering and completing the Buddha's act. It is in this that we find the necessity and inevitability of the Name as "great practice," that practice which, arising from shinjin, is the Buddha's act and holds the Buddha's virtues. It is but another aspect of what is symbolized by light, for, as stated in the tradition, "one says the Name of the Tathagata in accord with the Tathagata's light, which is the embodiment of wisdom."[47]

Further, although the Name is said to resound throughout the ten quarters, it must be communicated to us directly, and this requires personal contact with the teaching. Shinran states, "If you should come to realize this practice and shinjin, rejoice at the conditions from the distant past that have brought it about."[48] These conditions include prior encounters with the Buddhist teaching and acts which have led to present hearing of the Vow. Most concretely, contact is brought about through the work of historical figures and living people who have transmitted the teaching of Amida, and Shinran regards such people as manifestations of the Buddha. From the stance of his realization of shinjin, he reveres those who have embodied Amida's activity toward him from the infinite past, including Shakyamuni (manifestation of Amida), those who occasioned Shakyamuni's teaching of the Pure Land (Vaidehī, Ajataśatru, etc.), Prince Shotoku (manifestation of Bodhisattva Avalokiteśvara), and Honen (Bodhisattva Mahāsthāmaprāpta). Thus, the concept of manifestation of form from formless reality develops to include Amida and the Pure Land (light of wisdom), the Name, and the persons who have guided one to the teaching.

Finally, to respond to reality apprehended as interpersonal implies the emerging presence of oneself—the self of samsaric existence grasped by the Buddha's seeing—to oneself. This is the meaning of the two faces of "deeply entrusting mind": awareness of attainment of birth through the Vow and awareness of oneself as "a foolish being of karmic evil caught in birth-and-death."[49] Although birth is settled, the stance of egocentricity, of attachment and aversion, is not eradicated; thus, impulses toward a self-magnifying appropriation of the Vow may arise. Shinran was aware of such feelings in himself, and spoke of the lingering attachment manifested in an incident in which he embarked on a program of sutra recitation to benefit beings.[50] Hence the admonition by the compiler of *Tannisho*:

> If shinjin has become settled, birth will be brought about by Amida's activity, so there must be no designing on our part. Even when our thoughts and deeds are evil, then, if we thereby turn all the more deeply to the power of the Vow, gentleheartedness and forbearance will surely arise in us through its spontaneous working (*jinen*).[51]

In the mature phase, still, "our desires are countless, and anger, wrath, jealousy, and envy are overwhelming"; when such feelings arise, however, one should not seek to overcome and suppress them with an aim to making oneself good, but should reflect on the Vow, which has always been active from before. Shinran speaks of the experience of being "known beforehand."[52] In this way, one comes to recognize those impulses from beyond their stance, thereby allowing a true gentleheartedness to arise unwilled. Such is the unfolding of an interpersonal apprehension of reality.

Teleological Perspective: Aspiration to Wisdom-Compassion

A person's attainment of birth in the Pure Land is settled with realization of shinjin; at that point, the bonds of birth-and-death are severed. Complete transcendence of samsaric existence and realization of Buddhahood, however, remains in the future, at death in this world. Thus, it is said that shinjin is itself aspiration for enlightenment. Here, the teleological vector of desire for the transcendent, which is the original impulse in the initial phase, is reborn—or rather, it arises for the first time as aspiration for what is truly transcendent and not merely an extension of mundane attachments. Shinjin is the seed that will unfailingly result in enlightenment (being the mind pervaded by dharmabody), and it is also aspiration for that enlightenment (being fused with the self of samsaric existence). Further, such aspiration is invariably bidirectional; it is both teleological and interpersonal, being desire for enlightenment and at the same time desire to save all living things:

> True and real shinjin is none other than the aspiration to become a Buddha. . . . This aspiration for Buddhahood is none other than the wish to save all beings. The wish to save all beings is the wish to bear all beings across the great ocean of birth-and-death. This shinjin is the aspiration to bring all beings to the attainment of supreme nirvana; it is the heart of great love and great compassion. This shinjin is Buddha-nature and Buddha-nature is Tathagata.[53]

Just as awareness of the certainty of birth includes awakening to one's distance from enlightenment, so shinjin as the mind of compassion is pervaded by an awareness of the distortions of one's vision, the tenacity of self-attachment, and the limitations of one's powers. Nevertheless, it is a seed that will flower fully when people enter the Pure Land; at that point, "with great love and great compassion immediately reaching their fullness in them, they return to the ocean of birth-and-death to save all sentient beings."[54]

Deliberate yet selfless exercise of compassionate action lies in the future, with return from the Pure Land. Nevertheless, even in the present the Buddha's mind may become, in beings, an emerging awareness both of themselves and of others, and with deepening immersion in the mind of the Vow, a vision like that expressed by Shinran may arise: "All living things have been my parents and brothers and sisters in the course of countless lives in many states of existence. Upon attaining Buddhahood in the next life, I must save every one of them."[55] Here, we see that the egocentric stance of the self has been broken through and transcended.

In the mature phase, then, while one has realized shinjin that is the mind of Buddha, one remains a being of temporal existence. On the one hand, "one has already attained what one shall attain" and is the "equal of the Tathagatas." On the other hand, one recognizes Amida's working toward one in the past and grasping one in the present, and is filled with gratitude, and at the same time aspires to attain enlightenment and allay the pain of beings entangled in samsaric existence in the future. With such an integration of interpersonal and teleological modes of apprehending the transcendent, Shinran delineates a remarkably consistent and thorough vision of reality as love or compassion, one which is fully consonant with Mahayana conceptions of nondiscriminative wisdom.

Conclusion: The Creative Work of the Nembutsu Practicer

At immediate issue for practicers in the Pure Land path is less the acceptance of certain metaphysical assertions than the nature of conceptual constructions of the world, and how apprehension of reality is possible that is not ultimately shaped and motivated by the attachments of the egocentric self and the historical and cultural circumstances in which its desires and aversions have been nurtured. I have sought to show, through formulations of the teaching in disparate but sequential modes of engagement, that this is not a mere regression, in which one accepts as dogma that the self is delusional and the world impermanent. The problem is to come to a coherent and intelligible understanding of oneself and the world that ignores neither the historical and emotional boundness of the self nor the variety and worth of experience. The Pure Land path functions to guide practicers to such awareness.

A thoroughgoing penetration of ordinary conceptual life by an apprehension of its own limitations and distortions is not possible simply through the adoption of one further conception, but only as a new mode of conceptuality. Truth here is not proposition or conceptual construct, nor an emptiness in which all conceptions are rendered uniformly meaningless or conceptual thought itself transcended. It may be said to be a mode of perception and action in which the self is self-aware from the stance of the transcendent, or the transcendent is self-aware from the locus of the practicer's life. Self-awareness, since it emerges as an element of human life in the world, implies conceptuality and language. But where the content is the practicer's life together with others, this awareness involves the permeability of such conceptuality by its own inevitable inadequacy and distortion, and where the content is the transcendent, it is pervaded by a dimension of inconceivability in which awareness is the transcendent itself. In both cases, conceptuality fused with the transcendence of its horizons and dualisms allows for the growth of awareness, which ceases to be repetition of prior attachments and becomes genuinely creative activity in the world.

The practice of the Pure Land path is not to determine good and evil, accomplish good, and eradicate evil, for the permeability of conceptuality implies the collapse of any stance for an absolutized subject to view, judge, and impose its will on itself and the world. This does not mean, however, that the world is perceived as a morally homogeneous flatland or that the practicer is merely passive. The terrain is newly marked, not by determinations of gain and loss or right and wrong that shore up the righteousness of the self, but by a heightened and acute sense of both pain and gratitude—the pain visited on other living beings and the expenditure of life-energy borne by the closely interwoven world that is the cost for one's own existence, and the joy in and gratitude for one's own life as the locus of the activity of wisdom-compassion that arises in one's acts from beyond the delusional horizons of the self. Out of such awareness emerges the vocation of the Pure Land practicer, which is the call to see and experience the self and the beings of the world anew, not objectified, but with ever greater breadth and clarity.

In terms of the teaching, this is to live by Amida's Name and light. The Shin practicer's job of work is to hear and say the nembutsu. This is for one's self and world to become manifest to the self; it is for one to come to speak what is true within ordinary words and to enact what is real within the contexts of daily life. The obligation of the Shin path is above all to know the self and world by the exercise of such awareness, for such knowing allows for the arising of a world of action in which the reified self is no longer absolute center.

When banished from the capital during a persecution of Honen's nembutsu teaching, Shinran could both condemn the injustice that had been perpetrated by court and ecclesiastic authorities and express joy that his exile afforded an opportunity for the people of the countryside to encounter the dharma. As Nishida comments, he "looked to the dharma and not who a person was."[56] The failure of Shin institutions to develop, among Shin practicers, this transsocial sense of awareness and responsibility of the decentered self may, ironically, be indirectly ascribable to one of Shinran's radical innovations: the delineation of his own mode of existence as a nembutsu practicer as "neither priest nor worldly." In concrete terms, this meant that he wore monk's robes and taught the dharma, but at the same time abandoned monastic precepts and adopted family life. Though a fundamental break with tradition at the time, married priesthood has become the accepted norm in Japan in temples of almost all Buddhist schools,[57] indicating not the embracing of Shinran's evaluation of monastic practice, but rather the adoption by temple complexes of generational inheritance and hierarchal structures typified by the emperor system. The intrinsic social conservatism of such practices is obvious.

In Shinran, also, we see the impulse to rely on family ties, especially in his decision, in old age, to dispatch his son to the distant Kanto region to settle doctrinal disputes. But when his son abused his relationship with Shinran in order to assert his own authority, Shinran disowned him. This disownment, which is commonly described in Japanese scholarly literature as a "tragic" event of Shinran's last years, may be seen not as merely an accident of history, but as manifesting an aspect of his own religious path, one which has transformation rather than simple transmission as its core.

Perhaps the first great lesson learned by Shin Buddhists from Christian traditions is an institutional practice seen in the United States. There, Shin temples are not passed down from resident priest to son, as in Japan, but are held by the community. There is no question that it has been the often self-sacrificing dedication of generations of priests in Japan that has ensured the preservation of temples and traditions in times of hardship. Nevertheless, if Shin communities abroad are able to overcome the defensive and ingrown leanings that tend to dominate the temple institution, it may be there that a genuinely contemporary formulation of the practicer's existence as "neither priest nor worldly" will eventually be born and nurtured.

Notes

1. *Church Dogmatics* (Edinburgh: T. & T. Clark, 1961), vol. 1, 2: 342.

2. I use the romanization of the term *shinjin* 信心, usually translated "faith" or "trust," in order to avoid misunderstandings of Shinran's usage that might result from employing a term from Western tradition. Shinran's distinctive understanding of shinjin will be clarified in the body of this chapter.

3. Pure Land writings in Chinese and Japanese, including Shinran's, in general lack gender-specific reference. Dharmakara, the bodhisattva who becomes Amida after aeons of practice in the narrative of the Primal Vow, is male (former king); Shinran also speaks of Amida using the image of compassionate mother. For most Shin Buddhists, Amida is probably apprehended as possessing both fatherly and motherly characteristics.

4. From the English translation of *Church Dogmatics*. Cf. my translation in *Tannishō: A Primer* (Kyoto: Ryukoku University, 1982): "Even a good person can attain birth in the Pure Land, so it goes without saying that an evil person will" (section 3).

5. *Church Dogmatics*, vol. 1, 2: 342. Romanization adapted; emphasis added.

6. James Dobbins, *Jōdo Shinshū: Shin Buddhism in Medieval Japan* (Bloomington: Indiana University Press, 1989), p. 2 (emphasis added). It should be noted that although Shinran states that shinjin is the cause of birth in the Pure Land, the equivalent of "salvation through faith" in terms of expressive power to epitomize the path is "birth [in the Pure Land] through the nembutsu" (*nembutsu ōjō*), in which nembutsu is the practice of verbal saying of the Name of Amida Buddha. As discussed below, the element of practice remains central in Shinran's thought, despite the significance he gives to shinjin.

7. Dobbins, p. 160.

8. In *Beyond Dialogue: Toward a Mutual Transformation of Christianity and Buddhism* (Philadelphia: Fortress Press, 1982), especially chapter 6, "The Christian Witness to Buddhists."

9. *Teaching, Practice, and Realization*, "Chapter on Practice," 100, in Dennis Hirota et al., trans., *The Collected Works of Shinran*, 1: 67–68. A version of the following section originally appeared as Dennis Hirota, "Breaking the Darkness: Images of Reality in the Shin Buddhist Path," *Japanese Religions* (Kyoto) 16, 3 (January 1991): 17–45. A Japanese version appears in my book, *Shinran: Shūkyō Gengo no Kakumeisha* (Kyoto: Hōzōkan, 1998), pp. 13–57.

10. See *Teaching, Practice, and Realization*, "Chapter on True Buddha and Land," 39, in *The Collected Works of Shinran*, 1: 203.

11. That such problems troubled Shinran's followers is clear from letters in which he answers direct questions: "Although we speak of Vow and of Name, these are not two different things. There is no Name separate from the Vow; there is no Vow separate from the Name" (*Lamp for the Latter Ages*, letter 9, in *The Collected Works of Shinran*, 1:536); "Although the one moment of shinjin and the one moment of nembutsu are two, there is no nembutsu separate from shinjin, nor is the one moment of shinjin separate from the one moment of nembutsu" (*Lamp for the Latter Ages*, letter 11, in *The Collected Works of Shinran*, 1: 538).

12. In the enumeration and portions of the analysis of these two models— teleological and interpersonal—I draw on Gordon Kaufman, "Two Models of Transcendence," in *God the Problem* (Cambridge: Harvard University Press, 1972), pp. 72–81. I follow Kaufman in considering these as the principle models of apprehending the transcendent and as developing from bases in ordinary human experience. How far "teleology" as a Western philosophical concept is appropriate in a Pure Land context may be open to debate. My chief concern, however, is with the dialectical tension that develops between the interpersonal and teleological as general modes of engagement with transcendent reality in the Pure Land path. It should be noted, therefore, that my usage differs from that of Kaufman, who argues for the superiority of the interpersonal model as genuinely transcendent, pointing out that another person always transcends our direct experience and can be known only by acts of self-revelation, while the transcendent as teleological must in actuality be apprehended on the basis of present experience. From a Buddhist perspective, it might be said that the more basic problem is objectifying conceptual thought, and that this problem remains whether the object is viewed as a person or a thing. Concerning the teleological mode, I have also referred to Huston Smith, "Beyond the Modern Western Mind-set," in *Beyond the Post-Modern Mind* (New York, 1982), 153.

13. Kaufman, "Two Models of Transcendence," p. 77.

14. *Teaching, Practice, and Realization*, "Chapter on Practice," 84, in *The Collected Works of Shinran*, 1: 61.

15. Kaufman, "Two Models of Transcendence," p. 74.

16. E.g., David Tracy describes two kinds of "limit-situations in the world of the everyday": "'boundary' situations of guilt, anxiety, sickness and the recognition of death" and "'ecstatic experiences'—intense joy, love, reassurance, creation," in *Blessed Rage for Order* (New York: Seabury Press, 1975), p. 105.

17. In *Zen no kenkyū*, chapter 32. For a translation, see *An Inquiry into the Good* (New Haven: Yale University Press, 1990), pp. 173–76. There is also a translation and discussion of relevant passages in Dennis Hirota, *Wind in the Pines: Classic Writings of the Way of Tea as a Buddhist Path* (Fremont: Asian Humanities Press, 1995, pp. 105–116.

18. *Tannishō*, Postscript and section 2.

19. *Teaching, Practice, and Realization,* "Chapter on Shinjin," 52, in *The Collected Works of Shinran,* 1: 108.

20. *Teaching, Practice, and Realization,* "Chapter on Practice," 101, in *The Collected Works of Shinran,* 1: 68.

21. Transformed Buddha-bodies and transformed Buddha lands are discussed in the final chapter of *Teaching, Practice, and Realization.*

22. An outline of these stages may be found in *The Collected Works of Shinran,* 2: 66–69.

23. *Lamp for the Latter Ages,* letter 17, in *The Collected Works of Shinran,* 1: 548.

24. Dennis Hirota, "Shinran's View of Language: A Buddhist Hermeneutics of Faith," *Eastern Buddhist* 26, 1 (Spring 1993): 50–93, and 2 (Autumn 1993): 91–130. See also chapter 6 below. In Japanese, see my articles "Shinran no Gengo-kan," *Shisō* (Iwanami Shoten) 871 (January 1997): 54–80; and "Shinran Shisō to Kaishaku," *Nihon Kenkyū* (Kokusai Nihon Bunka Kenkyū Sentā and Kadokawa Shoten) 17 (February 1998): 47–86; and my book *Shinran: Shūkyō Gengo no Kakumeisha* (Kyoto: Hōzōkan, 1998).

25. *Notes on 'Essentials of Faith Alone',* in *The Collected Works of Shinran,* 1: 461.

26. Ibid.

27. Shōkū (1177–1247), Shinran's contemporary and fellow disciple of Hōnen, also identifies two dimensions of Buddha. However, basing himself on *The Awakening of Faith,* he adopts the distinction of "unchanging suchness" *(fuhen shinnyo)* and "suchness manifesting itself according to conditions" *(zuien shinnyo)* and identifies Amida with both. That is, unlike Shinran, he regards Amida not only as Buddha manifesting form from suchness, but also as formless reality itself. This tendency of thought, traceable to esoteric teachings, emphasizes an interpersonal over a teleological model, and results in an assertion of the nonduality of practicer and Amida Buddha in acts of temporal existence. See my article, "Religious Transformation in Shinran and Shōkū," *Pure Land* 3 (December 1987): 57–69.

28. Quoted in *Teaching, Practice, and Realization,* "Chapter on Shinjin," 61, in *The Collected Works of Shinran,* 1: 111.

29. *Notes on Once-calling and Many-calling,* in *The Collected Works of Shinran,* 1: 474.

30. *Teaching, Practice, and Realization,* "Chapter on Shinjin," 65, in *The Collected Works of Shinran,* 1: 112.

31. The tract "On Attaining the Settled Mind" (*Anjin ketsujō shō*), influential in the Shin tradition since the fourteenth century, asserts the simultaneity of Amida's attainment of enlightenment and beings' attainment of birth; for my translation, see *Eastern Buddhist* 23, 2 (Autumn 1990): 106–21 and 24, 1 (Spring 1991): 81–96. For a recent treatment of the ramifications of such a concept, see Nishitani Keiji, "The Problem of Time in Shinran," trans. Dennis Hirota, *Eastern Buddhist* 11, 1 (May 1978): 13–26.

32. *Teaching, Practice, and Realization,* "Chapter on Shinjin," 116, in *The Collected Works of Shinran,* 1: 138.

33. *Lamp for the Latter Ages,* letter 2, in *The Collected Works of Shinran,* 1: 526.

34. *Notes on the Inscriptions on Sacred Scrolls,* in *The Collected Works of Shinran,* 1: 513.

35. *Notes on Once-calling and Many-calling,* in *The Collected Works of Shinran,* 1:474.

36. Ibid.

37. *Teaching, Practice, and Realization,* "Chapter on Shinjin," 78, in *The Collected Works of Shinran,* 1: 115.

38. *Tannishō: A Primer,* section 2, p. 23, and also The Collected Works of Shinran, 1:662.

39. *Notes on 'Essentials of Faith Alone',* in *The Collected Works of Shinran,* 1: 453.

40. *Hymns of the Dharma-Ages,* hymn 40, in *The Collected Works of Shinran,* 1: 408.

41. *Lamp for the Latter Ages,* letter 4, in *The Collected Works of Shinran,* 1: 529.

42. *Notes on Once-calling and Many-calling,* in *The Collected Works of Shinran,* 1: 481.

43. *Lamp for the Latter Ages,* letter 3, in *The Collected Works of Shinran,* 1: 528.

44. *Sutra of the Tathagata of Immeasurable Life,* quoted in *Teaching, Practice, and Realization,* "Chapter on Shinjin," 23, in *The Collected Works of Shinran,* 1: 96.

45. *Hymns of the Pure Land,* 82, in *The Collected Works of Shinran,* 1: 347.

46. *Teaching, Practice, and Realization,* "Chapter on Practice," 72, in *The Collected Works of Shinran,* 1: 54.

47. Vasubandhu's *Treatise on the Pure Land,* quoted by T'an-luan, in "Chapter on Practice," 19, in *The Collected Works of Shinran,* 1: 27.

48. *Teaching, Practice, and Realization,* Preface, in *The Collected Works of Shinran,* 1: 4.

49. Shan-tao, in "Chapter on Shinjin," 13, in *The Collected Works of Shinran,* 1:85.

50. Described in a letter of his wife Eshinni, *Eshinni Shokan,* letter 5, in *Teihon Shinran Shōnin Zenshū* (Kyoto: Hōzōkan, 1973) 3: 196.

51. *Tannishō: A Primer,* section 16, p. 40, and also *The Collected Works of Shinran,* 1: 676.

52. *Tannishō: A Primer,* section 9, p. 27, and also *The Collected Works of Shinran,* 1: 665.

53. *Notes on 'Essentials of Faith Alone',* in *The Collected Works of Shinran,* 1: 463.

54. *Notes on 'Essentials of Faith Alone',* in *The Collected Works of Shinran,* 1: 454.

55. *Tannishō: A Primer,* section 5, p. 25; also *The Collected Works of Shinran,* 1: 664.

56. In "Gutoku Shinran," *Shisaku to Taiken* (1915), in *Nishida Kitarō Zenshū* (Tokyo: Iwanami Shoten, 1966), 1: 407–409. For a translation, see my article, "On Nishida's Gutoku Shinran," *Eastern Buddhist* 28, 2 (Autumn 1995): 231–44.

57. Exceptions in which celibacy is required include, for example, the Fuju-fuse sect of the Nichiren school.

2. Understanding Amida Buddha and the Pure Land

A Process Approach

John S. Yokota

Experience tells us that the world is a supportive and enjoyable abode and, at the same time, that it is a frightening and excruciating hell. These two intuitions of reality are mutually contradictory, and yet they work paradoxically to correct and balance one another. Shin Buddhism affirms the ultimately compassionate character of the world, calling it Amida Buddha, and yet it also recognizes the reality and corruption of evil. What then does it mean to say that Amida Buddha is compassionate—indeed, compassion itself—in light of this evil? In this chapter on Amida Buddha and Amida's Pure Land we will venture rarely articulated views on how we can and should regard Amida Buddha in relation to this religiously plural world in which we live. The challenges to traditional formulations offers an opportunity to extend our horizons beyond our respective historical, social, and ethnic limits to a more comprehensive vision of reality.[1]

Regarding Amida Buddha, I touch on two major aspects: the pathos of Amida, and the relationship between Amida Buddha and Shakyamuni Buddha. The first, what I call "the pathos of Amida," intends to draw out the basic implications of why Amida is called compassionate. Here, the process notions of the consequent nature of God, or God's receptive characteristic and divine persuasion, or how God acts in and on the world come into play and serve as my reference points in reflection. The second, the relationship between Amida Buddha and Shakyamuni Buddha, intends not only to clarify the nature of Amida Buddha, but also to confront the mythical foundation of the Pure Land tradition. It is asserted that a correct understanding of Shakyamuni's position in the Pure Land tradition would portray him as the concrete actualization of Amida's compassion.

There is a twofold purpose to our thinking on the Pure Land. First, we need to make sense of birth in the Pure Land upon physical death in light of modern assumptions of death and rebirth. Second, we need to clarify what is meant by the Pure Land to see how the claim of Amida's compassion is brought to fulfillment by Amida's gathering us in and transmuting our evil karma into that karma one with Amida's. Here, the categories of objective and subjective immortality in process theology were useful guidelines in my reflections.

The Pathos of Amida

The phrase *pathos of Amida*, was inspired by Jewish thinker Abraham J. Heschel's term *God of pathos*.[2] The primordial characterization of Amida as compassionate has obvious implications for what Amida is and how Amida acts upon our lives. If compassionate, then Amida feels and gathers in the feelings and desires of all existence; that is, Amida cannot be dispassionate toward what happens in the world. Further, the pathos of Amida means that Amida must be affected by what is happening in the world; in short, Amida has to grow. Finally, as to how a compassionate entity like Amida should act upon others, the general notion of power must be considered with special attention to the Shin Buddhist notions of self-power and other-power.

Divine Pathos

In Heschel's use of the term *pathos*, God feels and has concern for the world. God is not dispassionate but is in constant and intimate relation with the world.[3] This image of a receptive and active God is most explicitly expressed in the passage in Exodus where God tells Moses to lead the children of Israel out of bondage:

> Then the Lord said, "I have observed the misery of my people who are
> in Egypt; I have heard their cry on account of their taskmasters. In-

deed, I know their sufferings, and I have come down to deliver them from the Egyptians, and to bring them up out of that land to a good and broad land, a land flowing with milk and honey. . . . The cry of the Israelites has now come to me: I have also seen how the Egyptians oppress them. So come, I will send you to Pharaoh to bring my people, the Israelites, out of Egypt." (3:7–10; New Revised Standard Version)

Here, God exists in dynamic relation with the world. God observes, hears, and knows what is happening and then actively responds to it. Heschel's thesis and its biblical background are not without problem, however, which Heschel directly confronts in addressing the issue of anthropomorphism.

Anthropomorphism

Heschel resolves the problem of anthropomorphism or anthropopathy by asserting that we are not humanizing God (anthropomorphism) but that God is theo-gizing us (theomorphism).

> Absolute selflessness and mysteriously undeserved love are more akin to the divine than to the human. And if these are characteristics of human nature, then man is endowed with attributes of the divine. God's unconditional concern for justice is not an anthropomorphism. Rather, man's concern for justice is a theomorphism. . . . The language the prophets employed to describe that supreme concern was an anthropomorphism to end all anthropomorphisms.[4]

The *imago dei* metaphor is here being understood, as was its original intent, to indicate that our humanity is ultimately our divinization, partial though it may be. Admittedly, this interpretation is not without its critics. On the other hand, the issue of theomorphism well highlights the perennial problem of how to understand a savior figure who is an "other" distinct from us in a definitive and qualitative sense, versus one who is a savior and creator that is intimately concerned about our welfare. In classical terms, this is the problem of transcendence and immanence.

Transcendence and Immanence

To resolve this dichotomy is to express the need to affirm a dual quality in God where otherness is maintained simultaneously with a basic relatedness. For Heschel, it is clearly this relatedness, an I-Thou relationship of mutuality yet distinction, that he hopes to express with his notion of divine pathos. This simultaneous assertion of opposite characteristics in God and its fundamental rationality is discussed by Charles Hartshorne.

> The formula "dual transcendence" is mine. The basic idea is in Whitehead and still others, but in some respects less sharply formulated. The criticism, made for instance by a conservative English theologian, that it is contradictory to attribute both finitude and infinity, for example, to the same deity is nothing but the neglect of an elementary logical truth, which is that the description of something as both P and not-P (where P is some predicate or property) is contradictory only if the predicate and its negation are applied in "the same respect" to the something in question. And dual transcendence does not make or permit such an application. Moreover, it offers a definite explanation of how the difference in the two respects is possible. The absolute, infinite side is abstract and concerns the divine potentiality or capacity to have values, while the finitude or relativity concerns the divine actuality. If you or I had made different decisions, God would have enjoyed (or suffered) these other decisions. Anything that could be actual God could divinely have, but what God actually has depends partly on creaturely decisions. This is the social structure of existence. The primacy of love means that there is no possible value that any being could have simply in and by itself, or simply by its own decision.[5]

In Whiteheadian terminology, dual transcendence corresponds to the notions of the primordial and consequent natures of God.

> But God, as well as being primordial, is also consequent. He is the beginning and the end. He is not the beginning in the sense of being in the past of all members. He is the presupposed actuality of conceptual operation, in unison of becoming with every other creative act. Thus, by reason of the relativity of all things, there is a reaction of the world on God. The completion of God's nature into a fullness of physical feeling is derived from the objectification of the world in God. He shares with every new creation its actual world; and the concrescent creature is objectified in God as a novel element in God's objectification of that actual world. This prehension into God of each creature is directed with the subjective aim, and clothed with the

subjective form, wholly derivative from all-inclusive primordial valuation. God's conceptual nature is unchanged, by reason of its final completeness. But his derivative nature is consequent upon the creative advance of the world.[6]

In process thought as articulated by both Whitehead and Hartshorne, God is characterized as having a twofold, complementary nature. The timeless or transcendent aspect is the basis for all existence and fundamentally characterizes all moments of existence and as such is very much "part of" each moment of existence. In its primordial nature, God may be transcendent in the sense of being foundational to all existence and as such timeless, yet it is clearly not separated from any one element of existence. Nevertheless, it is clearly the consequent nature of God which emphasizes the mutual relationality of God to other entities of existence through the assertion of the influence of what happens in the world on God. Yet relationality does not go far enough in describing this mutuality, since there is a definite indwelling of God in the world and the world in God. It is here that process thought goes beyond the traditional I-Thou relationality that is the basis of Heschel's divine pathos and suggests the emptiness of Buddhism where interpenetrating mutuality is made possible. It is in this reality of interpenetrating mutuality between God and the world that one can go beyond the simple dichotomy of transcendence and immanence and talk meaningfully of God in the human terms of care and concern, in short, of feelings. Moreover, this mutual ingressing can best be described in the very human and here fully apt terms of love and compassion.

Pathos and Change

As the above process elaboration develops the theology of pathos beyond the I-Thou relationship, so too will a process elaboration clarify the inherent quality of change that must accompany this emotional openness of God. In the Hartshorne and Whitehead passages cited above, it is clear that God, in its consequent nature, is dependent on what happens in the world. There is a contingent element in God, since God is a different God depending on how any one entity of existence responds to the world around it. What makes any one entity of existence what it is, is largely the influence of preceding entities as integrated by the arising entity guided by the sheer force of the creative process and the organizing ideal given to it by God which includes among other ideals the sometimes conflicting notions of harmony and novelty. Since God does not dictate how to integrate the past but suggests the ideal by introducing it into the creative process, God too can be surprised by what happens. The point is that with each new integration of the past that is the arising entity of existence, God grows. It need not be a qualitative growth but merely a quantitative one, since most new integrations mirror the past or do not heed the ideal and disharmony and stagnation are what the new integration actualizes. Nevertheless, all is taken in by God and as such God changes and grows with each new addition.

The theology of pathos necessarily leads to the conclusion that God changes as God responds to what happens in the world. This point, while implied in Heschel's discussion, is not explicitly asserted. It is especially with the notion of the consequent nature of God that process thought can help draw out the implications of the theology of pathos. It is of course this aspect of process thought that is a point of contention for more orthodox theological traditions, but it also marks its distinctive contribution to the discussion. It seems to be a rather straightforward contention that since one holds that God takes in what happens in the world, God must be affected by it and so is changed by the world. Hartshorne makes clear in his discussion of dual transcendence that the changing or growing aspect of God need not negate the timeless, primordial aspect of God. Thus, what process thought does with dual transcendence or the primordial and consequent natures of God is make logically consistent two assertions of the faithful: that God is timeless and the foundation of our existence, and yet simultaneously, that God is not merely aware of our existence but also positively concerned and responsive to it.

It is especially this last point of the change or growth within God that will be emphasized as the doctrine of Amida is discussed in light of the theology of pathos and its process elaboration. It is here and in the basic contention that a God of love is open to its creation that can be helpful to a reconsideration of Amida and the notion of compassion.

Compassion and Pathos

It is my contention that the process modes of thought outlined above could well augment the Buddhist discussion of compassion. All too often, however, enlightenment/wisdom is characterized as passion-less and detached. This can lead readers to the mistaken conclusion that the compassion flowing from it is somehow colorless and unfeel-ing. This perception of an apathetic compassion is further fueled by the ideals of equanimity and stoic aloofness from the vicissitudes of life that mark the common notion of the enlightened one.[7]

Buddhism characterizes reality as compassionate, thus a pivotal issue is to recognize the soteriological context of Buddhist compas-sion.[8] Whether in the early literature centering on the life of Shakyamuni or in the later literature centering on bodhisattva practices, invariably they are related in the context of the salvific activity that aids another's enlightenment. In the Pure Land Buddhist context, the story of Amida—both at the causal stage related to Dharmakara (Dharmākara) Bod-hisattva's practice, and at the fulfilled or recompensed stage of Amida Buddha—centers on those activities that will bring enlightenment to all existence. Thus, Buddhist compassion is fundamentally that con-cern and care toward others expressed in those activities that will bring them to actualize themselves spiritually. This experience can be partially described as a self-awakening to one's true and real self and the true and real world that supports this self.

To aid another to realize enlightenment—the fundamental mean-ing of Buddhist compassion—cannot merely mean to be concerned about that other's spiritual needs divorced from the person's physical needs. Compassion then is concern for the whole person. This concern is manifested primarily as an awakening to and actualization of suchness, where one is caused to see oneself and the world in their suchness, and through this seeing one is caused to become this suchness. Suchness, then, is not a passive acceptance but an active becoming of this suchness.

Here, an integral element to understanding suchness is the inter-penetrating unity of all entities of existence where both individuality and unity are maintained simultaneously. The Indra-net metaphor of the Hua-yen tradition expresses this well. Each individual entity of existence includes the whole of existence in this very individuality. We see the whole of reality in any one individual and the individual in the whole of reality. This interpenetrating unity means that there is a basic openness of all entities of existence toward all other entities, a basic and inherent freedom and equality of all entities of existence. This is how the world should be, for, in the end, there is a basic preference for this actuality. The spiritual element is obvious, yet the physical or socio-political element must be as obviously apparent. There are both spiritual and socio-political structures of existence which impede or negate this suchness and so must be addressed if concern for the actualization of suchness in any one entity and the world as a whole is indeed the goal of compassion.

Compassion, then, while used in a specific Buddhist sense, also can and must be used also in its general and normative sense. Moreover, if the interpenetrating unity noted above is an integral element in the Buddhist vision of reality, then the sense of compassion as openness and concern toward the other has to be an inherent element of this suchness. In short, an apathy toward or dissociation from others is anathema. If Amida is to be primordially characterized as compassionate, then there must be a real concern and openness toward all elements of existence—what I call the pathos of Amida.

If we recognize the pathos of Amida, then with it comes our acknowledgment of Amida as being intimately related to all aspects of our lives. As we individually struggle to answer the call of Amida to actualize our true and real selves in the true and real world, we take in all we can from the world and give back to it freely and openly. In short, Amida compassionately takes in all our struggles, triumphs, and defeats and is thereby enriched, or lessened, by our responses. Amida is affected by how we react to the world and Amida's call to compassion. In this, Amida calls us to actualize a compassion not unlike the compassion that Amida embodies.

Power and Pathos

As the process notion of the consequent nature of God makes clear, not only does God change and grow because of the response of each entity of existence, God does not know what this response will be. God does not control the actions of any entity of existence. In this declaration of the intrinsic freedom of all entities of existence to exercise this power of choice within the limits of the conditions they find themselves, we find a limit, if you will, to the power of God over the entities of existence. It is from this fact of existence that process thought talks about the persuasive rather than coercive force in the activity of God. In the same vein, it is best, then, to talk of the Other Power of Amida as a persuasive power rather than a coercive power. Moreover, this persuasive power inherently acknowledges the inviolable quality of individual freedom. Thus, the power that emanates from the self cannot be simply negated, requiring us to reexamine the Pure Land notions of self-power and Other Power in this light.

The sheer opposition between the doctrines of self-power and Other Power leaves no room for contingencies. Ever since Shinran emphatically declared his "faith alone" position, any possible efficacy of self-power was thrown out; Other Power alone was what mattered in the end. While this standard rhetoric sounds plausible, the need to negate selfish orientation in a religious setting being understandable, is it really the case that self- and Other Power are mutually opposed? Here, rather than adopting the straight self-power/Other Power dichotomy, I have found it fruitful to think in terms of empowerment by Other Power. In this empowerment paradigm, Other Power neither negates nor overpowers self-power; it becomes, instead, a new source of power for the self, such that Other Power empowers the self. This empowerment by Other Power is a persuasive empowering in which, through a variety of life experiences, we are cajoled to accept the truth of our lives and thereby transform ourselves to conform with that truth.

Other Power shows us what is real, and this becomes the persuasive force for us to actualize this reality. Other Power forcefully makes its argument by having the real self and real world break into our imaginings of who we are and what the world is. Forced to open up to ourselves and to the world we inhabit, we are forced to feel and experience and be true to that feeling and experience. The openness and concern that Amida exemplifies should in the end corroborate with how we relate to ourselves and to our world, imperfect though it may be.

The persuasive power of Amida is this constant incursion of real life into our fabricated view of life. But the truth of the matter is that we rarely heed the call to a life of openness and concern. That call is made repeatedly, in hopes that, should the opportunity arise, it will be there to beckon us toward the truth.

Amida and Shakyamuni

The importance of Shakyamuni to Shinran is that Shakyamuni in the Pure Land sutras relates the story of Amida. From a historical-critical perspective, this view is untenable, since the story of Amida is an ahistorical myth. For Shinran, however, the Amida story is historically true, and it was important for him to anchor Amida in the historicity of Shakyamuni. In the latter half of this section we will attempt to elucidate this sense of history, or remembering, into our views of Amida and Shakyamuni, without subverting our modern critical sense.

Shinran centers his thoughts on Amida as dharma-for-us,[9] a Buddha ever concerned with enlightening all existence. For Shinran, the dharma is nothing but dharma-for-us. Shinran rarely talks about the historical actualization of Amida, although it is not altogether absent. In his hymns Shinran identifies Shakyamuni and Honen (Genkū) as actualizations of Amida.

> Amida, primordially established,
> Feeling compassion for the foolish ones of the five defilements
> Actualized himself as Shakyamuni
> And appeared at the castle of Kapilavastu.[10]

> The Tathagata Amida, transformed,
> As master Genkū actualized
> Conditions expended,
> He returns to the Pure Land.[11]

Further, there is a sense of remembering, a sense of history in Shinran as he talks of Amida Buddha and Dharmakara Bhiksu in the causal state before becoming Amida. In Shinran's "Hymn of True Shinjin," for example, he relates the story of Dharmakara establishing the Vows and, in their fulfillment, Amida embracing all existence in the glow of its light, as well as Shakyamuni and the Pure Land masters proclaiming the wonder of Amida's compassionate intent.[12] This story of Amida, in particular the establishing of the Vows, had historicity for Shinran.

It is obviously an error for contemporary interpreters of Shinran to bring their own mindset into the hermeneutical process and make claims about his understanding of problems from that viewpoint. However, it is equally erroneous to assume that a person of medieval Japan could not have conceived of matters in a contemporary vein. That is, it is not totally impossible that Shinran thought of the Amida myth and of Dharmakara raising the Vows in the existentialistlike manner of the collapsing of time in the now-moment of faith, and in his writings there are suggestive passages that lend themselves to such an understanding: "Pondering the mind of true entrusting of oneself to Amida, this mind of entrusting has one-moment. One moment expresses the moment of entrusting as being the ultimate point of time."[13] On the other hand, he talks about events as events in history which evoke a sense of remembering. Is it not our contemporary prejudice against historical apprehension of a mythical event that prevents us from recognizing that Shinran literally believed the story? But if he talked about the historical actualizations of Amida, and if he had this sense of remembering, this sense of history, then we cannot ignore it when considering his treatment of the Amida myth. This does not mean we must adopt a stance of literal belief in the myth and throw out recent critical research. It simply means we must acknowledge the role this sense of remembering played in Shinran. This sense of remembering supported his faith, allowing him to secure the subjective reality of faith in the objectivity of history.

The story of Amida with its mythic language of kalpas (eons) and kotis (infinite distances) is obviously symbolic, and this, I believe, has been the way it has been understood by the faithful in all ages. This explains the lack of resistance toward the critical research that came to Asia at the turn of the twentieth century, and why, to a large extent, the findings of such research were really never confronted. But believers in general, and Shinran in particular, also took the story at face value and saw it as relating an event occurring in the primordial past. This attribution of some sort of historicity to the myth, however, is something that we cannot honestly share.

The Actualization of Amida in History

When the myth of Amida is viewed critically, the parallel with the life of Shakyamuni is obvious. The Amida myth can be seen as modeled after the life of Shakyamuni and amplifies themes of compassion in his life. This critical historical interpretation is probably true, but this is not the historicity that Shinran had in mind. Shinran saw Shakyamuni as the communicator of the story of Amida. Shakyamuni's prime function in the world, according to Shinran, was to proclaim the Vows of Amida. This is expressed in the "Hymn of True Shinjin and the Nembutsu," wherein Shinran states: "The Tathagata appeared in this world only in order to declare the reality of Amida's Primal Vow."[14] His position as the first teacher is evident in a widely noted *Tannisho* passage:

> If the Vow of Amida is real, the teachings of Shakyamuni cannot be
> false. If the Buddha-teachings are true, the commentaries by Shan-tao
> cannot be false. If the commentaries of Shan-tao are true, how can the
> teachings of Honen be false? If the teachings of Honen are true, how
> can the heart of what I, Shinran, say be false and empty?[15]

The above passages explicitly center on the fact that Shakyamuni taught the reality of Amida's Vow, hence his importance to the Pure Land tradition. The earlier cited hymns relating Shinran's belief that Shakyamuni and Honen were actualizations of Amida can be interpreted to mean that Shakyamuni and Honen proclaimed the reality of the Vow. The actualization of Amida in history focuses on the teachings of Shakyamuni and Honen and, by extension, the teachings of the other Pure Land masters. The fact that Honen spoke of Amida's Vow cannot be denied, but the fact is that Shakyamuni said nothing of Amida.

It is impossible to be certain as to the core of Shakyamuni's teachings, but it is clear that he did not speak of Amida and Dharmakara's raising of the Vows. Indeed, while the teachings of the Nikaya and Agama literature are clearly related to Shakyamuni, the Mahayana sutras' relation to Shakyamuni is tenuous, to say the least. As a result, Shinran's view of Shakyamuni is based on the erroneous assumption, shared by all Buddhists of his time, that Shakyamuni was the source of all sutras. One cannot fault Shinran for being a person of his times, but one cannot accept this assumption today. Thus, the position attributed to Shakyamuni in the Pure Land tradition centers on a now erroneous and unacceptable premise. As religious traditions must revise themselves in accordance with contemporary historical knowledge, this fact that Shakyamuni could not be the source of the Amida myth must be acknowledged. Nevertheless, the intuition of Shinran to secure the reality of Amida's Vows in the historicity of Shakyamuni is correct. A problem arises how can this be done while being both faithful to this intuition and to the historical-critical results of contemporary Buddhist Studies.

There is no question as to the existence of Shakyamuni. Inscriptions commissioned by the Indian emperor Asoka verify Shakyamuni's existence and influence. A core of his teachings can be discerned with caution, and it includes no explicit discussion of the saving and compassionate reality of Amida. Indeed, his teachings tend to avoid any hint of the notion of grace. His death scene includes an exhortion to the disciples to secure their own salvation. There is a hint of grace or compassion in the stories of the acts of Shakyamuni, and a closer look at the teachings to discern positive discussion of the compassionate intent may be worthwhile. Nevertheless, it is impossible to secure Amida's Vow specifically on what can be historically known of particular sayings and deeds of Shakyamuni.

There is, nevertheless, the undeniable fact of Shakyamuni's teaching to and gathering of followers. The traditional biography of Shakyamuni states that he gained enlightenment at the age of thirty-five and spent the rest of his life teaching. He spent thirty-five years searching for the dharma and forty-five years teaching the dharma. Whether this chronology is exactly accurate is unimportant. There can be little doubt that after some years of struggle, he came to see reality as it is and began to talk of his realization and thereby influence people. This is the undeniable, historical fact of Shakyamuni's life. Shakyamuni is said to have encountered many temptations and hindrances as he sat under the bodhi tree in his final attempt at fathoming reality. This inner struggle is personified in the stories of the temptations of Mara. The "last temptation" is that of remaining in the meditation of wisdom and fulfilling his goal of ultimate enlightenment (parinirvana). Moreover, he is told by Mara that even if he were to teach, no one would understand. Shakyamuni denies himself the full satisfaction of ultimate enlightenment and disregards the probability of people not accepting or understanding his teachings. He gets up from the seat of enlightenment and goes forth to preach his first sermon at the Deer Park. It is in this act of going forth from the seat of enlightenment to teach that the dharma-for-us is actualized in history. The Buddha Shakyamuni seated under the bodhi tree fully actualizes himself in the getting up from that seat of enlightenment and going forth. It is to this act that Shin Buddhists can turn to and secure the ahistorical Amida in the flow of history.

Unlike Shinran, we cannot look back to Dharmakara establishing the Vows nor can we look back to Shakyamuni telling the story of Amida. Nor is it possible or desirable to do so from our modern perspective. What we can look back to is the fact that Shakyamuni rejected full enlightenment for himself to tell others of this enlightenment experience and how they too could partake of it. It is in this rejection of enlightenment that, paradoxically, Shakyamuni fulfills enlightenment and actualizes in history the compassion that is enlightenment. Amida is actualized in history by Shakyamuni going forth to teach others. Amida is not actualized by the Amida story or by Shakyamuni telling of the Amida story, because neither is a historical event. Amida is actualized by the act of ultimate compassion that is Shakyamuni getting up and going forth from the seat of enlightenment.

The Amida myth is not the abstraction of Shakyamuni's compassionate act. As Shinran says in the earlier cited *Tannisho* passage, the reality of Amida's Vow is the basis of the teaching of Shakyamuni. The myth of Amida reveals the primordial reality of the compassionate and caring dharma-for-us. It is *this* that is actualized and made concrete by the act of Shakyamuni getting up and going forth.

There are two practical implications of this recognition of the actualization of Amida in history through this act of Shakyamuni. On the level of popular worship, it is easier to talk of Amida or dharma-for-us in terms of a historical person and a historical act. Moreover, the founder of our tradition is reincorporated into our development of that tradition in a historically critical way. The second point is that once this is recognized, one can no longer ignore the historical/social context in which one lives. No longer can one say that the subjective state of the mind of entrusting alone is all important. The mind of entrusting while ever subjective and therefore ahistorical is nevertheless in history. Thus, the flow of history in which one finds oneself cannot be ignored.

Objective Immortality and Birth in the Pure Land

The Pure Land and how we are to understand birth in the Pure Land ought to be problematic for the modern thinker. Too often, however, the treatment of such notions does not go beyond traditional formulations. This is especially the case with this central reality of birth in the Pure Land where the usual explanations tend to be ambiguous. There are those who are content to look at birth in the Pure Land merely as a metaphor for spiritual awakening. My thesis does not deny such an understanding, but I would contend that birth in the Pure Land is more than just that. In the following, we will first discuss the Shin Buddhist treatment of the Pure Land and birth in the Pure Land. We will then attempt to interpret birth in the Pure Land in light of the process notion of objective immortality. Finally, we will discuss the advantages of this process interpretation as well as indicate how such a novel interpretation develops certain implications already present in the Shin tradition.

The Pure Land and Birth in the Pure Land

Applying the logic of the middle path, where both extremes are refuted, I would contend that the language of birth in the Pure Land is neither literally descriptive nor merely metaphorical. As modern beings, we cannot accept a literal understanding of the Pure Land as a physical or spiritual realm existing an infinite distance to the west where we are reborn upon death. Not only is the notion of the Pure Land as an otherworldly realm anathema to the present-day mind, it is anathema to the Buddhist philosophical tradition. To affirm Shin Buddhism does not mean we must affirm this kind of literal notion of the Pure Land.

Nor can we understand birth in the Pure Land simply as a metaphor for spiritual rebirth, where birth in the Pure Land represents the culmination of one's personal journey toward fulfillment during one's lifetime. This seemingly viable alternative to understanding Pure Land birth is widely shared, and though I would be loathe to deny it unilaterally, this leaves unanswered certain basic questions as to how to understand this notion of birth in the Pure Land, in particular, what becomes of us upon physical death and rebirth? The Shin Buddhist position is that, upon death, we do not become as if we never existed, but rather we partake in the timeless reality of Amida; thus in some basic way we remain forever. How are we to understand this?

Classical Pure Land texts present a dearth of descriptions of the Pure Land that implicitly convey its character. In the *Larger Sutra*, the central scripture of the tradition, the story begins with a mythical bodhisattva who, in preparation for the establishment of his own Pure Land, surveys a myriad of pure lands so he can choose the best elements of all existing ones for his own. He then summarizes these elements in a series of forty-eight Vows that express the conditions for his own enlightenment. After an aeon of practice, he perfects these Vows and establishes his Pure Land an infinitude to the west.

Of these forty-eight Vows only two positively describe the Pure Land and another negatively, while the rest describe the quality of Amida's enlightenment or the conditions for those born into this Pure

Land. The negative description states that there will be no hellish realms existing in the land (First Vow). The positive descriptions state that the land will be so pure that it will illuminate all the innumerable Buddha Lands (Thirty-first Vow) and be bedecked in all its areas with a myriad of jewels as well as emit sweet fragrances that perfume all directions and cause all bodhisattvas who inhale them to engage in practices that lead to Buddhahood (Thirty-second Vow).[16]

The Pure Land described above is ultimately one that functions as a realm of enlightenment where those who are born into it or even merely touched by it—that is, all existence, since its light of purity and the fragrances of its teachings[17] reach into infinity—partake in the enlightenment of Amida, where purity, light, and bliss (sukha, the antonym of duhkha, suffering) are all symbols of enlightenment or nirvana. As a concrete symbol of enlightenment, the Pure Land's enlightening activity includes not only activity in our present life, but also, and perhaps more importantly, continued and consummating activity in the future after our physical death. As an untiring activity bringing about the ultimate enlightenment of all existence, the Pure Land is thus a symbol of hope that all existence will one day fulfill itself in the timeless reality of Amida's enlightenment.

The Chinese Pure Land master T'an-luan, in his *Commentary on Vasubandhu's Treatise on the Pure Land (Wang-sheng-lun-chu)*, speaks of the Pure Land as a placeless place where birth into that land must be a birthless birth; indeed, even the production of that land must be a productionless production.[18] Negating the notions of the Pure Land as being anything like a physical or spiritual place, such as a Heaven, he demythologizes the Pure Land through a Madhyamika treatment of emptiness that ultimately identifies it with emptiness itself; that is, it is a place that is no place toward which there can be no desire for birth, since it is a birthless birth. The identification of the Pure Land with nirvana is simply to convey the fact that birth in the Pure Land is nothing short of entering the realm of enlightenment.

Shinran carried on this tradition of seeing the Pure Land as a realm of enlightenment and had a conscious appreciation of the concrete descriptions of the land as symbols of the enlightened nature and enlightening activity of the realm. His creative contribution to the tradition did not include a rethinking of the notion of the Pure Land,[19] since he was in agreement with this demythologized interpretation, but revolved around how to understand birth in the Pure

Land and the central place of the faith-mind, the mind of entrusting, to gain this birth.

Shinran's Dual Usage of Birth

In a widely read series of articles, Yoshifumi Ueda, an eminent Mahayana scholar and Shin Buddhist thinker, clarified this somewhat vague aspect of Shinran's thought.[20] Treating the discontinuous continuity aspect of Shinran's thinking within general Buddhist thought and in the Pure Land Buddhist context, his articles center on the contention that Shinran used the term *birth in the Pure Land (ōjō)* in two distinct ways: (1) as the traditional Pure Land notion of birth in the Pure Land upon death, and (2) as birth in the Pure Land at the decisive moment of insight that occurs when the mind of entrusting emerges in the seeker. In his careful reading of Shinran, Ueda supported the latter interpretation, which can be understood as looking at birth as a metaphor for spiritual awakening in this life. This latter usage marks Shinran's unique position in the Pure Land tradition, for it is at once his departure from the Pure Land tradition up to then and his point of reentry into the mainstream of the general Buddhist tradition with its emphasis of the transformative insight in this lifetime, in this case, the moment of awakening that occurs when the mind of entrusting emerges. The emphasis on insight in this lifetime that lies at the core of the general Buddhist path is thus seen in Shinran's second usage of the term.

As Ueda makes clear, Shinran's dual usage of the term had an explicit rationale. For Shinran, the appearance of Amida at one's deathbed was not determinative of birth in the Pure Land. To die without the insight of the mind of entrusting would only mean further endless drifting within the cycle of birth-and-death. What determined birth in the Pure Land was not physical death but our taking leave of the realm of samsara by rising above the cycle of birth-and-death. This transcendence of our existence was achieved only by a true insight into our humanity; that is, we realize we are totally the opposite of enlightenment, and yet through the mind of entrusting we have been accepted as we are, and have fully actualized entrance into the realm of enlightenment, to be finalized upon physical death. Thus, birth in the Pure Land through the awakening of the mind of entrusting is characterized by a paradoxical identification of opposites.

Ueda is careful to note that this insight is not to be understood as the insight of enlightenment but as the insight of the faith-mind, the mind of entrusting. Faith-mind points to that fundamental insight into the depths of our evil and passion-ridden existence which causes us to totally entrust ourselves to the compassionate power of Amida. It is at this moment that we gain birth in the Pure Land, which the hour of death only finalizes.

While the notion of birth in the Pure Land upon death is not to be denied, the problem of how we are to understand birth in the Pure Land upon physical death remains. Indeed, birth in the Pure Land upon physical death remains the fundamental meaning of birth for the entire Pure Land tradition, notwithstanding the second meaning Shinran gives it. Although the Shin tradition makes it perfectly clear that talk of the Pure Land with its many adornments is metaphorical and that it indicates enlightenment itself, there are no doubt many dedicated Shin Buddhists today who still think of birth in the Pure Land in terms of going someplace upon death. The problem is not how to understand birth into an otherworldly realm upon death, but rather how to understand birthless birth into the realm of enlightenment at the time of death as well as at the moment of the awakening of the mind of entrusting. One perspective on this problem is gleaned from the process notion of objective immortality which articulates both this spiritual rebirth as well as this sense of everlastingness after death.

Objective Immortality

In the process notion of objective immortality, all events do not merely disappear after the immediacy of their coming to be. Though it is undeniable that all events perpetually perish, all live on in the future through the influence they have on all subsequent events. All subjects become objects of later subjects and thereby gain an everlastingness beyond their ever real perishing.[21] As the notion of objective immortality makes clear, process thought, for all its emphasis on becoming, sees a context of basic continuity in which this becoming occurs. Something that has been remains forever something that is in its incorporation in the events that follow it. It is in such a context of continuity or influence on the future that the becoming of perpetual perishing occurs. This incorporation into the future is partial at best and fades with the passing of time. If this is the extent of the immortality of an occasion, then the term *immortality* hardly seems appropriate.

This problem of partial and fading retention through the processes of coming to be is recognized by process thinkers and is a primary reason they see for the necessity of God. It is God's full and continually vivid retention of all events that grounds objective immortality. While Whitehead is explicit in his expression of this position,[22] Hartshorne, especially, develops this understanding.[23] This aspect of God is particularly evident in the process notion of the consequent nature of God or God's responsive and retentive qualities. All that happens makes a difference to God since all is taken in by God.[24] The tradition is unanimous in its understanding of God as this final and unifying repository of all events: God is the keeper of the past. The nature of this retention becomes a point of conjecture and contention for process thinkers, however, and has much to do with the suggestive language of Whitehead on this point.

Hartshorne's position marks one end of the spectrum. He holds that without God, the full significance of our activities would slowly but surely fade away and be essentially lost with the passing of time. It is in God's total and vivid gathering in of our activities just as they are that our acts do not go for naught. The point for Hartshorne is that the retention by God is of our acts just as they are. What we have done is what we have accomplished nothing more or less, and it is this that is retained forever in the mind of God. A person's whole life is indeed preserved in the mind of God. Thus, not only are the joys, accomplishments, and fulfillments of a person felt by and preserved in the mind of God, but the pain, failures, and incompletenesses of our existence are also as strongly felt and retained by God. This retention of the entirety of our lives in the mind of God is the extent of immortality for Hartshorne. He sees no reason to believe that a personal or subjective immortality can be posited or that this social or objective immortality can take a form in which a finalizing or completion of one's humanity takes place in God after our death. In short, the orthodox eschatology of the Christian tradition is denied. In its place, Hartshorne posits a straightforward, unsentimental, and almost empirical notion of immortality that emphasizes the vital, "once-in-a-lifetime" quality of our actions as we make ourselves during that lifetime. In this sense of simplicity and unsentimental honesty, Hartshorne's position is quite satisfying.

The emotionally unsatisfying quality of his position (though there are no doubt many who would find the position quite satisfying emotionally) for more orthodox Christians as well as not-so-orthodox Christians can be summarized concisely in that such a sense of immortality is not really immortality.[25] As noted above, however, even among other process thinkers Hartshorne's position seems to be the most uncompromising, while others to a greater or lesser degree attempt to speculate on the possibilities of something more.

Subjective Immortality

Marjorie Suchocki tentatively develops a thesis of subjective immortality and concisely summarizes the ongoing debate within process circles in a work on evil and eschatology.[26] She proceeds to speculate on the existence of subjective immortality in a twofold discussion. First, the notion of the creative act, the coming to be of the occasions of existence, must be seen as an ongoing process that upon a pause in activity in the coming to completion of an occasion of existence does not merely become a passive factum for a new occasion but actively gives to the future occasion as well and thereby actively continues the creative process beyond itself into the future. The creative process does not descend upon an occasion of existence as it is coming to be only to leave it as it comes to completion. It is not something that can be abstracted from the occasion but must be identified with the occasion itself. The lingering effect of a thing on the future is not merely as a condition to be gathered in by the thing coming to be, but is also the future thrust of the creative process that is the occasion as it gives itself to the future occasion. The second aspect of the discussion centers on the complementary character of the subjective and objective. In the usual process explication, all occasions save for God incorporate the past as objective datum, notwithstanding the creative impulse given to them by these past occasions. For God, this objective quality of the occasion is always incorporated with the subjective character of that same occasion. However, to incorporate the occasion itself (as object) would have to entail incorporation of the subjective feeling of the occasion at the time of its coming to being and its fulfillment. Thus, while God may incorporate the subjective feeling of the occasion fully, all other occasions too incorporate the subjective as well as the objective aspects of the occasion to some degree. The entire process of coming to be has within it a creative impulse that thrusts itself toward the future in which not only the occasion as object but also as subject is preserved. The point for Suchocki is that not only is the occasion preserved as both complementary subject and object but also because of the creative impulse being ever open to and ever entering the future, the occasion is open to the possibility of transformation and not mere preservation as is.

Suchocki understands Hartshorne as essentially agreeing with her thesis of the complementary character of the objective and subjective aspects of an occasion yet readily recognizes their differences in regard to the possibility of transformation, although she sees no inherent reason why Hartshorne's basic position could not support such a possibility.

My reading of Hartshorne does not necessarily disagree with Suchocki's, but while I agree that Hartshorne understands God as taking in all of an occasion, including the feeling of feelings, and thus the subjective as well as objective aspects of the occasion, this sense of subjective immortality, while it is indeed subjective immortality in a very precise sense, hardly seems to answer the reservations of those who hold a more usual notion of personal immortality. The complementary character of the objective and subjective aspects of an occasion is undeniable. However, with a less technically precise sense of subjective immortality, it seems to be more appropriate to recognize this complementary character in terms of objective immortality. Applying the phrase *subjective immortality* to what Hartshorne seems to be saying confuses the issue a bit. There is no sense of personal integrity with active subjectivity after losing the physical body at death, which the usual sense of personal immortality implies and which both Hartshorne and Suchocki deny.

These reservations aside, what is noteworthy of the above thesis is the possibility of transformation that Suchocki outlines. It is here that the eschatological fulfillment so central to Christian thought can be more forcefully upheld. If what Suchocki claims about Hartshorne's basic position is true, then this emotionally satisfying element is part of Hartshorne's position. However, Hartshorne himself is quite explicit about there being no such possibility for transformation.

It is precisely this possibility of transformation that calls for the retained entity to be called subjective rather than objective immortality. Suchocki sees the phrase *objective immortality* as being a fixed nugget of the past evoking no sense of a possibility for change, leading her to this preference of the phrase *subjective immortality* to describe what she has worked out.

A further point that Suchocki makes, which is relevant to the topic at hand, is that all occasions of existence save for God are initially concentrating on the past and that grounds their anticipation of the future. Most occasions, then, look to the past as they go forward to the future. For God, the reverse is the case. God initially looks to the possibilities of the future and this grounds God's incorporation of the past occasions. Thus for God, it is always to the future, rich with the possibilities of the undetermined, that God gazes upon. It is this sense of openness and the pull to novelty that God gives to the creative process that is the context in which things come to be.

Objective Immortality and Birth in the Pure Land

From a Buddhist point of view, what is first quite obvious about the above discussion of objective immortality is its similarity to the general notion of karma. The continuity within the flux of existence is also noted by Buddhists in this doctrine that sees all present activity affecting to a greater or lesser degree all future activities. The thesis of an earlier work considering aspects of Hartshorne's concept of God in contrast with aspects of early Buddhist thought develops this notion of continuity within flux.[27] The major difference noted therein between the two positions is the existence of God as the final and complete repository of all past occasions for process thought. It is, of course, this notion that must be considered here.

Again, the basic sense of objective immortality is articulated already in the general Buddhist notion of karma. An occasion of reality, a dharma, influences all succeeding occasions of reality and is thereby objectively immortal in succeeding occasions. This alone leaves only a partial and fading retention of the occasion in each succeeding occasion. The problem noted above is also present here. Does Buddhism have anything inherent within its various strands that tries to resolve this problem of partiality and fading retention? There do seem to be a number of notions in the tradition that can be seen as resolutions to this problem whether they were developed for that purpose or not. The first suggestive notion is developed in the Buddhology of the developing tradition. Here one often encounters discussion of the omniscience of the Buddha especially in terms of knowing all past lives of beings, that is, the entirety of a person's karma with the clear implication that this full retention will be preserved forever. As the tradition develops, one encounters the notion of *alayavijnana* or the storehouse consciousness that is comparable to the collective unconscious. It is the storehouse of all karma and as such the vital pulse of creativity. It is interesting to note that the Shin Buddhist scholar Soga Ryōjin equated Amida with this storehouse consciousness.[28] Hua-yen, in many ways the most philosophically developed school of Buddhism, has the notion of the dharma realm *(dharmadhatu)* in which the interpenetrating mutuality of all occasions of reality is vividly retained and unified yet with its diversity intact. Admittedly, these doctrines have been attacked in Buddhist circles as substantializing, hence contradicting, the inherently empty reality Buddhism advocates. Nevertheless, the emptiness that grounds all these notions is clearly declared in careful articulations of these doctrines. These so-called substantializing doctrines indicate the back-and-forth movement of the tradition in articulating reality not only as impermanence but a coming to be and "continuity" that recognizes the need to resolve the problem of perpetual perishing.

Turning to Shin Buddhism and the notion of birth in the Pure Land, we have seen that the Pure Land can be understood as the realm of enlightenment and as such is neither a physical nor spiritual realm that is literally entered upon death. It is emptiness and enlightenment itself and can thereby be identified with Amida itself as well. The land and the Buddha are identical, since the quality of both is enlightenment. Thus, to enter the Pure Land is to enter into Amida itself or into the mind of Amida. It is this image that will be developed in the following as a way to understand birth in the Pure Land.

As the discussion of objective immortality noted, it is in the incorporation into God of the entirety of an occasion in all its vividness and completeness that the evil of perpetual perishing is resolved. Amida too is seen as taking in the entire person in that the karma of that person is taken on by Amida in its entirety with the proviso that the karma of the person is all evil karma that must be transformed into and through the enlightenment of Amida. The image of rivers entering into the ocean and being gathered in just as they are yet transformed into the same salt water of the ocean that Shinran uses so effectively in his hymns evokes this sense of total yet distinctive incorporation (individuals they remain and not a mere mass) that objective immortality articulates.

Yet as the above indicates, this incorporation must provide for the possibility for transformation. That is, while the karma of a person is gathered in and preserved just as it is, the evil karma of the individual must be transformed into the karma of and for enlightenment. Hartshorne's explicit position does not allow for this, while Suchocki's position of the ongoing creative activity does. The notion of transformation in Buddhism and in particular Shin Buddhism is complicated and remains in need of thorough explication.[29] However, put in process-influenced terms, the karma of an individual is incorporated as the experienced karma of the individual (the feeling and experience of the karma by the individual is felt and experienced by Amida—in Suchocki's expression, subjective immortality is achieved) but there is an objectification of the karma in that it is taken on by Amida and through the power of Amida's own enlightenment transformed into karma of and for enlightenment. It is through this enlightening power of Amida that transformation takes place. The creative activity does not merely continue of its own force, though that is a major presence, but Amida, through the power of enlightenment, helps create the ongoing coming to be of the person's past actions into enlightenment itself. Here, we can see the connection between the birth into the Pure Land identified with the awakening of the mind of entrusting and birth upon death. In the awakening of this mind we touch and are touched by the enlightenment of Amida so that this transformation takes place, and upon our physical death, since our actions have stopped, the finalizing of this transformation can occur.

Here, however, a question becomes apparent. Is birth in the Pure Land dependent on the awakening of the mind of entrusting? The transitional or provisional birth in realms bordering the Pure Land are for those who are unable to awaken the mind of entrusting and thus still have a mind centered on oneself. With no thought of enlightenment that the awakening of the mind of entrusting witnesses to, one has made no condition for or connection with enlightenment. Therefore, incorporation by Amida of that person's karma means that there is a distance from Amida's enlightenment and from the enlightening activity that finalizes the individual's karma. Through a long process of muted activity upon death, however, the individual's karma will be brought closer and closer to the karma of and for enlightenment until real completion is attained. We are, as it were, upon birth in these borderlands, made to journey on through a vale of enlightenment-making as a continuation of our journey, much ignored during our lifetime. The above is a play on Hick's own "vale of soul-making" theodicy.[30] If there is no resolution of the evil we are and do and the evil that is and is done in the world, then the claim of the ultimate compassion and wisdom of Amida cannot be easily upheld. Here, the continuation of the creative process is evident in the need for ultimate transformation and fulfillment.

Yet Hartshorne's words haunt me in their straightforward honesty and similarity with the stark realism sometimes evident in Ch'an/Zen. Why must we think that our activities in this lifetime will be transformed after we are done with it? If the vale of enlightenment-making is not traversed now, then no matter how much we are beckoned upon our death we will no doubt still not walk it. Amida takes in our karma, but since we have not taken that karma seriously ourselves, then why should we hope that Amida will? In the end, there may be no real resolution to the problem of evil, and the compassion of Amida will remain a mystery.

Neither this hardy realism nor transforming liberation from the past alone is enough. We must live as if this time is our only chance, and yet in the hope that the wrongs and evils of this time will be transformed in the processes of the ever becoming reality of ourselves and God/Amida. Evil is not only that which we perpetrate but that which has been perpetrated upon us for no obvious reason. The Pure Land must have this power finally to transform these evils of life, or what is the use of it? This power to transform has been the lure of the Pure Land tradition for ages and needs to be rearticulated so that the tradition can regain its power to attract and thereby transform people and again impart hope to those whose lives are filled with despair.

Notes

1. This chapter developed in light of parallel reflections on God and eschatology in process theology. My general attitude toward interreligious dialogue, as well as more specific reflections using modes of thought articulated in Process Theology, owes much to the thought of John B. Cobb. See his *Beyond Dialogue: Toward a Mutual Transformation of Christianity and Buddhism* (Philadelphia: Fortress Press, 1982).

2. Abraham J. Heschel, *The Prophets*, volume 2 (New York: Harper and Row, 1962), pp. 269–72.

3. Ibid., pp. 1–11.

4. Ibid., pp. 51–52.

5. Charles Hartshorne, *Omnipotence and Other Theological Mistakes* (Albany: State University of New York Press, 1984), p. 45.

6. Alfred North Whitehead, *Process and Reality*: Corrected edition. David Ray Griffin and Donald Sherburne, eds. (New York: Free Press, 1978[1929]), p. 345.

7. Needless to say, the extinguishing of self-preoccupied desire that is nirvana is necessary to actualize our real selves. This extinguishing of desire, however, is not a freedom from the world but rather a freedom to seize the world, to see it for what it is. Thus, rather than closing one off from the world, this actualization of our true self that is enlightenment opens us up to the world unhindered by what we want to see in it and lets this world come into ourselves just as it is.

8. The word *compassion* does have a specific and technical meaning in its Buddhist usage, and this must be asserted. It also has a more general meaning that cannot be ignored unless one wants to use the word totally isolated from this meaning. Then, of course, one must ask why use that word at all. If one asserts that reality is fundamentally compassionate, then that should mean a certain thing and have certain implications.

9. The phrase *dharma-for-us* is a free translation of *upāya* (compassionate means) and is often used as an abbreviation for *upāya dharmakāya* (the dharma-body of compassionate means), a synonym for Amida Buddha. The translation attempts to convey the dynamic, saving activity of reality as it issues out of itself for our sake. It is this central insight into the character of reality that highlights Shinran's view of reality.

10. *Shinshū Shōgyō Zensho* 2: 496.

11. *Shinshū Shōgyō Zensho* 2: 514.

12. *Teaching, Practice, and Realization*, "Chapter on Practice," 102, in *The Collected Works of Shinran*, 1: 69–74.

13. *Teaching, Practice, and Realization*, "Chapter on Shinjin," 60, in *The Collected Works of Shinran*, 1: 110–11.

14. *Teaching, Practice, and Realization*, "Chapter on Practice," 102, in *The Collected Works of Shinran*, 1: 70.

15. Dennis Hirota, *Tannishō: A Primer* (Kyoto: Ryukoku University, 1982), p. 23; adapted.

16. For a rather free translation of the vows, see: D. T. Suzuki, "A Miscellany on the Shin Teaching of Buddhism" in *Collected Writings on Shin Buddhism*, Eastern Buddhist Society, eds. (Kyoto: Shinshū Ōtaniha, 1973[1949]), 43–49. For a discussion of the Pure Land based on this scripture which emphasizes the continuous hearing of the dharma by those born there, see: Ryūkyō Fujimoto, *An Outline of the Triple Sutra of Shin Buddhism*, vol. 1 (Kyoto: Honpa Hongwanji Press, 1955), 87–103. For a short but comprehensive discussion of the concept of buddha lands and Amida's Pure Land see Yoshifumi Ueda and Dennis Hirota, *Shinran: An Introduction to His Thought* (Kyoto: Hongwanji International Center, 1989) pp. 122–25.

17. The Chinese character for hearing is used for the inhaling of fragrances.

18. See Roger Jonathan Corless, *T'an Luan's Commentary on the Pure Land Discourse* (Ann Arbor: University Microfilms, 1973), pp. 32–36.

19. It should be pointed out that the Pure Land tradition was probably from the beginning a target of other schools who accused it of being unorthodox precisely for holding to a belief in the Pure Land. In China and Japan one major point of contention especially with the Ch'an or Zen schools was this notion of the Pure Land as a heavenlike realm or afterlife, which was popular among Pure Land followers and no doubt a large number of the clergy. While this strand of the tradition in the popular worship of the majority of followers and clergy cannot be denied, the more thoughtfully inclined strand of Buddhists of the same tradition must be recognized as resolving this problem of thinking of the Pure Land as a literally existing realm through the demythologizing process of emptiness, where one is embraced by the wisdom and compassion of Amida.

20. "Shinran no Ōjō no Shisō" [Shinran's Concept of Birth in the Pure Land] in *Shinran Kyōgaku*, 13 (1968) 97–117 and 14 (1969), 105–28; and "Shinran no Ōjō no Shisō ni tsuite [Regarding "Shinran's Concept of Birth in the Pure Land"] in *Jōdokyō no Shisō to Bunka* (Kyoto: Bukkyō Daigaku, 1972), 37–60.

For an adapted and expanded English version, see Dennis Hirota, trans., "The Mahayana Structure of Shinran's Thought," in *The Eastern Buddhist*, n.s. xvii: 1 (1984), and xvii: 2 (1984). With Ueda's approval, Hirota restructured and augmented the article to articulate the underlying unity of the two meanings of birth and the continuity of the resulting concept with general Mahayana patterns of thought.

21. Whitehead, op. cit., xiii–xiv; 29; pp. 222–23.

22. Ibid., pp. 346–51.

23. Hartshorne, op. cit., pp. 32–37 and Charles Hartshorne, *The Logic of Perfection* (LaSalle, Ill.: Open Court, 1962), pp. 245–62.

24. John B. Cobb, Jr., and David Griffin, *Process Theology: An Introductory Exposition* (Philadelphia: Westminster Press, 1976), pp. 121–23.

25. John Hick, ed., *Classical and Contemporary Readings in the Philosophy of Religion*, 2d ed. (Englewood Cliffs, N.J.: Prentice-Hall, 1970 [1964]), pp. 544–45.

26. Marjorie Hewitt Suchocki, *The End of Evil* (Albany: State University of New York Press, 1988), 81–96; pp. 165–69.

27. John S. Ishihara, "Continuity and Novelty: A Contribution to the Dialogue Between Buddhism and Process Thought," *Charles Hartshorne's Concept of God*, Santiago Sia, ed. (Dordrecht, the Netherlands: Kluwer Academic Publishers, 1990).

28. Ryōjin Soga, "Dharmakara Bodhisattva," *Eastern Buddhist* n.s. I, 1 (1965). Soga's combining Amida (Dharmakara Bodhisattva) and storehouse consciousness is an intuitive one, and has no precedent in Buddhism.

29. For a discussion, see Yoshifumi Ueda and Dennis Hirota, *Shinran: An Introduction*, pp. 56–90 and pp. 152–54.

30. Stephan Davis, ed., *Encountering Evil: Life Options in Theodicy* (Atlanta: John Knox Press, 1981), pp. 39–68.

3. Mandala Contemplation and Pure Land Practice: A Comparative Study

A Buddhological Approach

Musashi Tachikawa

Act and Time

The World in Process: Arising, Growth, and Demise

Religious practice as conceived in Hinduism and Buddhism is closely related to the biological and cosmological process by which things arise, develop according to their inherent programming, and then perish. This is not to say that either Hinduism or Buddhism already possessed cosmological or astronomical knowledge concerning the birth and demise of the solar system or the galaxy. Both Hindu and Buddhist thinkers constructed their religious theories on their observation that the world of phenomena repeated the pattern of "birth, development, and death" and that their own lives and bodies were not exceptions.

Hinduism and Buddhism lacked "scientific knowledge" of the objective world, the world grasped by the senses, as an autonomous, unified body of movement. Even though there was the awareness that the phenomenal world or the various elements of which it is composed repeat a pattern of birth, development, and demise, there was no recognition of the entirety of the objective world of "nature" as an

Translated by Dennis Hirota

organic, self-determining, unified whole. Of course, it has been in this century that we have come to possess this kind of awareness, and it is not now possible for religious thought to ignore it. At the same time, however, the attitude of ancient Indian thought, which recognized the world as reconstructed through the senses, still remains appropriate in certain respects.

Three Elements of Action

It is action, including movement, that gives evidence of life. Further, movement may be understood as a function of time. Let us say that a person X is moving from point A to point C, and at present is at point B (figure 3.1). Here, the movement or action of going from A to B and further to C is best represented not in terms of three points A, B, and C, but by the line from A through B to C. What is essential here is extension. Further, in movement represented by extension, it is possible to consider directionality. In the case of X moving from A to B, the energy of movement possesses a direction from A to B. The amount of energy having direction may be called its "vector," and the religious action that we are considering also clearly possesses direction and may be grasped as a vector. Moreover, all acts have a purpose or goal. In cases where no specific goal is apparent, it may be said that acts possess goals that are nearly indistinguishable from the means of attainment. The act of not doing or thinking anything has the aim of rest or alleviating fatigue.

Acts may always be seen as possessing three elements: (1) recognition of present conditions, (2) purpose, and (3) means. In the figure mentioned before, X departs from A and moves to C. In this case, it

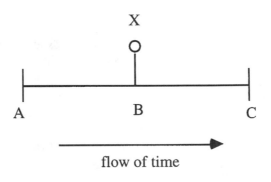

flow of time

FIGURE 3.1   The Movement of X

may be that X has something to do at point C, or has as an aim walking to C. In either case, before reaching C, X has established reaching C as the goal. In religious acts also, the power to determine the result before the act has begun or been completed is important.

There is a continuity between (1) the recognition of present conditions and (2) goal in the case that X decides to move from A to C. Let us take, as an example, the case in which, on receiving news that a tidal wave is approaching point A, X has moved as far as point B on his way to point C in the hills. In this case, it is easy to identify the three elements in the act. The recognition of present conditions is the awareness of danger at point A. The goal is to flee to safety. The means may be by going on foot or by vehicle.

What I wish to emphasize here is that the apparently simple act of X moving from one point to another in fact manifests the fundamental model of religious practice. Although we may not know the length of time living things have, it is certain that the life activity will end. X reaches point B from point A and is proceeding to point C; this schema applies to the fundamental structure of all human life activity. Religious acts also exist in time and are undertaken while according with a continuity that can be represented by a line. There is, however, a difference from general acts in that, in seeking change from present actuality, they are attempts at emancipation from time.

Whatever the nature of movements faster than the speed of light, movement on Earth occurs in the irreversible flow of time. Time in this case is physical time, not time as grasped psychologically. When X, thinking that a tidal wave is approaching, has moved to point C, rather than experiencing the ordinary sense of passage of time, he probably was more strongly aware of it, whether he thought it longer or shorter. Or, wholly preoccupied with fleeing, he may have had no awareness of the passage of time at all. In any case, whether he was aware of the passage of time or not, physical time has passed for the living body. Further, when we are aware in our acts, we become aware that we are encompassed within that which transcends our own powers.

Process and Acts of Living Things

All things, including both living things and inanimate things like atoms, are moving bodies. Further, they repeat the pattern of origination, development, and demise. We do not know, however, for what purpose they repeat this process. It is probably impossible to raise the question of purpose. At the least, it is probably meaningless to introduce the concept of purpose with regard to the process of origination, development, and demise in the cosmic structure. In this pattern of conjectured repetition in the universe there is nothing that may be called an "act." An act is undertaken by an agent with a set goal. In the case of the universe as a whole, it is impossible to consider that a particular agent performs an act by setting a goal and selecting a means. At most, it can be called a "process."

We ourselves as biological beings follow the process of origination, development, and demise. We do not know whether this process itself has a purpose. Nevertheless, while following this biological process and existing within the advance of physical time, we set goals in response to various aspects of our lives' tasks and perform acts. The aims of our acts are diverse. As bodily beings we perform acts that aid the programming for maintaining our physical structures. Most of our acts are related to the biological functions of the living body. If we do not eat regularly, the body will perish. We know from experience that if we take food appropriately, our bodies will function smoothly for a certain period.

We do not know for what purpose all things of the universe are developing and perishing. Nevertheless, it is a fact that, for example, our physical bodies seek to grow for a certain period. It is not that a physical body continues to grow fortuitously because food happens to be taken regularly. It demands food for the continuation of its life according to its own programming. To this extent, it is possible to introduce a kind of concept of purpose for the period that the activity and life of our physical bodies is maintained. I cannot take up here the problem of how far this concept of purpose may be applied to the world of nature or, further, even to only the case of human bodies. It is necessary for us to consider here only on the low level of our physical bodies that we possess "the desire to live."

We do not, however, perform only acts that are appropriate for maintaining the life of the body. At times, people perform acts resulting in the destruction of their own healthy bodies and in ending their lives. Further, human beings are capable of performing this with feelings of excitement. There are also many who find their supreme joy in destroying the bodies of others. Even apart from the extreme cases of suicide and murder, human beings frequently perform with pleasure acts that clearly contradict activity considered to promote the health of the natural, living system that is our bodies.

If we acted wholly in accord with the natural programming of our physical bodies, religion would not have arisen. Human beings exist within the processes that biological life must conform to, and at the same time can go counter to those processes. Religion is the action of interpreting those processes as opportunities for achieving one's own goals.

Goals involve the anticipation of the future. Without the recognition of present conditions and the delineation of an image of the future surmised on the basis of the present, it is impossible to possess a goal. Although we speak of "recognition of present conditions," needless to say this involves the presently existing circumstances in relation to the past and the future. Here, "recognition of present circumstances" may be rephrased as worldview. We construct a consistent theory with regard to the world that opens forth before us, establish goals for the sake of our lives, and select means.

Space and Time

Dependent Origination and Time

At the foundation of religious acts lies an awareness of the impossibility of being satisfied with present conditions and circumstances or of remaining in them. There are cases in which, becoming aware that the physical body is gradually dying, one seeks that which is unperishing. The thought that it is necessary to change present conditions is the starting point.

The fundamental nature of religion is action. All religious traditions arise from action. Religious action possesses three elements:

1. the recognition of the necessity to address and change present conditions through some action;

2. the result, which is the goal attained through such action;

3. the action as the means for attaining the goal.

These three elements have traditionally been termed the "cause" (in), the "result" (ka), and the "path" (dō).

The teaching of dependent origination (*pratītya-samutpāda*), which is the core of Buddhist thought, is a guide to action seeking the spiritual salvation termed "enlightenment"; hence, it includes these three elements. Although the details of the teaching of dependent origination taught by Shakyamuni himself are not known exactly, it is clear from extant texts that his teaching of it included the three elements: the necessity of the recognition of both the "world" he conceived—the world of mind and body—and enlightenment; liberation from "pain" through enlightenment; and the means by which to attain that goal.

One influential version of the Buddhist teaching of dependent origination is the twelve-link concept formulated by Vasubandhu in his *Abhidharmakośa*, the most basic compendium of Buddhist scholastics. Here, I will take up two points concerning it: its consideration of the biological movement of the living body and its exposition of the process of practice as the means of attainment in the form of an inverted perspective. Here, the theory concerning the arising and structure of the world traverses a path that contradicts going against the causal relationship. On the one hand, according to the view of the regular order of the twelve-link dependent origination, depending on the first link of ignorance, the second link of volition arises; depending on volition, consciousness arises, and so on. This is a theory concerning the origination and structure of the world. On the other hand, according to the reverse order, if there is no eleventh link of birth, there is no final link of aging and death; further, if there is no tenth link of existence, there is no birth. This method of thought continues down to the disappearance of the second link of volition through the eradication of the first link of ignorance. This view of reverse order indicates the path by which one reaches the eradication of ignorance or enlightenment. The teaching of dependent origination, while recognizing that human beings live according to the inescapable law of movement from birth to death, anticipates the painful end of death that will occur in the future and seeks the sacred by reversing that natural movement.

Dependent Origination and Emptiness in Nagarjuna

Nagarjuna (Nāgārjuna, fl. c. 150–250) also adopted the concept of dependent origination as the core of his thought. In his *Middle Stanzas (Madhyamaka-kārikā)*, 26, he treats the twelve-link dependent origination emphasized in Abhidharma Buddhism, but his concept of dependent origination is broader, and is deeply connected with language. For him, "that which arises dependently" is that which is expressed in words. The world is not something that exists apart from our senses;

rather, we temporarily establish its existence through words. For him, the goal of religious practice is attained when we realize that this world is temporary, and further that it is empty or lacking in substantial existence. The means he selected for reaching emptiness in *Middle Stanzas* was the demonstration that the words used in our daily life, in the final analysis, cannot be established as meaningful.

When considering Pure Land faith and esoteric Buddhism, it is illuminating to compare them with dependent origination in Middle Stanzas. In this work, the following three are all termed dependent origination:

1. the phenomenal world expressed by language and propositions;
2. true reality that transcends language; emptiness;
3. language that is reborn after being negated, and the world it indicates.

These three kinds of dependent origination also express the process of religious practice. The first meaning indicates the world of ignorance in which unenlightened beings live, that is, the profane. The second meaning describes the manifestation of the wisdom of enlightenment, that is, the sacred. The third meaning, the "world of provisional speech," indicates the mode of existence of that which has been brought to death through negation and been reborn through the power of the sacred. In Nagarjuna, three stages or moments may be distinguished, and all three are referred to by the term *dependent origination*:

a. advance from the profane toward the sacred;
b. the instant in which the sacred manifests itself;
c. the sacred giving its power to the profane.

These three stages or moments indicate the structure of religious practice in Nagarjuna's thought, and may be illustrated as in figure 3.2. A and C represent the level of the profane, while B represents the level of the sacred. Time flows from A toward C, with the movement from A to B representing the advance from the profane with the sacred as the goal. B represents emptiness, and the movement from B to C represents the profane being reborn through the power of the sacred.

In the movement from A to B, intentional acts are performed repeatedly over a set period of time; the movement from B to C, however, is instantaneous.

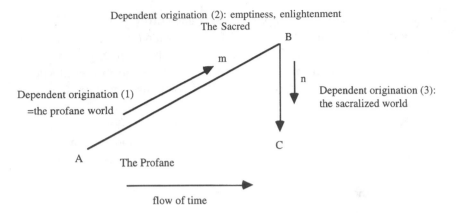

Dependent origination (2): emptiness, enlightenment
The Sacred

Dependent origination (1)
=the profane world

Dependent origination (3):
the sacralized world

The Profane

flow of time

m: Going from the profane to the sacred requires a long period of time.

n: The sacralization of the profane by the sacred is instantaneous.

C is a higher point than A because the sacralized C is closer to the sacred.

FIGURE 3.2   The Structure of Dependent Origination in Nagarjuna

In the case that the world at C has lost the power of the sacred and fallen back to the status of the profane, it must be brought once more to extinction. Nagarjuna's exposition of practice is thus founded on a circulation of energy that is established through incessant negating action.

Nothingness of Time and Temporary Exposition

In the formulation of practice found in *Middle Stanzas*, there is first an understanding of the theory concerning the structure of the world or of language, then advance toward "understanding that originally the world does not possess a structure." Emptiness lies beyond these gradually advancing practices. After the wisdom of emptiness has been attained, the practicer does not dwell within "nothingness" but rather in the world of provisional speech "that has been revived through the working of emptiness." In Nagarjuna's *Middle Stanzas*, this revived world of provisional speech is discussed frequently. As we will see later, in esoteric teaching, this "revived world of provisional speech" is the arena of practice.

Nagarjuna thoroughly rejects language as profane. The rejection of the reality of the phenomenal world is for him the rejection of the activity of using words and further of the plurality (idle speech) that language necessarily possesses. The operation of negation that he employs exempts nothing, but brings everything to nothingness. In *Middle Stanzas*, he does not even use the term *prajnaparamita*, the wisdom of enlightenment. Further, he holds in disdain the notion of emptiness as really existing, for emptiness is that which is attained only within the operation of incessant negation.

Nagarjuna does not take up for discussion the process of birth, development, and demise that unfolds before us in the natural world. For him, the world is always that which individuals construct from the data received through the senses and which they shape as the system of language. He does not regard the references of words as real existents, but grasps them as meaning. In essence, the world for him, in contemporary terms, is a code system.

Nagarjuna of course knew that the things he saw around him followed a process of origination, development, and demise. Almost all the chapters of *Middle Stanzas* are, in a broad sense, observations of movement. For example, the main topic of the first chapter is arising, that of the second, going. He asserts, however, that "arising" or "going" is originally nonexistent. To deny movement in this way is to deny the flow of time. To collapse the time that flows in the code system of language and lead the world into the nothingness termed "emptiness"—in other words, to attain emancipation from time—is the aim of the religious action advocated by Nagarjuna. After time is destroyed comes the rebirth termed "provisional speech."

Emptiness and Pure Land

The Working of Emptiness

As I have stated, emptiness is attained only within the operation of incessant negation. It is not an eternal and unchanging substance. It possesses a working, however, and it is precisely for this reason that the revival of language as provisional speech is possible. *Middle Stanzas*, 24, states, "Dependent origination is called emptiness." Dependent origination, which originally includes the meaning of arising, possesses an affirmative side, and in the same way emptiness does also. For those seeking to cope with the perishing of the living body, this positive, affirmative aspect of emptiness represented salvation.

How is it possible for the operation of incessant negation to have an affirmative aspect? It comes about not through the character of the operation itself, but through the nature of the locus in which that which is negated exists. In other words, language (world), while being negated, is gradually brought to the stage of new birth. What is important for us is that the working of emptiness may possess human character, which implies that it is possible for us to address it. An interaction may be established between the working of emptiness and ourselves. The Mahayana Buddhist tradition has called the personal working of emptiness by various Buddhas' names. Those which are related to our concerns here are *Amida* in the Pure Land tradition and *Vairochana* (Vairocana, Dainichi Nyorai) in esoteric traditions.

Emptiness and Rebirth

It is impossible to halt the physical process of arising, development, and demise and to turn it back in the opposite direction. Many people have believed, however, that the repetition of this pattern may occur for the same person. This is the concept of transmigration, which assumes a "soul" or "spirit" dwelling in the physical body; when the body grows old, "just as in shedding and discarding old clothing and putting on new" (*Bhagavadgītā*), it abandons the old body and takes up residence in a new one. This concept of transmigration includes two elements that, at first glance, may appear mutually contradictory. On the one hand, as long as we remain within the cycle of transmigration, there is no ultimate liberation for us. To transmigrate is to wander in the world of the profane. On the other hand, if there were no possibility at all for transmigration or change through birth, human beings would realize that there was no possibility of emancipation, and would be even more greatly filled with despair. Shakyamuni states repeatedly that "all is painful." His teaching is not, however, pessimistic. "Pain" here is not ordinary suffering, but may be interpreted as "adverse" (*du÷*) "chance" or "happenstance" (*kha*); it indicates something unavoidable. Shakyamuni was clearly not, however, expounding a fatalism.

The working of emptiness promises us a rebirth at death. The negation of the profane is a deliberate, intentional act of human beings, and has no direct connection with the process of the biologically living body advancing to its demise. Nevertheless, when the various activities that take the physical body as their foundation are grasped as "the profane which should be negated" and something spiritual is sought after the death of the body, then the moment the physical body as the biological life-system dies becomes the unique opportunity for attainment of spiritual bliss. While aware that their allotted time is nearing an end, human beings seek to make a plunge or leap, with the thickness of the brief time remaining to them as their springboard. Trained Tibetan monks and Indian yogis, at the moment of death, all at once extract their breath (*prāṇa*) from the tops of their heads, thus liberating their spirits or souls from their bodies, and die. This method of practice is called *pho bo* in Tibetan and *saṃ krānti* in Sanskrit. In brief, the meaning is "drawing out and passing over [of breath]."

While there are differences in degree, at the point of death, we who have not accumulated practice in such methods also seek to make a leap. This leap or plunge is a matter of devoting the energy available through burning all at once the time left to the self and, as though using it to pay the cost, seeking to obtain something that differs from the self up to that time. I have used the word *leap* with the sense not of soaring but of leaping from the cliff's edge into a valley, or hurdling oneself into a bottomless chasm. Even while facing death and falling as though into an abyss, one wishes that one's life undergo a rebirth. This is surely an expression of profound greed. Nevertheless, if one were not falling so, one would be unable to change the self existing up to then. To seek to change the self only when dying may seem meaningless. When we are conscious of death, however, we begin for the first time to reject the self's previous mode of existence.

Nothingness and Pure Land

There are people who, like the practicers who suddenly draw out their spirit-breath, courageously cast their entire existence into the abyss. Such people may be said to possess Pure Land faith. One cannot know with certainty that, after casting oneself into the abyss, rebirth is assured. No matter what sage or saint may appear in the world, or what sort of intellectual or physical training one may go though, this is something that will remain uncertain. It can be known only by those who have cast themselves into the abyss, and those who have not can only conjecture. Further, though the former may wish to transmit that experience through words or gestures, this is of course impossible.

People who cast themselves into the abyss possess a personal relationship with the working of emptiness. They believe that the place they are going is the land where Buddha lives. As mentioned before, there is no proof that they will be born in a Buddha land. At the very least, however, at the moment they cast themselves into the abyss, they have a relationship with Amida Buddha, their personal savior, and they entrust their own later existence to that personal figure. After they have entrusted themselves to the Buddha it is difficult for them to do anything for their own salvation, for they themselves can do nothing but fall. Paradoxically, for Pure Land Buddhists, whether the Pure Land itself exists and whether they can be born there are not issues. They believe that although it may be possible to catch a glimpse of the Pure Land, it is impossible for them to reach it. The moment they glimpse it and cast up their entire existence to attain it, their eyes no longer function.

Thus, the attitude of Pure Land Buddhists is indeed active. Before they have made their crucial resolution, they are not Pure Land Buddhists. The term *Other Power* is used because they have entrusted completely to the personal Buddha. Because they constantly negate the existence of the self by entrusting to the other, it is said that they abandon all personal designs and calculative thinking.

Moment and Pure Land

Up to now, I have spoken of the period, usually requiring several decades, of the aging and demise of the physical body as a biological life-system following its stage of growth. Within the overall, decades-long process of a person's physical origination, growth, and death, certainly this same process may be seen as recurring on a smaller scale numerous times. An infant's tooth follows such a process in a few years. Hair and nails go from origination to death in a shorter period. With blood, sperm, and ovum within a body, this process goes on repeatedly. Thus, the process toward demise does out occur only once, but is repeated many times within the body. We are constantly in the process of being born and constantly dying. In infancy and adolescence, our bodies are as a whole young, but in old age, they are already dead in various parts. We do not die for the first time when our hearts stop.

On the one hand, our bodies repeatedly undergo a process of arising, development, and demise, and on the other hand, our consciousness and awareness of death is various and multilayered. We cope with death not only as the ceasing of the heart, but as death that is inflicted on us daily and gradually. Hence, we become aware of ourselves as leaping daily into the abyss of nothingness. It may be that our lives are a continuation of the process of arising, developing, and perishing occurring momentarily. The period we think of as one year or as decades, when considered in relation to the cosmos, is an exceedingly brief unit of time, but from the perspective of the mechanism of the life-system, it possesses a length that is cosmic. Considered in this way, it may be said that we transmigrate moment by moment. If this is so, our death comes moment by moment, and moment by moment we can glimpse the Pure Land. Continuously, with each moment, we see the Pure Land as though through a crack in the door, and seeking to go there, deliver over the self. In the moment of delivery, however, the self is no longer the self. This is the nature of Pure Land faith.

Self and Pure Land

To the extent that such religious action is action, as mentioned above, it possesses the three elements of recognition of present conditions (worldview), purpose, and means. In this case, the recognition of present conditions is the consciousness that the self should be reborn; the aim is the rebirth of the self; and the means is the entrusting of one's entire existence to the working of emptiness as personal. In Pure Land faith, however, it is not permitted the practicers of religious action to judge for themselves the extent to which their goal has been attained. Let us consider once more the situation of the person X going from point A and passing point B on the way to C. While standing at point B, X is able to ascertain that he has to some extent accomplished his goal of reaching C. Further, he realizes that in order to achieve his goal, there is no means apart from walking by his own will. Nevertheless, to think that while walking under one's own power one is nearing the goal is extremely dangerous. From the moment practicers begin to think in this way, they are relegated to a realm completely unrelated to Pure Land faith. For them, what is required and sufficient is that they discard even their own aims and entrust themselves completely to the personal Buddha.

In this formulation of practice, no systematic knowledge of the structure of the world is gained; at very least, it is not positively sought.

The self and the world are the profane that is to be rejected, and knowledge of their structure is, in comparison with the aim of rebirth, scarcely of value. In this connection we may note that in Japanese Pure Land thought, the desire to construct a system of knowledge regarding the structure of the world may be said to be completely lacking. This tendency is particularly clear in Shinran, but in Japanese intellectual history in general, the construction of a system of knowledge concerning the world, which was a focal concern of philosophers in India, was utterly abandoned. From the opposite perspective, it may be said that Pure Land faith was easily adopted and embraced by the Japanese.

Pure Land and Mandala Practice

The Starting Point of Esoteric Practice

In Indian thought, the sacred that is the goal to which religious practice aims is commonly believed to be attained as the result of long and rigorous training. An Indian classic declares, "One may be reborn a thousand times, but attainment of emancipation is uncertain." *Abhidharmakośa*, after expounding a detailed theory regarding the structure of the world, sets forth a minute process of ascent by which the wisdom of enlightenment is attained through training. The traditional path for the monk who has abandoned householding life includes observing precepts, gaining systematic learning relating to the makeup of the world and the self, performing spiritual control (meditation), and gaining the goal of enlightened wisdom.

Another process of practice, however, is also possible. If what is aspired to does not first enter the field of vision as the result of long and arduous cultivation, but is already beside us from the beginning, then the situation differs from the classical stages of training. This is the stance of esoteric teachings. Let us consider the case of X once more. Let us say that he is not moving from A to C, but has already reached the goal of point C. Further, he sees that what he sought, for example some ore, is abundant there. He intends to refine it for utensils. Here, X need not travel further in search of ore. What is necessary is that he recognize that the ore is present around him, and that he know how to turn it into utensils. In recognizing that the sacred already lies right beside one, esoteric and Pure Land teachings are similar. Between them, however, there is a fundamental distinction. They seek to abide in different dimensions. In Pure Land teachings, one is not permitted to assert that one hears Amida Buddha's voice or is saved by Amida. Such assertions express no more than self-conceit. In esoteric Buddhism, however, such "conceit" is necessary. "The self is fundamentally the wisdom of emptiness itself," or "I am none other than Vairochana Tathagata," is the actual starting point of religious practice. In Indian and Tibetan monasteries, only those already familiar with exoteric forms of teaching and practice were allowed to study the esoteric teachings. This prior preparatory practice made possible the "self-conceit" that is the actual beginning of esoteric training.

Esoteric practice may be said to "begin at the end." It seeks to create a more effective form of practice by reversing the general process of religious training. One example of this apparent reversal may be found in the Tibetan *Book of the Dead*. According to this work, immediately after the moment of death, persons see a great light. This light shines for a time and encourages the dead to leap into it, much in the fashion of Pure Land faith. Fearing the radiance, however, the dead hold back. The light then takes the form of Buddha and, appearing before the dead, urges them to come to his abode. But the dead fear the Buddha also and cannot go. Next, gentle bodhisattvas appear. Even then, the dead only stiffen with fright. Finally, fierce figures of Myōō appear and scold the dead, but they still hold back. If the dead could cast themselves into the Buddha's dwelling, they would be liberated from transmigration, but failing to accord with the Buddha's encouragement, they return to transmigration. In other words, it is determined that the spirits of the dead will again enter physical bodies. The Tibetan *Book of the Dead* describes the inability of the spirits separated from physical bodies to go to the abode of the light or the Buddha during a period of forty-nine days and their search of their next physical bodies.

In this narrative, first the sacred at its most exalted level, then at increasingly lower levels, appears. In other words, the goal that is to be aspired to and the possibility of attaining it are offered first, then goals of lesser worth are presented. In the common formulation of practice in exoteric teachings, one begins at a lower level and advances toward that of higher value. In esoteric teachings, while first one attains the manifestation of the sacred as in the *Book of the Dead*, the formulation of consciousness after that is quite different. The practice recommended at the time of death in the *Book of the Dead* provides a link to the esoteric configuration of practice, but it cannot serve as a model for esoteric thought in general. The most typical among esoteric practices is mandala contemplation. In the early stages of mandala contemplation, practicers gain a realization that the sacred and the self have become one, but afterward they deepen their experience of the sacred. After an hour or two of mandala contemplation, the consciousness of the practicer returns to everyday consciousness, but through continuing such practice over a number of years, ordinary consciousness is gradually purified.

The Structure of Mandala Contemplation

Mandala contemplation takes emptiness as its starting point. Pure Land Buddhists entrust themselves to the personal Buddha that manifests the working of emptiness, and the *Book of the Dead* also encourages one to give up oneself into the radiance of emptiness. By contrast, in the thought of Nagarjuna, emptiness is instead the goal. With Nagarjuna also, however, the stance of provisional speech first becomes possible by taking emptiness as the point of departure. It may be said that mandala contemplation developed with greater complexity the conception of provisional speech in Nagarjuna. In this sense, it is possible to view mandala contemplation as encompassed within the movement of dependent origination that Nagarjuna expounds (see figure 3.2). Dependent origination refers to the unfaltering flow of the energy of practice, and emptiness is the terminal point of the energy of that action.

There are three stages in mandala contemplation:

1. One contemplates the personal being that the working of emptiness manifests and realizes that one is that.

2. One contemplates the mandala, which focuses on the personal being manifested in the first stage, and takes the mandala as a symbol of the world that has been sacralized.

3. Through yoga, one realizes that the mandala and the self are one.

It should be noted that mandala contemplation shows variations depending on the period and the particular streams of the tradition; I outline here one method occurring in the later esoteric tradition.

Contemplation of the Central Figure of Veneration in the Mandala

In the first step of mandala contemplation, the practicer attains the wisdom that is emptiness. Wisdom has "acting on others" as its fundamental nature, but it may also be said that this wisdom brings the self to manifest itself. It is taught that the wisdom of emptiness is apprehended as light. It is unthinkable, however, that practicers who perform mandala contemplation see the light of emptiness whenever they perform the practice. Such a fundamental experience probably occurs only a small number of times in a lifetime and each time continues for only two or three seconds. In this sense, practicers of esoteric teachings who realize the self to be the fundamental nature of the wisdom of emptiness must be said to experience the wisdom of emptiness itself only after arduous training.

Mandala contemplation is a method of religious practice, and must be performed repeatedly. Even when they cannot experience the light of emptiness directly, practicers produce before their eyes the nucleus of contemplation as the "shadow" of the working of emptiness. This is a supplementary means contrived in order to gain contact with the light of emptiness. In contemplation, the nucleus for forming the image is essential. Just as a snowflake crystallizes around a nucleus of slender, hairlike filament, the constructive powers by which the figure is formed require a starting point for the development of the image to begin. Most texts on contemplative methods prescribe starting with something small like a letter and developing complex images, such as Buddhas, from it.

In the first stage of mandala contemplation, practicers see the figure of the personal being. Calling to mind the special iconographic characteristics of the venerated figure, they progressively add them to the still partial Buddha figure standing before their eyes until finally the image is complete. This procedure, however, is followed by those who have yet to become accustomed to contemplative method. The practicer who has reached a certain level of accomplishment sees—that is, forms—a perfect figure of a Buddha instantaneously, however complex it may be.

Mandala contemplation itself is a ritual, a form of action undertaken to create a distinction between the sacred and the profane. By following predetermined forms, we can enact the sacred meaning that has been given them. In the performance of ritual, one's consciousness often is not that of everyday life. In mandala contemplation, because practicers see the figures of Buddhas immediately before them, their consciousness is not the haphazard and multifarious one of ordinary life. It is concentrated like that of one performing a dance or singing in a loud voice. In fact, in mandala contemplation in general, in calling the Buddha before one, one recites the *mantra* of the Buddha and forms the hand postures *(mudrā)* that symbolize the Buddha. To the observer, this resembles singing and dancing performed in self-forgetfulness. The practicer does not lose ordinary consciousness, however. As Mircea Eliade states repeatedly in *Yoga*, the yogic practicer does not lose regulatory self-consciousness. In other words, in seeing the mandala or Buddhas before them, they have such awareness as "I am now seeing a mandala" or "It is dangerous if I lie down here." Such ordinary consciousness, however, is quite faint, and the consciousness for the most part is absorbed with the image of the mandala. Ordinary consciousness is overwhelmed by the mandala or other images, and difficulty is felt even in such normally effortless actions as shifting seated posture.

In this way, practicers first encounter the Buddhas manifested before them, then come to realize that the Buddhas are themselves. Realizing this involves the same difficulty as with entrusting oneself to Amida and plunging to the Pure Land. Practicers must have the courage to look on the frightening—because sacred—being before their eyes and believe that they themselves are that. This method of practice probably cannot be accomplished in one or two years. Practicers must seek the light of emptiness and envision the shadow of emptiness hundreds of times. Mandala contemplation is this kind of deliberately, purposively repeated ritual.

In the second stage of mandala contemplation, the practicer contemplates the mandala that has as its focus the Buddha that emerged in the first stage. Contemplation of the mandala is involvement in the world. The mark of birth or arising is action, and action is none other than involvement with others. The realm in which self and others exist is the world. In exoteric teachings, one first seeks awareness of present conditions or systematic knowledge of the structure of the world. The second stage of mandala contemplation corresponds to awareness of present conditions (worldview) in exoteric training.

Mandala as World Picture

The image of the mandala has undergone various changes over the centuries. The earliest image was probably a lotus with open petals and several Buddhas sitting in its center. It appears that the mandala is related to the Hindu Yantra, in which a triangle with an angle upward and another with an angle downward were joined within a lotus. Later, a square was drawn within a circle, and the square was divided in complex ways, giving rise to the mandala as seen today. Until about the eleventh century, the mandala was thought of as a three-dimensional figure composed of light rays. This three-dimensional figure embraced within it all the material elements of the universe—earth, water, fire, wind—and mountains, sun, and moon. It may be called a picture of the cosmos. Further, stupas were often built as three dimensional mandalas.

Later mandalas depict the four great elements of earth, water, fire, and wind as the materials of the world, and Mount Sumeru as the world axis. They are sufficiently complex to be labeled pictures of the cosmos. Nevertheless, leaving aside later Jain and Hindu mandalas, Buddhist mandalas are not world maps or three dimensional models representing actually existing continents, countries, and geographical features. Such features are symbols of Buddhas. The mandala signifies the cosmos, but the image of the cosmos in this case is not that of a map.

Nevertheless, in its historical development the mandala gradually reached completion as a three-dimensional picture of the cosmos. Whether or not the mandala was three-dimensional in the beginning, the image that evolved corresponded closely with the Indian image of the cosmos. This image held the potential for becoming a structural model of the continual world process of birth, development, and demise, and in fact it came to be understood in this way. The temporal world is like a small egg that grows and then withers. Since awareness of the flow of time inevitably involves foreknowledge of death, some method is sought to retain existence even after demise. Such activity is also expressed in the mandala.

In the mandala, energy circulates from the center to the periphery, and from the periphery back to the center. The interrelationships of the elements and Buddhas depicted in the mandala express this. It is a world of embodied energy that circulates giving concrete expression to death and rebirth. The mandala is a moving body. There is nothing stagnant in the world. This is true of course of thoughts and concepts, but all things, whether animate or inanimate, are dancing within time. The mandala as the cosmic dance of energy beckons us and our life into this dance.

A minute and elaborate image of the structure of the world—one that rivals in fineness of detail the esoteric model and depicts a repeated process of birth, growth, and demise—is already present in Abhidharma philosophy. The sutras of the esoteric tradition learned much from the Abhidharma world-picture. *Abhidharmakośa*, however, does not speak of the world as a mandala, for it does not give the world the value of the sacred. What is central for Abhidharma philosophy is how human beings can eliminate the blind passions we inherently possess. In the nothingness of the practicer possessed of blind passions lies the sacred. Here, the world as the environment for human life possesses no religious value of profane or sacred. Further, although the world as environment may undergo birth, development, and demise repeatedly, this temporality is unrelated to the subjective practice of the person seeking the wisdom of enlightenment.

In the later tradition of the mandala, not only human beings but also the world that is the human environment are laden with the electric charge of the sacred. There is no distinction between human beings and their environment; heavenly bodies and mountains and rivers are grasped as the same in nature as humans. The entire life system possesses the significance of the sacred.

When the mandala as the sacred reflects the world, the world appears adorned. It becomes a life-system embellished with a solemnity not seen in ordinary life, a loftiness that draws our life upward, and a pristine and harmonious beauty. With the mandala depiction—the adornment—before us, we inspect the actual world, and the world is sacralized by the energy that flows forth from the adornment. The adornment of the mandala not only sacralizes our world and profane time; the world that has ceased to be profane grants us energy that moves the self toward the adornment. In the practice that takes the mandala as its medium, a cosmic dance is produced by the vector moving in two opposite directions, from the adornment to the world and from the world to the adornment. This dance follows a process in which first the sacred manifests itself, thereby sacralizing the profane world, and then, through this sacralization, the world returns and enters into the sacred.

Just as in the first stage of mandala contemplation, this sacralization of the world takes the form of ritual and is performed with nonordinary consciousness. In general, practicers are aware of being in the center of the mandala. Let us imagine sitting in the center of a room in which figures of Buddhas and bodhisattvas are depicted on the four walls and the ceiling, and on the floor also many Buddha images are side by side in an orderly fashion. Practicers can call this room vividly to mind even with their eyes closed. Gradually, their subjective space becomes the state of the room, and they come to have the consciousness of being the room itself. As in the first stage of mandala contemplation, in this second stage as well, they must perform the appropriate mantras and mudras when calling each Buddha and bodhisattva before their eyes.

The mandala that emerges is gradually compressed to the size of a mustard seed, and practicers contemplate it as in front of their noses. It is thought that this is the condition of the mandala that has reached death and awaits its next birth. How this mandala is reborn is understood variously according to historical period and tradition. The rebirth occurs in the third stage of mandala contemplation.

Self and Mandala

In the third stage of mandala contemplation, the oneness of the mandala and the self is realized. The compression of the large mandala to the size of a mustard seed is preparation for achieving oneness with the self easily and effectively. Here, the self is thought of as taking the limited space of the physical body as its basis. Hence, the realization of the oneness of mandala—the world turned into symbol—and self takes place in the locus of the physical body.

Understandings differ according to the period and specific tradition concerning how the tiny mandala is fused with the self's subjective space that each individual practicer conceives on the basis of his own physical body. In one tradition, the reduced mandala is returned to original size and the practicer's consciousness dissolves into the expanding mandala. In another tradition, the minute mandala is carried into the body by the breath and circulates inside. In yet another tradition, unity is experienced when the venerated one (intelligent being, *jñāna-sattva*), which was thought to exist outside the self, is beckoned into a framework (being of promise, *samaya-sattva*) prepared by practicers beforehand in their own subjective space.

The actual content of mandala contemplation is yoga accomplished through mental functioning so strengthened and sharpened that practicers can form before their eyes Buddha images that appear to be alive. In the yoga of esoteric Buddhism, it is thought that innumerable invisible veins run throughout the body, and that the mental functioning passes through these veins. More precisely, the body itself is a composite of veins taking the shape of the body. This is called the "subtle body." The veins are passage ways through which the breath runs, being drawn or expelled. Breath is the transporter of the mental functioning, and by it, the tiny mandala circulates throughout the "subtle body."

The aim of the third stage of mandala contemplation lies in attaining repose through bringing about the oneness of mandala and self. This sense of repose or bliss is felt in the "subtle body" that has replaced the self. In this way, the mandala symbolizes three levels of cosmos: the universe, the body, and the self.

Conclusion

At the foundation of Pure Land faith lies the concept of emptiness, or the entrusting of oneself to a personal being who is the working of emptiness. People must cast themselves into emptiness, abandoning not only the attainment of knowledge of the structure of the world, but even the wish for rebirth. Borrowing terms from the diagram of Nagarjuna's conception of dependent origination (figure 3.2), it may be said that when Pure Land practicers who are climbing the slope from A to B are about to reach point B, they cast themselves to the point where emptiness (B) works upon others. They abandon hope of attaining the wisdom of emptiness itself, or at least do not believe they themselves have attained it.

If figure 3.2 is recast to depict the structure of Pure Land faith, the result is figure 3.3, where point B is indicated by a small circle. The curve of movement from A to B just touches this point, indicating that the wisdom of emptiness itself is normally not attained. The curve from B to C is broken because the practicer's actual action is represented by the curve from A to B, and only the vector of the leap into

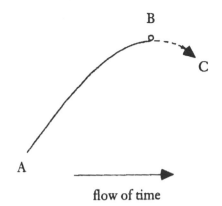

FIGURE 3.3   The Structure of Pure Land Faith

the working of emptiness, seeking to touch B, is indicated. To the very end, the practicer remains within the profane.

In mandala contemplation, there is a period of time during which—whether falsely or ritualistically—practicers entrust themselves to the working of emptiness. Even though they cannot attain the wisdom of emptiness itself, they devote one or two hours to seeing directly the working of emptiness color the image of Buddha and also to seeing the mandala emerge as the sacralized world. The practicers' consciousness in this situation is almost wholly dominated by the sacred and is not ordinary awareness. Even when the oneness of mandala and self is attained through yoga, practicers are dominated by the sacred consciousness, but when the ritual ends, they gradually return to ordinary consciousness.

The structure of mandala contemplation may be depicted as in figure 3.4. In the same way as in figure 3.3, emptiness is indicated by B (circle mark), and the curve ABC touches it. The actual starting point of mandala contemplation is quite close to B. At a point extremely close to B, a curve is drawn from the wisdom of emptiness (B) toward C. This curve is an unbroken line because practice is performed while being conscious of time from within its passage. This curve from B to C does not descend to the same level as A because, in the same way as in figure 3.2, practicers remain at a more sacred level than before practice. The practice indicated by the curve from A to B is preparatory training in mandala contemplation.

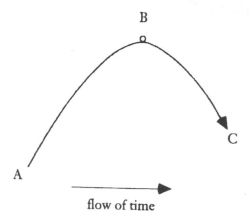

FIGURE 3.4   The Structure of Mandala Contemplation

Above, I have shown that it is possible to delineate a consistent understanding of the concept of emptiness, Pure Land faith, and mandala contemplative methods within the outlines of dependent origination in Nagarjuna's thought. Pure Land faith emphasizes the negation of self as the profane as its crucial moment, while mandala contemplation emphasizes the sacralization of the world and the self. They may be grasped as consonant by viewing them from the perspective of dependent origination and emptiness.

PART TWO

Responses from Two
Western Religious Thinkers

4. Pure Land Buddhism Today

Some Mythodological Issues in
Recent Revisionist Interpretations

Gordon D. Kaufman

I have been asked to comment on chapters 1, 2, and 3, in which fundamental themes of Pure Land Buddhist reflection are presented in terms that are intended to be intelligible and meaningful to a fairly wide circle of readers in today's intellectual world. I am not in any sense an expert on Pure Land Buddhism or any other form of Buddhism (though I have been engaged in Buddhist-Christian dialogue for a number of years); and, therefore, I am not qualified to make judgments about the adequacy of these chapters with respect to their interpretations of Pure Land (or other Buddhist) traditional themes, or, for that matter, about the relationship of these chapters to other contemporary interpretations of Buddhism. My comments will be based, therefore, entirely on what I see in these three texts themselves, as I read them from my standpoint as a Christian theologian and philosopher of religion.

One way that an outsider like myself may be able to make some helpful comments on these chapters is through focusing attention on some of the methodological issues that appear to be posed by the approaches taken in them. Though all three authors are seeking to set their discussions of Pure Land Buddhist themes in a wider perspective than has often been done, they clearly approach this project in different ways, proceeding on the basis of significantly different presuppositions as they define the problems they are seeking to address. The chapters thus move in distinctly different directions, and comparative examination of them can bring to our attention aspects of what is going on that might otherwise not be noticed, and can thus facilitate better assessment of what is to be learned from each of them. Those interested in moving further with interpretations of Buddhism along one or another of these lines should thus be helped, by this sort of analysis, to do so with greater methodological self-consciousness and thus with greater effectiveness. That is, at any rate, my hope about the remarks I shall make.

The three chapters are exceedingly rich in their proposals for fresh interpretation of Pure Land Buddhist themes. I would like to comment on many of these, or at least be able to give my own summaries of the overall arguments presented. Constraints of space, however, make that impossible; and I must turn immediately to the several methodological issues to which I wish to call attention in order to develop them properly.

I

In pursuing a methodological approach here, one could say, I am taking seriously a point made by Mr. Tachikawa in his analysis of human action in the first section of his chapter. All acts, he points out—and this would of course include the act of writing papers of this sort—"exist in time"; they are movements brought about by agents, and they have at least these three features: (a) recognition by the agent of certain present conditions that need to be attended to; (b) the agent's purpose in performing the act; and (c) the means undertaken by the agent to execute that purpose (p. 102). This means that our acts are our human attempts to change something in the world, to bring about a state of affairs that did not previously exist; they are efforts to construct or create something that was not there before. It is possible, thus, to examine scholarly papers (like those we have before us) not only in terms of the explicit themes that are developed in them, but also as expressions of human purposive action, in which a writer brings into being a way of thinking or understanding that did not previously exist; they are acts of what I call "imaginative construction" of new ways of thinking. Methodological analysis of the sort that I will pursue here attempts to bring to light aspects of this imaginative constructive (or reconstructive) activity that the author may not have made explicit or may not even have been aware of. If the analysis is successful, it should assist readers in deciding whether the issues taken up in these chapters are important ones that truly need attention, whether the author's way of pursuing these issues is indeed a fruitful one, or whether other moves (that can be imagined) would be better targeted and more effective. In my methodological analysis I will not attempt to systematically set out, with respect to each of the chapters, the three features of action that Tachikawa has identified for us, but I will be seeking to uncover some aspects of the imaginative constructive acts of the authors that will (I hope) enable us to see more clearly just what is going on in each chapter.

I think it is possible to see the approaches of our three authors to the reinterpretation of Pure Land Buddhism as falling on a continuum. At one end is Tachikawa's chapter; in the middle is Hirota's; and at the other end is Yokota's. Tachikawa seeks to illuminate contemporary Pure Land Buddhism largely by looking backward to some of its historical roots (particularly in Nagarjuna) and outward to some other forms of Buddhism, attempting to show lines of connection and of difference that will enable today's Pure Land Buddhists to get their bearings in the wider (Buddhist) world in which they find themselves. To accomplish this objective he utilizes methods and concepts developed in modern history of religions and comparative religions, but he says little or nothing about the significance of his use of these modern academic ways of thinking, or about the extent to which this methodological approach can be considered an appropriate and justifiable way to interpret Pure Land Buddhism today. These things he seems simply to take for granted.

Hirota also adopts materials from outside traditional Buddhist resources in his interpretive work. Indeed, he goes considerably beyond Tachikawa: for he not only employs modern history of religions' procedures to help place Pure Land Buddhism in its larger (Buddhist) historical context; he also picks up concepts and methods of interpretation invented by modern Christian theologians—as they have attempted to understand and reconstruct Christian thinking in ways intelligible and meaningful to persons living in the twentieth century—employing these in his own attempt to explain and interpret today's Shin Buddhism. He is aware that his efforts to "modernize" and even "demythologize" Pure Land teachings in light of modern ideas may appear illegitimate to many fellow practicers, so he devotes much of his chapter to showing that such demythologizing or interpretation in terms of wider, more general (philosophical) concerns has in fact been going on for many generations—at least as far back as Nagarjuna and many of his successors, among whom he apparently regards Shinran as virtually definitive. The movement from ordinary, limited, commonsense ways of thinking to more universal categories is a principal part of the path to "enlightenment." So contemporary reconstructive work (such as demythologizing and reinterpreting important traditional concepts) should be understood as a response to a central demand of the tradition itself.

Yokota, in his reconstructive work—though not as self-conscious as Hirota on the importance of methodological reflection about these matters—goes the furthest with this procedure of employing ideas drawn from nontraditional resources. Unlike Hirota—who seems to feel that his task is largely the hermeneutic one of simply reinterpreting for today's world and today's ways of thinking the central ideas of the tradition (especially as articulated by Shinran)—Yokota regards the modern twentieth-century awareness of the great diversity of religious and cultural traditions around the world as itself an "opportunity" for interpreters and teachers of Shin Buddhism to "extend our horizons beyond their historical, social and ethnic limits to a *more comprehensive vision of reality*" (p. 73, emphasis mine). There is, he suggests, much in the outside world of religious practice, experience, and reflection that can benefit adherents of Pure Land Buddhism—not simply through providing concepts and methods for more adequately interpreting tradition (as with Tachikawa and Hirota)—but through presenting significantly *new insights* into the basic situation and condition of human life in the world, insights that will call attention to and can help correct deep-lying distortions and prejudices in the tradition, thus enabling it to grow in significantly new, more fruitful directions as it moves into the future. At a number of points in his chapter he mentions some of the changes in the basic standpoint of Pure Land thinking that he believes need attention: any conception of enlightened wisdom as utterly "passionless, detached" (p. 79), with a concomitant understanding of compassion as "somehow colorless and unfeeling" (p. 79) is unacceptable; a full recognition of "*socio-political structures of existence* which impede or negate . . . suchness," and a rejection of "apathy toward or dissociation from others" (p. 80, emphasis mine) is important; failure to adequately interpret and properly value "self-power" needs to be corrected (p. 80f.); and, perhaps underlying all these points, a much fuller realization of the significance of the basically historical character of human existence is badly needed (pp. 81–85). Although both Hirota and Tachikawa employ *historical* methods and concepts in their analysis and interpretation of Pure Land Buddhism, they do not seem to give history and historicity the all-pervasive importance in their overall conceptions of human existence that Yokota does.

In what follows I shall try to develop further, and examine more fully, these contrasts among the three chapters before us.

II

As just noted, Hirota and Yokota appear to differ somewhat from Tachikawa in their willingness to utilize themes, ideas, and methods developed in Western religious and philosophical reflection, as they work out their own interpretations—or, more precisely, their *reconstructions*—of certain Pure Land practices and ideas. It is not that Tachikawa completely rejects modern Western thinking and practices in his work: in at least two important respects he has adopted Western ways of working and thinking (without, however, calling specific attention to this point). (1) His very attempt to orient contemporary Pure Land thinking through historical analysis and reconstruction presupposes that he regards human beings and human life as in some significant respects *historical* in character, as developing in and through *time* (his interest in human agency is further evidence of this); and for this reason it is important to him to engage in *historical reconstruction* (as methodologically worked out in the last two centuries or so) in his own attempts to understand particular religious or other historical movements (such as Pure Land Buddhism). It is not entirely clear just how Tachikawa reconciles this methodological commitment to time and history with his express contention that what Buddhism (indeed, all religious activity) is really all about is "emancipation from time" (pp. 103, 109). Perhaps he is not concerned with this question at all, being interested only in giving an adequate *description* of historical religious movements; his chapter is confined almost entirely to that. But if he has religious commitments of his own to "emancipation from time," one cannot but wonder how or why he would suppose that

presenting a temporal/historical picture of Buddhism could be properly illuminating. Why would he not regard this sort of approach as
thoroughly misconceived?

(2) Historical analysis and reconstruction can, of course, be pursued from many different points of view and with quite different sorts
of emphasis. Tachikawa himself appears to find the conception of
religion that utilizes the polar contrast of what is called "the sacred"
with what is called "the profane"—a conception indebted to the work
of Rudolf Otto, Mircea Eliade (who is mentioned once, on p. 118), and
others—particularly illuminating; for he uses this contrast as a principal analytical tool (p. 107ff.), as he sets out what Pure Land Buddhism
is and how it should be understood. It is interesting to note that though
both Yokota and Hirota seem as committed to the use of historical
methods as Tachikawa, neither makes any use at all of the sacred/
profane contrast in their reconstructive proposals. They seem to regard religions, rather, as having the function of orienting women and
men in precisely the wider ("secular") world and life in which they
find themselves; as Hirota puts it, "The problem is to come to a coherent and intelligible understanding of oneself and the world that ignores neither the historical and emotional boundness of the self nor
the variety and worth of experience" (p. 65f.). Instead of thoroughly
rejecting the modern world as utterly "profane"—in contrast with the
"sacred sphere" to which humans should be fleeing—they appear to
expect human religiousness to be relevant to major dimensions of
modern existence; so both present ways and respects in which Pure
Land Buddhism can orient practicers effectively in today's world (an
issue which Tachikawa does not directly address). Yokota adopts
conceptions developed in Whiteheadian process theologies to work
out his reconstruction of a number of Shin Buddhist notions; Hirota
uses some ideas from my work (and that of others) as he analyzes and
demythologizes what he calls the "mythic-narrative terms" (p. 52) characteristic of traditional Pure Land thinking.

These procedures of Hirota and Yokota may seem in significant
respects sharply different from the stance characteristic of traditional
Pure Land Buddhism (which Tachikawa, with his more "objectivist"
historical approach does not seek to move beyond, except through
pointing out historical roots and connections). One can argue, however, that Shinran's radical conviction (a) that all men and women
throughout their lives remain utterly bound up with their commit-

ments to "this world," and (b) that the whole point of trusting in Amida's Vow is that this enables practicers to live with this condition, can be interpreted as providing a significant basis for the sorts of reconstructive accommodating moves proposed by Yokota and Hirota (as both suggest). Tachikawa, if he is himself personally committed to the kind of Buddhism he describes (something not clear in his chapter), may regard all such compromises with the "profane" (as he might be inclined to put it) as unacceptable.

We have, then, some points of agreement in approach among our three writers—particularly, it would seem, on the understanding of human existence as historical (at least in certain respects), and the necessity, therefore, to utilize the tools of modern historical science to understand, interpret, and properly grasp human religious movements, activities, and standpoints. There are also some sharp differences regarding what religion (or at least Buddhism) is all about, and regarding what our historical understanding actually teaches us concerning Pure Land Buddhism and how it should be reconstructed (that is, *constructed anew*) for practicers in today's world.

Keeping these points in mind, let us turn to a closer look at the proposals of Yokota and Hirota, both of whom make significantly new imaginative moves in their constructions of Shin Buddhism, moves which, however, lead them in different directions. As we have been noting, they both apparently accept modern ideas about human historical development and historicity—ideas which can certainly be related to traditional Buddhist notions of the world and human life as incessantly changing, but which differ from those notions by emphasizing *human creativity* in the ongoing historical process and significant *human responsibility* for the directions in which that process has moved in the past and may move in the future. (It might be interesting to bring these latter notions into direct connection with traditional ideas about karma. Some of Yokota's remarks about karma [94 ff.] seem somewhat relevant, but he does not bring out clearly their pertinence to these issues.) This modern historical perspective apparently leads them both (a) to understand Pure Land Buddhism as itself a movement that has not only developed in the course of a particular history, but one that is—precisely now in this present—continuing to change (along with the rest of the human world in which it finds itself); and (b) to believe that contemporary Pure Land Buddhists should actively participate in this ongoing change by seeking to create or construct versions of Shin Buddhism more relevant to and appropriate for life in today's world, in this way taking deliberate responsibility, as far as possible, for the future of this religion. (Though similar presuppositions about history may also, in certain respects, underlie Tachikawa's claims and proposals, he does not appear to have drawn these sorts of conclusions about their significance.)

Both Yokota and Hirota seem to regard what they call the "mythical" (Yokota, 74) or "mythic-narrative" (Hirota, 52) character of Pure Land traditions to be a problem that needs address today; and both present interpretations of those traditions in analytical and/or philosophical terms and approaches (what Hirota calls "more general frames of reference," Hirota, 53) developed with the help of ideas proposed by contemporary Christian writers seeking to deal with similar "mythic" elements in traditional formulations of Christian faith. Just as the polarity of "sacred/profane" (not used by Hirota or Yokota) provides Tachikawa with an important way to focus the major issues he wishes to address in his chapter, so the notion of "myth" (not mentioned by Tachikawa) appears to be taken for granted by Hirota and Yokota as they seek to identify the issues to which they wish to attend. ("Myth" has functioned similarly in "demythologizing" interpretations of Christianity going back at least as far as Kant.) What is "myth," and why does it have this sort of importance? What does it identify in traditional forms of religious speech and thinking that requires special attention and significant reformulation in today's world?

Myth (from the Greek word meaning simply "story") became a technical term for nineteenth-century European writers seeking to designate what seemed to them—with their modern scientific and historical perspectives—to be "fabulous" tales about "primordial times" or faraway "imaginary places," a category of stories found in many of the literatures and preliterate traditions of cultures around the world. "Myths" or "mythical ideas" or "mythic modes of thought" were regarded as standing in sharp contrast with modern scientific and historical knowledge and methods. They were fictive tales and notions, creations of the human imagination, that had now become (as some believed) completely superseded in the modern age of "positive" scientific knowledge (Comte and other "positivists"); or (as others held) which presented, in narrative and anthropomorphic terms, important insights into, or "kernels" of truth about, human existence and the world (the German Romantics, Hegel, and their successors). According to this latter group, these truths could be made accessible and helpful to modern educated folk if they were carefully analyzed and reinterpreted in ways that took into account modern scientific, historical, and philosophical understandings of the world and of human life. Both Yokota and Hirota employ the conception of myth as a point of reference helping them to ascertain and bring into focus (some of) the issues that need to be taken into consideration in the constructive and reconstructive work they think contemporary Pure Land Buddhist thinking needs. (Yokota does not directly define what he understands by "myth"; Hirota offers his characterization on p. 53.)

Yokota appears to regard it as obvious that "the mythical foundation of the Pure Land tradition" must be confronted (p. 74); and from the first page on he develops his paper—in which notions and ways of thinking worked out in Christian process theology are frequently employed—on that largely unexamined presupposition (he later suggests that "demythologization" was what was actually going on in the traditional "Madhyamika treatment of emptiness," 88f.). Hirota, however, refrains from introducing the concept of myth until page 53, and even then he uses it in a cautious and carefully qualified way. It is not until he has set out a good bit of the Pure Land understanding of human life in the world—analyzing and explaining traditional conceptions such as "Pure Land," "Buddha's Vow," "the world of the five defilements," and the like with the aid of a distinction between "teleological" and "interpersonal" transcendence (adapted from an essay of mine)—that he finds himself in a position to make clear the full significance of another illuminating distinction of his own: between "Initial Engagement" with Pure Land practice and "Fulfilled Engagement." With the first of these terms he is calling the reader's attention to a period on the Pure Land path during which "practicers tend to conceive of the real either in terms of a theistic being (Amida) who works for their salvation . . . or as the power of the Vow that functions like a universal law to effect the birth of beings who accord with it" (p. 50). When the reader has that picture, and its meaning, fairly clear in mind, Hirota reminds us that this "mythic-narrative" (p. 52) way of thinking is, of course, only "provisional"; and that it is not until "the second phase . . . when a person has broken through the frames of reference of the first" (p. 52), that it becomes appropriate (or even possible) to move beyond this modality to a more mature understanding.

In this way, by suggesting that each of these terminologies and conceptual frames hás its own distinctive role to play as practicers move down the Shin Buddhist path toward enlightenment, Hirota is able to justify—in terms of Shin Buddhist understandings themselves—both (a) the sharp differences between "mythic-narrative" ways of speaking/thinking and more sophisticated and refined patterns, and (b) the necessity to move beyond the former to the latter in order to attain adequate understanding (today) of what is at stake in Pure Land practices and commitments. Though Hirota does not himself directly discuss the appropriateness of his use of the notion of myth, the analysis in his chapter (in my opinion) provides a way in which he could address that issue fairly easily. Indeed, his entire chapter can be seen as (a) a demythologizing of the traditional Pure Land message, and (b) an attempt to show that demythologizing of this sort is not only implicit in the message, but is itself a significant part of what the message is about; namely, that the Shin Buddhist path is a movement from the illusion and error of samsara (in which practicers regard familiar mythic stories to be presenting them with *realities*) to a more (or fully?) adequate awareness of reality. In this more adequate awareness practicers see and acknowledge the delusional reified character of the world in which they live; and yet, in precisely this seeing and acknowledgment, they are moved beyond this delusory character into an orientation of life that is in significant respects true to reality. Yokota also, I suspect, may find these features of Hirota's analysis useful for his purposes; for Hirota has shown that in Pure Land traditions and ways of thinking there are significant grounds for engaging in quite drastic demythologizing of traditional conceptions.

III

In my opinion this achievement moves the engagement between Christian theologians and Pure Land Buddhists to a new level.[1] For at least the past two centuries, Christian theologians have recognized that the linguistic/narrative forms in which the Christian message is presented in the Bible require rather drastic reconception and reinterpretation if they are to remain challenging and relevant for reflective people in the modern world. And much Western philosophical and theological reflection has been devoted to the difficult issues this poses for understanding what faith can be in modernity, how this modern faith is related to that of earlier historical periods, in what sense the Bible can continue to be regarded as normative for faith and life, and so on. Figures such as Descartes, Spinoza, Locke, Leibniz, Kant, Schleiermacher, Hegel, Strauss, Feuerbach, and Mill all devoted attention to these questions; and they have remained central in the work of every important twentieth-century theologian, with Rudolf Bultmann's "demythologizing" program perhaps focusing the debates most sharply. Throughout these discussions one of the most important and difficult issues was concerned with showing that and how proposed "new formulations" or "modern interpretations" of Christian faith maintained significant continuity with more traditional, particularly biblical, views. On this point, it will be remembered, Bultmann argued that the activity of demythologizing was actually as old as the Fourth Gospel—with its presentation of a picture of Jesus and the central Christian message radically different from most other New Testament writings. One can also argue that much post–New Testament Christian theological reflection has been largely an activity of ongoing appropriation of current philosophical and other concepts, ideas, and ways of thinking, attempting to reconceive Christian faith and the Christian message in terms of these (new) frames of reference.

However, as far back as the "Christian gnostics" of the second century (including such notable early theologians as Clement of Alexandria and Origen), there have been problems connected with demythologizing and reconception of this sort. Perhaps the most important of these concerned the claim that there are two levels of Christian understanding and faith: the level of most ordinary believers, who grasp their faith largely in somewhat crude mythic terms; and the level of the sophisticated intellectuals who believe that this way of understanding the *realities* of Christian faith is misleading, inadequate, untrue. Elitism of this sort is in significant tension with important strains in the Christian message toward an egalitarian leveling of all human beings as equally beloved children of God, and it has therefore never been fully accepted as a satisfactory way of dealing with the "mythic elements" (as the sophisticates saw them) in Christian traditions. It may be that the understanding—apparently central to Pure Land teaching (if I read Hirota correctly)—that different humans will likely be at quite different stages on the path to enlightenment, provides a satisfactory way for Buddhists to deal with this problem (though it does not seem to be easily appropriable by Christians). I would, however, assume that an elitism of the intellectuals must also present some serious problems for Buddhists—particularly Pure Land Buddhists.

IV

In the early part of his chapter, Hirota suggests that in interreligious discussions it is a mistake to assume that "the conceptions of truth [in different religious traditions] are the same," and that it is possible to directly compare "truth-claims" made in one tradition with those in another:

> If we begin by grasping the teachings in terms of "truth-claims," are we not already assuming features of religious traditions that limit too narrowly the kind of conversation that can develop? . . . we must pursue not only the reasons certain assertions should be regarded as true, or the broader, common frames of reference in which to interpret and evaluate traditional truth-claims, but what it means within a tradition to say that a statement is true, and the very nature of our engagement with the teachings. (p. 34)

He is undoubtedly correct in this observation, and he is completely justified, therefore, in devoting much of his chapter to showing that Shin Buddhist teachings are primarily concerned with moving the practicer along the path to enlightenment, not with making ontological "truth-claims"[2] (as he, along with many others, seems to suppose is the central issue for Christianity). Given this absolute significance of "practice in the immediate present" (p. 39) for Shin Buddhism, it appears that the criteria to be invoked in assessing the appropriateness of specific Pure Land teachings are largely pragmatic ("useful means," *upāya*): how *effective* are the practices, in any particular case, in moving men and women forward on the Shin path? This emphasis on the overriding priority of practice enables him, as we have seen, to deal very successfully with the mythic aspects of traditional Shin teachings. But does it really dispose of the question of truth? I think not. For the path of practice itself, as Hirota usually presents it, appears to be premised upon a very definite conception of the ultimate reality with which humans have to do, a conception of what the world really is, a conception (that is to say) of ontological reality.

Hirota suggests this a number of times in his chapter (here differing sharply from Tachikawa, who claims that "in Japanese Pure Land thought . . . a system of knowledge regarding the structure of the world may be said to be completely lacking," 114). Early on, he refers to "a conception of true reality [in Shin Buddhism] as love or wisdom-compassion" (p. 40); and toward the end of his chapter he sums up by interpreting the symbol "Amida Buddha" as implying that reality (apparently even as understood by the mature practicer) is a kind of personal active agency—"reality [is] inherently personal, acting toward and embracing beings, yet without judgment or discrimination" (p. 61)—and then referring again to "the nature of reality as wisdom-compassion" (p. 62, cf. p. 54; and also p. 40 where he interprets Shinran as holding this view). The Shin path, of course, is expected to move us beyond our normal and natural egocentric way of living and acting in the world, with "wisdom-compassion" gradually taking its place: that is what commitment to and entering into the practice of entrusting oneself to the Vow, aspiring for the Pure Land, and so on, are all about. But the plausibility and meaningfulness of this new way of acting and living seems to depend at least in part (according to his interpretation)—and this is why the symbol of Amida Buddha as an active agent is so important—on our taking the ultimate reality with which we humans have to do in life to be itself, in some significant sense, "wisdom-compassion," that is, quasi-personal. Yokota makes similar sorts of claims (e.g., 79, 94f.). The problem of ontological truth-claims—anthropomorphic (i.e., mythic) ones at that!—seems to be still with us here.

The picture drawn here by Hirota (and Yokota) is coherent enough as it stands, but I wonder if it is a full enough demythologization for modern practicers (just as I wonder if continuing Christian talk about God as "a personal being" can still be made plausible to many educated believers).[3] Making such notions as "wisdom" and "compassion" fundamental to our interpretation of ultimate reality seems to involve a projection onto the cosmos of a basically anthropomorphic vision of the universe—an increasingly dubious move, if one takes seriously scientific cosmological notions (of a "big bang" followed by an enormous evolutionary expansion of the universe) and evolutionary-biological ideas about the origins of life and of human existence. The same issue arises, of course, with the idea of God in Christianity: God is said to be ultimate reality, beyond all our conceiving or knowing, the source and ground of all that is, and so on—and at the same time God is (usually) taken to be purposive, loving, and forgiving.

That is, the basic reality with which we finally have to do is regarded as, in important respects, *humanlike;* and it is precisely this characteristic of ultimate reality in Christian traditional symbolism (and apparently also in Shin Buddhism) that grounds both faith and the aspiration to live our lives in loving kindness toward others. In some forms of Buddhism (e.g., Zen) there is an attempt to overcome such anthropomorphisms through the affirmation that it is finally "emptiness" alone in terms of which all life must be oriented. But moving too far in this direction can easily lead dangerously close to a perception of the world as what Hirota calls "a morally homogeneous flatland" with "merely passive" practicers, something that he declares the Pure Land path seeks to avoid (p. 66). (Yokota takes a similar position on this issue; see, e.g., pp. 78–80, 93.) Although Pure Land Buddhism may not wish to end up at a position of that sort, it does rely on the corrective (of tendencies toward anthropomorphism) which the doctrines of suchness, emptiness, formlessness and the like can provide (cf. Hirota, 54–56; Yokota, 87–90). It is not at all clear to me that we can have it both ways with this issue. To say that the tension of these highly abstract characterizations of "ultimate reality" with more anthropomorphic (and humanly attractive and meaningful) notions like "compassion" and "wisdom" is merely a function of the "initial" stages of engagement with the Pure Land way, and that this tension dissolves when more mature levels of understanding are reached (cf. Hirota, pp. 57–60), has a certain plausibility; but it seems to come dangerously close to being a merely verbal solution to an exceedingly difficult intellectual issue. Yokota seems to me to recognize more forthrightly the seriousness of this problem (p. 96).

My own thinking about these questions has been pursued largely in connection with the similar problems that arise (as it seems to me) with Christian theological conceptions of the world, God, and demythologization. Perhaps the most carefully thought-through (but highly controversial and clearly elitist) theory about these matters is Hegel's. Hegel argued (a) that traditional religious "picture-language" (*Vorstellungen*, "representations") is "true," but that what this "truth" really is can be ascertained only through articulating it in philosophical/conceptual form (i.e., only when, to use the language of this chapter, it is properly "demythologized"); and (b) that this philosophical conceptualization, moreover (however strange it might sound to the pious religious ear), is in fact *identical* in meaning to the traditional religious representational ("mythic") notion. This is an exceedingly interesting, but very problematic, proposal. It seems to me that the underlying issue at stake here—for both Pure Land Buddhism and Christian faith—is this: How can we humans relate to the cosmic or-der in which we appear to be situated—in all of its *im*personality (displayed vividly, for example, in modern scientific theorizing, which we certainly cannot ignore without sustained justifying argument) as well as its personal dimensions, in its *de*humanizing as well as its humanizing features—without falling into a cynicism and despair that are ultimately destructive of love and compassion? Do not (almost) all of us need some sort of mythic/anthropomorphic conception of a God/ Amida who loves/has compassion on us, and who draws us into a higher realm of life in which we too are enabled to live with compas-sion and care for all other creatures?

If that is so, and we feel that intolerable problems arise if we go all the way (in our demythologizing) to the ultimate formlessness or emptiness or abyss or mystery from which all things come and to which they ultimately return, it may be that we need to pose this whole issue of religious "truth-claims" in a somewhat different way: though a thoroughgoing demythologization is thought to represent our best human "knowledge of the world," it may not express a form of *wisdom* that is effective in overcoming human self-centeredness and in bringing forth genuinely self-sacrificing human compassion/agape for all creatures. (A distinction of this sort between "knowledge" and "wisdom" obviously involves giving moral pragmatic criteria greater weight than epistemic criteria, at least with respect to certain issues— e.g., about how life is to be lived.) With considerations of this sort in mind, I find myself agreeing with Hirota in his suggestion (early in his chapter) that it is a mistake to think of "religious truth" as consisting essentially of doctrinal "truth-claims" about the cosmos (as Western philosophers and theologians seem often to have done); we should instead proceed in terms of a much more pragmatic understanding of truth as that which enables us to go forward on the path to compas-sion/caring/love (cf. also Yokota, 96).[4] The "conversation" in which our various religious traditions need to be engaged, then, should be about the diverse "paths" they each propose: to what "goals" do each of these paths lead? how can these paths complement or supplement each other? what norms are available for assessing them? and so forth. Although (as I have suggested above), Hirota at some points seems to think claims about the ontological status of "wisdom/compassion" are necessary—and here his thinking (as well as Yokota's) bears a strong resemblance to Christian reification of personalistic God-imagery—in other places he can be interpreted as making a quite different, definitely pragmatic, proposal about religious truth: "The obligation of the Shin path is above all to know the self and world by the . . . awareness [brought about by hearing and saying the nembutsu], for such knowing *allows for the arising of a world of action in which the reified self* is no longer absolute center" (p. 66, my emphasis). Ultimately (he seems to be saying at this point) all doctrinal interpretations, including demythologizations, must be tested by the way they shape human action in the wide world of human experience. With this point I as a Christian theologian—and a pragmatist in my understanding of religious symbolism, knowledge, and truth—find myself in complete agreement.

V

In these chapters by Hirota and Yokota, the notion of myth, I have suggested, plays an important role: it provides a point of reference in terms of which one can discern why much traditional religious language often seems fanciful, irrelevant, perhaps even absurd to (at least some) Pure Land Buddhists who live out their lives largely in terms of the dominant conceptual frames of modernity. That is, it helps to identify a problem which, as Yokota suggests, religious teachers today should "confront" (p. 74). It does not in itself, however, provide much guidance on how to deal with this problem; and, if given a free leash (as we have just been noting), it may lead to quite unfortunate consequences. How, then, should one proceed at this point? Our three chapters (assuming for the moment that Tachikawa is also, in his own way, concerned with this issue) address it in three distinctly different ways, which I would like, now, to take up as I bring my comments to a conclusion.

Yokota suggests that Christian *process theologies* have developed ways of speaking and thinking that successfully integrate modern scientific thinking with a thoroughly Christian vision; and that much can be learned from these efforts as one seeks to demythologize and modernize Pure Land Buddhist practices and notions. (It is interesting in this connection that throughout his chapter Yokota takes over Christian thinking about God quite freely, as a basis for his discussion of the way in which Amida should be interpreted today; toward the end of his chapter he goes so far as to refer to the ultimate reality with which we have to do as "God/Amida" [97].) Hirota, in his middle position, seeks to construct a demythologized and modernized version of "mature or fulfilled engagement," with (on the one hand) the help of his refined and highly illuminating concepts of "teleological" and "interpersonal" transcendence, and (on the other hand) thoughtful reflection on the meaning of *shinjin* (especially in Shinran)—culminating (somewhat ambiguously, as we have noted) in an "understanding of reality as itself wisdom-compassion" (pp. 53, 67). Tachikawa apparently does not see his task as a modernizing one in the sense of demythologizing; rather, he presents a straightforward (and quite illuminating) historical exposition of the tradition in light of the polarity of the sacred and profane (a modern comparative religions' concept), not concerning himself much with the question of whether this is intelligible to moderns and can illuminate human existence today as well as in earlier times.

Though Hirota and Tachikawa appear to differ greatly in their respective concerns about the question of the intelligibility of traditional Pure Land symbols and concepts to modern minds, they each understand their task as essentially a *hermeneutic* one; that is, what they appear to be doing is giving updated *interpretations* of what they take to be basic features of Pure Land traditions. As nearly as I can tell, neither of them is interested in significantly changing these traditions: Hirota appears to take it for granted that the basic understanding of the human situation in the world found in them is correct and true, and his task is to bring this out in terms that make clear to moderns (a) just what that basic understanding is, and (b) why and how it can be regarded as correct and true. Tachikawa simply attempts to set out the "facts" of the matter in historical context. Both seek to translate into modern idioms and ways of thinking what Pure Land traditional texts present in linguistic forms that are no longer easily and immediately accessible to moderns. The translation efforts of these two men move in distinctly different directions, but their basic understandings of the procedures required to carry through their tasks—to *interpret* the essentials of traditional Pure Land Buddhism in modern terms, not to change them in any important respects—appear to be very similar.

Yokota, however, seems to understand his task somewhat differently. He is also engaged in interpretive work, of course, but he does not think of his efforts to modernize and demythologize as limited to hermeneutic activity: though he agrees that the basic insights and practices of Pure Land Buddhism have much to offer men and women living in today's world, he thinks certain traditional emphases must— in the light of (a) modern understandings and knowledges generally and (b) certain things that can be learned from other religious traditions (e.g., from Christian process theologies)—be regarded today as no longer useful or appropriate for orienting human life in the world, and therefore should be changed. (Earlier in this paper I listed a number of the items characteristic of [some] traditional Shin Buddhist understandings and practices that he mentions in this connection.) Yokota apparently sees his task, therefore, as involving not only (a) *interpretation* of Pure Land traditions; but also (b) *assessing* the adequacy of the various features of those traditions, deciding not only which are essentials and which of less importance and thus dispensable but also which must be judged misleading, misconceived, or even false; and then (c) *recommending certain changes* in thinking and practice that are necessary if adherence to Pure Land symbols is to shape and orient human life today in meaningful and effective ways. He never spells all this out explicitly, but he seems to regard the task of reflective thinkers and teachers of Shin Buddhism today to be as much an *imaginative constructive* one as a hermeneutic one; and in this he appears to be moving significantly beyond what Hirota and Tachikawa take themselves to be doing.

Yokota could defend his position (if he were to work out more thoroughly the methodological aspects of what he is doing) by arguing that all interpretive activity is in fact a matter of constructive reimagining—and is thus in significant respects a fresh re*creating* of religious ideas and ideals in terms and patterns significantly different from those found in received traditions. Interpretation of texts in a new situation, a new linguistic and cultural context, is always an act in which the tradition is actually being *transformed;* it is never a matter of simply reproducing what was already there. To the extent that it is creative of the new, it involves (a) *judgments* (by the interpreter) of what is of real importance in received traditions and what may (or should) be dispensed with or ignored, and (b) *imaginative proposals* of images, metaphors, and concepts, sometimes quite different from those that had previously been employed, to express these essentials in the most effective way possible in today's world. All of this, of course, changes the tradition in what are often highly significant (though perhaps unnoticed) ways—as later historians will be able to see clearly. Shinran radically changed traditions he received from Honen and others before him, though he may have thought of himself as only emphasizing what was truly important in those traditions; and Hirota and Tachikawa (as well as Yokota), precisely through their use of modern conceptual frameworks and ways of understanding and thinking, are also significantly changing what they have received—they are creating *new* conceptions of what Pure Land Buddhism is all about—though they may regard themselves as simply interpreters of what has always been there. From this point of view Yokota's work, with its critical, constructive, and creative features, really does not differ as much in principle from that of Tachikawa and Hirota as at first seemed to be the case: he is simply doing openly and explicitly—and thus, perhaps more boldly—what every interpreter does in more concealed fashion.

In my view this *creative* dimension of interpretive work should be more straightforwardly acknowledged than it often is—and then openly and explicitly taken on as part of the task for which one makes oneself responsible. To do that would be, of course, to move to a methodologically more self-conscious level than that evidenced by our three writers. To engage most effectively in the kind of work they are seeking to do (as Tachikawa's initial analysis of what is involved in action suggests), it is important for them to understand that this is what they are in fact undertaking. For only with a clear grasp of what is really involved in this sort of work will it be possible for them to think through clearly, and make clear to their readers, (a) the reasons why this sort of creative or constructive work is an unavoidable part of all translating, modernizing, and demythologizing activity; (b) why it is justifiable and important to engage in activity of this sort, and (c) the specific criteria and constructive principles being employed in the particular creative moves they are making.[5]

Notes

1. Hirota has taken on the major questions about Shin Buddhism (presented in my address at Ryukoku University in 1989 and outlined in the introduction to this volume) in a brilliantly illuminating fashion, making it possible to move the discussion between Christian theologians and Pure Land Buddhists significantly forward.

2. Neglect of this distinction, he shows in a very insightful and illuminating discussion of Karl Barth's interpretation of Jōdo Shinshū (pp. 35–37) and James Dobbins's understanding of Shinran (pp. 37–39), can easily lead to serious misunderstanding of what Pure Land Buddhism is all about.

3. My entire book, *In Face of Mystery: A Constructive Theology* (Cambridge: Harvard University Press, 1993), can be interpreted as grappling with this question; see esp. chs. 1 and 5, and pts. 3 and 4.

4. For a brief argument of mine along these lines some years ago, see "Christian Theology and the Modernization of the Religions" (*The Theological Imagination: Constructing the Concept of God* [Philadelphia: Westminster Press, 1981], esp. pp. 200–206). This "pragmatic" understanding of religious truth is central to my reconstruction of the Christian symbolic world in In *Face of Mystery,* and comes up repeatedly there. See esp. chs. 4, 5, and 16 (which emphasize, through developing the theme of "mystery," the unsurpassable limits of our "knowledge") and chs. 17–27 (which propose a movement through a series of "small steps of faith" toward what, in the context of this chapter, we might call "wisdom").

5. My own first attempt to set out clearly this imaginative-constructive conception of religious reflection and interpretation (developed in terms of my analysis of what actually goes on in specifically Christian theological work) is to be found in my *Essay on Theological Method* (published by Scholars Press in 1975; issued in a second edition in 1979; and recently reissued in a third edition, with significant revisions and a new preface outlining important changes in my thinking on certain points). My attempt to develop a full Christian theology in terms of this methodological understanding is to be found in the book, *In Face of Mystery,* mentioned in earlier notes.

5. A Christian Critique of Pure Land Buddhism

John B. Cobb, Jr.

The Point of View

I have been asked to provide a Christian critique of Pure Land Buddhism as presented in the three chapters with which this volume begins. It is important to underline the a. I cannot speak for Christians generally. No one can. And in my case I am committed to a form of Christian thought, process theology, that is highly critical of much of the Christian tradition.

Being critical of Christian tradition is not unusual today among Christian theologians, especially those in the old-line Protestant traditions. Protestantism began as a critique of tradition, and, although it has produced forms that absolutize the original critique and abandon the critical spirit, it also generates a critical attitude in many theologians. Each generation rejects, but also builds upon, the work of its predecessors, often retrieving elements of the earlier tradition that those predecessors had rejected.

As a Protestant who believes that this process of self-criticism, both personal and corporate, is an expression of faith and that every attempt to absolutize any given form of the tradition is idolatrous, one question I ask of other religious communities is whether they encourage this questioning and critical spirit. Do they seek to develop and transform their traditions again and again, or do they endlessly defend a past formulation?

147

In most traditions (certainly in Christianity as a whole), the answer is mixed. But the nature of the mixture varies from one community to another. In Buddhism, for example, there seems to be less "fundamentalism" in the sense of absolutizing particular formulations than in Christianity, partly because of the suspicion of concepts. There is also less attention to the historically conditioned character of all formulations and therefore to the need for change in new historical circumstances. However, Yokota's chapter is a model of openness to recast tradition in light of interaction with other contemporary movements of thought. Tachikawa is in some respects even more critical. His criticism tends to be more objectifying, more that of one who studies the Buddhist tradition as a scholar than of one who undertakes its revision as a participant. This is, of course, a common approach also in the Christian context. Tachikawa pursues it with extraordinary ability and insight, but it is less clear to me how it will affect his own formulations of Buddhist beliefs in general or those of Pure Land in particular.

Although it is not unusual for Protestant theologians to be critical of Christian tradition and to develop new formulations of the faith, the extent to which the criticisms by process theologians are similar to those directed by Buddhists against Christianity is unusual. For example, when Dennis Hirota writes that Shinran "avoids a voluntaristic . . . view of reality, with such concomitant problems as predestination, the need for a theodicy, and a substantialist understanding of reality or of self," I applaud Shinran and hope that the Christian tradition to which I belong succeeds equally well in these respects. On the other hand, I have deleted "or theistic" from this quote, because I use "theistic" in a much broader sense, regarding voluntaristic theism as only one of its forms. My use of "theistic" could apply to Shinran.

More broadly, I view all reality as constituted by momentary events, and I believe these events are well characterized as instances of pratitya-samutpada (*pratītya-samutpāda*, dependent origination). This stands in contrast with the dominant metaphysical traditions that have shaped both official Christian theology and much of popular piety. It is not, however, uncongenial to Biblical teaching; and the appropriation of this vision, so brilliantly worked out in Buddhism, can enable Christians to recover much in our scriptures that has been obscured in our tradition.

The Problem with Formlessness

My discomfort with much of the Japanese Buddhism I have encountered is that in dealing with pratitya-samutpada or emptiness or Buddha-nature, it accentuates its formlessness. I do not mean here to dispute the fact that dependent origination as such is formless and can, for that reason, assume any form. Also, I fully realize that no one questions that every instance of pratitya-samutpada has an absolutely particular form and that close attention to this particularity is characteristic of Buddhism. What disturbs me is that attending only to these two points leads typically to the view that the Buddha-nature or Emptiness is "beyond good and evil." It leads also to the disparagement of conceptual thinking. It leads to prizing wisdom above compassion, despite the acknowledgment of the importance of the latter. It leads broadly to an emphasis on what is always true at every historical point, and therefore to a depreciation of the importance of historical analysis.

My own "theistic" view is that among the many that come together in each act of dependent arising, there is one that provides an impetus toward enrichment. This means that concretely, in each moment, the Buddha-nature includes a dependable form. Abstractly we may describe it as formless, but as it works to constitute each new actual instance in the world, it is always characterized by compassion. It is the compassionate form of Buddha-nature to which we ideally, moment by moment, conform.

I have used Buddhist language in formulating my own Christian convictions. It may misrepresent my views in some ways, but I believe it shows how close my Christian vision is to some formulations of Pure Land Buddhism. I am led to great appreciation for the subtle ways in which Pure Land Buddhism both distinguishes the other-power from self-power and also avoids a dualistic juxtaposition. The senses in which Amida is and is not "personal" are helpful to me in wrestling with the question of whether to speak of God as "personal." Of course, I detect differences on this point among Pure Land writers and find myself more drawn to some than to others. I am also impressed that in Pure Land imagery Amida as personal does not have the strongly patriarchal character that God as personal retains for most Christians.

I indicated above that my use of Buddhist terminology at some points may misrepresent my own Christian view. This focuses on the use of *compassion* instead of the more usual Christian term *love*. Christians certainly include compassion as a form of love, and process theologians especially emphasize compassion in just that way that Yokota has described and appropriated for purposes of expounding and expanding Pure Land thought. But, at least in English, *compassion* identifies a receptive feeling-with rather than an active going out to the other in specific ways. For the latter we often use the New Testament Greek word *agape*. This focuses on disinterested action for the good of the other.

Something like this is surely contained within Amida's compassion that works unceasingly for the enlightenment of all sentient beings. Hence there may be no problem. But there may be a difference between the way Amida is understood to work in each instance of pratitya-samutpada and the way I understand God to do so. I raise this question because the extent to which Pure Land Buddhism overcomes what I find to be a limitation in Mahayana Buddhism generally depends, in my view, on the answer.

I understand God to be that one, among the many that participate in dependent origination, that introduces alternative possibilities and calls for the realization of that possibility that is best both for that instance and also for the future. The "best" in some instances may be defined by movement along the path to enlightenment, but in many instances this will be incidental. In the human case, the best may usually have more to do with thinking clearly, acting generously, enjoying fully, relating sensitively, or listening openly.

The constitutive presence of this divine lure in each moment does not determine what will happen. It does determine that in that moment there will be a decision among alternative possibilities. The decision may be, ideally, the full realization of the lure. Usually the decision falls short of this, sometimes drastically so.

Viewed in this way, the call of God (the Primal Vow?) and the decision of the human occasion may coincide. They do so when the decision is to embody fully the call. But they remain distinct. If we associate the self with the decision, then the self is never simply identical with God. The relation is certainly not dualistic. The human self is brought into being in each moment by the call of God. It is not a substance, but rather only a momentary response to that call. It is called to conform to that call. But it is not compelled to do so.

I have sketched my own position in hopes that this will clarify the questions this analysis leads me to address to Pure Land thinkers. These questions are two.

First, I find in Pure Land rhetoric, as in Buddhism generally, a strong focus on enlightenment as the one goal worthy of pursuit, recognizing that it can occur only when it is no longer sought. It is clear that once enlightenment occurs, one can expect compassionate actions from the enlightened one. It is also clear that moral behavior is important as a precondition for the movement toward enlightenment. My question is whether we may consider that Amida works quite directly for other goals as important and worthy in themselves.

To explain why this question is so important to me, I need to clarify further my own concerns. At this point in history I am much more concerned for the salvation of the planet, and especially of the human species, from the misery and destruction we are now bringing upon it than for personal salvation. Of course, if the self-destruction of the species is inevitable, I prefer that as many individuals as possible find personal salvation despite the encompassing horrors. But I find preoccupation with our inner states an inappropriate response to our global historical situation.

Preoccupation with personal salvation has characterized most Christians through most of history. I do not want to raise my concerns about Buddhism without emphasizing that these are concerns about Christianity. Nevertheless, the idea of salvation in the Bible is by no means limited to the inner achievements of individuals. It often refers to what happens to the Jewish people as a whole. On Jesus' lips the "Realm of God" that constitutes his vision of salvation refers to a world in which God's will is done.

Through Christian history there has been a tension between the aim at realizing justice and righteousness within history and personal salvation either in this life or after death. In the twentieth century the social gospel and the liberation theologies have continued the prophetic emphasis on concrete historical change. Hence, when, as a Christian, I state my belief that God is calling us today to repent of those practices that are leading to the destruction of Earth and its inhabitants, I find myself in a supportive tradition.

I do not see a comparably supportive tradition in Mahayana Buddhism as a whole. By that I do not mean that there are no themes or points of contact for accenting global responsibility of this sort. Buddhists have certainly taken the lead in deploring violence and working for peace. But on the whole the analysis of what now works against peace still tends to underplay the concrete historical factors that are currently so threatening. The tendency is to contrast the general human condition with enlightenment and to see enlightenment as the way to peace.

In Theravada Buddhist countries where Buddhism has supplied the public philosophy, the points of contact are more apparent and the emphasis easier to ground. There are Buddhist social movements in both Sri Lanka and Thailand that are, from my point of view, models of religiously motivated social analysis and action from which Christians have much to learn. So I judge that what seems a weakness in Mahayana Buddhism is rooted more in its particular history than in fundamental Buddhist teachings. Nevertheless, the limitation concerns me.

Despite Tachikawa's apparent disagreement, I continue to find in Pure Land the most promising basis available among the Mahayana schools for moving in the direction of historical particularity. Passages in Hirota encourage me in my belief. But I am especially influenced by what Yokota has taught me earlier and because of his interpretation and development of Pure Land Buddhism in this chapter. Indeed, he has thematically developed the idea of compassion in just the way for which I call, so that his answer to my questions is clearly affirmative. I press the question since I do not know how other Pure Land thinkers respond to Yokota's proposals.

Can we quite unequivocally understand Amida's compassion as directed to the salvation of the world in a corporate way as well as toward the enlightenment of the individuals who make up the whole? Can we understand Pure Land Buddhists to be called to develop human societies that will cease to be destructive of one another and of the other sentient beings with whom we share the planet? Can this call be made convincing to Pure Land Buddhists as continuous with some aspects of their tradition? Or is my wish that this might happen a Christian wish with little resonance among Pure Land Buddhists?

My second question is more narrowly theological. Is my typically Christian need to maintain the distinction between self and God to the end, even in the fullest and final attainment of oneness, alien to Pure Land Buddhism? No doubt the answer is already offered me in each of these three chapters, but the subtlety of the formulations leaves me uncertain. For most Christians, however fully God indwells the creature and the creature indwells God, God is not the creature and the creature is not God. For Buddhists generally, I gather, there is less discomfort about affirming an identity between the self and Buddha nature. As a process theologian I understand that one may realize one's identity as an instance of pratitya-samutpada and thus as an embodiment of the Dharmakaya. But in relation to Amida or the Primal Vow a distinction seems to me appropriate even in the fullest unity. Again, I find such a distinction clearly present in Yokota, but I am less sure of other formulations.

I hope my concern can be understood from what I have said above. I share the ideal that in each moment one constitutes oneself according to pratitya-samutpada as characterized by compassion or the Primal Vow. But in my view this way of constituting oneself never becomes automatic. Even when human habits are most ideally attuned to the divine call, human decision remains. At this point I part company with the strict Calvinist view that there can be no falling from grace, and I am troubled by what seems to be an analogous doctrine in Shinran. Are we to believe that there is a state of *shinjin* that, once established, does not need to be renewed moment by moment by a human act of conformation. Are self-power and other-power so perfectly merged that there is no longer any possibility of self-power functioning in tension with other-power?

I trust I have made it clear that this is not a question of differences between Christianity in general and Buddhism in general. It is a debate within Christianity, and it may be a debate among Pure Land Buddhists as well. To me it is important to recognize that spiritual growth leads to more demanding challenges, that there is no assurance that our attunement to God's call will lead us to respond fully to those challenges. It is also important to see that subtle distortions in the saintly life may be as destructive as vicious rejections of God's call by grossly unspiritual people. In Christian language, the belief that one is beyond temptation, or beyond the danger of yielding to temptation, is a dangerous one.

Faith and Practice

From these chapters and from other contacts I have had with Pure Land Buddhism, I sense that there are disagreements as to how to understand the relation of faith and practice. There are, of course, similar disagreements among Christians. I shall first spell out my own Christian view as a basis for clarifying the questions I address to Pure Land Buddhists.

In my view, faith is independent of practice and not attained by practice. It arises by grace, or what I called above "the lure." The lure calls us to trust it. If we trust it, it is because of the efficacy of grace. But there is no trust without decision.

There is no spiritual condition or state to which faith is a means. There is no Christian goal higher than trusting God. Of course, some receive spiritual gifts of various sorts, and these are to be prized. But they do not constitute a normative condition for all Christians.

Although the lure works in us always, its effectiveness is affected by our context. If we are surrounded by a community that seeks to be sensitive and responsive to grace, our response is more likely to be positive. If the presence of this grace and the importance of our decisions are highlighted and emphasized, the chances of a positive response are heightened. If the trustworthiness of grace is affirmed and demonstrated, that, too, enhances our prospects. In the Christian tradition, this means that participation in the life of a worshiping community provides the "means of grace."

Despite the independence of faith from practice, practice is not unimportant. The lure may call us to attend to it consciously and to develop particular disciplines. For Christians, in addition to active participation in the church, personal prayer and the study of the Bible are typical practices. But we must beware of supposing that faith is given to us as a result of these practices. Faith can exist without them, and they can, and often do, occur as means of gaining merit and thus rejecting grace. The practices by themselves can be "works righteousness" as easily as expressions of faith through which faith is deepened.

Faith frees us from the need for special practices. It also frees us to take part in practices that we find beneficial either for ourselves or others. I believe, for example, that Christians are entirely free to adopt and adapt Buddhist meditational practices as long as they do not suppose that they need these for their salvation or that engaging in such practices lifts them to a higher spiritual level than their fellow Christians who do not do so.

Faith expresses itself most consistently in love of the neighbor, understanding that all other creatures are neighbors. This love is embodied in actions favoring the well-being of these neighbors, including, but by no means limited to, their spiritual well-being. This well-being may be sought either directly for individuals who are at hand or indirectly through social and ecological analysis and action guided by it. This love is also compassion, feeling with others, and truly hearing them.

From this perspective I ask my questions. Can I understand *shinjin* as trusting the present working of the Primal Vow and deciding to be conformed to it? Or is it a spiritual condition or secure state attained as a result of meditational practice? Of course, I include the nembutsu and contemplation of the mandala as meditational practices.

The question arises for me because in Buddhism generally it seems that the concern is to attain a spiritual condition or state and that the means of doing so is primarily meditational practice. If *shinjin* is a spiritual state attained through meditational practice, then this understanding of faith and practice is quite different from my Protestant one. On the other hand, there are passages in Shinran and in these pages that give such priority to *shinjin* that it does not seem to be necessarily dependent on practice. It seems to come to us by the power of the Primal Vow. This does not preclude recitation of the nembutsu, but this is more response to the gift than a means of attaining a desired spiritual condition. It is this impression that makes Shinran so attractive to Protestant theologians. Have we taken him out of his Buddhist context and projected our ideas upon him? Is trusting Amida for Buddhists simply a step toward the attainment of a higher spiritual condition in which such trust is no longer needed?

In asking these questions I am not assuming that all Pure Land Buddhists speak with one voice. In Tachikawa's chapter, faith as trust seems clearly subordinate to meditational practice. In Hirota's they seem to be held in dialectical tension. Yokota's work can be interpreted in a way that is closer to my form of Christianity. Nevertheless, I would press for as much clarity as I can get as to whether there are significant differences here between Honen and Shinran and among the disciples of each.

Amida and Christ

Hirota quotes Karl Barth's emphatic statement that Christianity is bound up with the historical figure of Jesus Christ. I believe Barth is correct in this respect. I do not agree with him that doctrines in other communities similar to Christian ones lack similar effects. His position here follows from his supernaturalistic view of Jesus Christ, a view I do not share. If faith and practice similar to that of Christianity have emerged independently of Jesus Christ, then I would expect them to have similar salvific efficacy.

Hirota points out that the emphasis on similarity abstracts from contexts that are very different. In the previous sections I have been exploring the extent to which the different contexts lead to different conclusions on points that are important to me. Here I want to ask whether the historical connection to Shakyamuni plays the same essential role for Pure Land Buddhists as the historical connection to Jesus Christ plays for Christians.

Some Buddhists seem to answer negatively. Buddhism, they say, has to do with the attainment of enlightenment rather that with a historical connection to a particular Enlightened One. The historical context and tradition within which one becomes enlightened is secondary. Some Buddhists have affirmed this difference between Christianity and Buddhism as displaying Buddhism's greater openness and freedom from exclusivity.

These Buddhist arguments led me at an earlier point to propose that in the further development of some forms of Buddhism it would be possible to relate Buddhism to figures outside the Buddhist tradition equally with those within it. I thought this might be particularly appropriate for Pure Land. My argument was that Pure Land Buddhism identified its founder with a mythical figure, Dharmakara, that there are advantages in connecting one's tradition to historical reality, that the emphasis on other power or grace is clearer in the Christian tradition than in most Buddhism, and that Jesus could function as an historical embodiment and teacher of grace.

I realized, of course, that this was not a step that many Pure Land Buddhists were ready to take. And on the whole the proposal has been greeted by silence. However, Yokota has taken it seriously and gone to some length to reject it. He agrees that connecting the act of compassion to an historical figure is desirable, but he shows that this can be done with Shakyamuni. He apparently holds that since this is possible, there is no reason to consider other embodiments of compassion outside the Buddhist tradition.

His point that the Pure Land emphasis on the compassion of Amida can be grounded in Shakyamuni's life and practice is well taken, and I am interested in the response of other Pure Land Buddhists to his proposal. Is there recognition of the advantage of locating the act of compassion historically, or are most Pure Land Buddhists content with a mythical account recognized as mythical?

Nevertheless, I continue to wonder whether the embodiment of compassion *must* be found in the Buddhist tradition? Is this a point of disagreement among Buddhists? To sharpen my question, I again revert to an account of Christianity.

I have said that virtually all Christians understand Christianity as inherently, essentially, related to Jesus Christ. Many do not agree with Barth that salvation is effective only through this one historical event, but they then typically argue that God works salvifically outside of Christianity as well as within. Christianity is tied to the historical event even though the salvation to which Christianity witnesses need not be.

I am asking whether the relation of Buddhism to Shakyamuni is similar to that of Christianity to Jesus despite the statements by many Buddhists that there is a difference. Specifically in Pure Land Buddhism, must faith be directed toward figures reverenced in traditional Buddhist teaching in order for it to be Buddhist faith? If faith in the grace manifest in Jesus Christ had the same form and the same effect as faith in the compassion manifest in Gautama or the mythical vow of Dharmakara, would this be *shinjin*, and would it be Buddhist?

To answer negatively is certainly not to make oneself vulnerable to Christian criticism. It *is* to clarify that being Buddhist is being part of a community and tradition initiated historically by Gautama. It then can be discussed whether one can realize Buddha nature or enlightenment apart from being Buddhist, and here, I assume, most Pure Land Buddhists would take the same position as many Christians, namely, that Amida's compassion works independently of the Buddhist community and tradition. Would others take a position analogous to Barth's, namely, that apart from the nembutsu there can be no *shinjin*, whatever the formal similarities?

Language and Metaphysics

Until recently the great majority of Christian theologians assumed that their language about God and Christ and grace had a referent, that in this sense it was metaphysical. I continue to think and write in this way. However, in the past few decades many Christian thinkers, recognizing the difficulty of supporting claims about cosmic realities, have emphasized the symbolic character of all such language. Taken to its extreme, this means that each of the symbols has its meaning only in its interconnections with the other symbols, that there is no reference beyond the linguistic system.

Buddhists in rather different ways have also taught us to suspect our concepts and to empty them. They have refused to provide a cosmological account in answer to speculative questions. Thus there seems to be some agreement between Buddhism and the direction in which Christian theologians have been led by the linguistic turn and its current deconstructionist form. One alternative to the linguistic school is the phenomenological. Tachikawa works chiefly in this mode. This assumes that we have access to the phenomena not mediated by language.

On the other hand, I have interpreted pratitya-samutpada as a statement about how all entities or events are in fact constituted; namely, nonsubstantially, through relationships. That means that, in my language, Buddhism involves a metaphysical assertion of insubstantiality and nondualism. The most important application of this assertion is to the human soul or self, but I have taken it to have universal application. It is in this metaphysical sense that I share and affirm this Buddhist vision.

I realize that many Buddhist accounts emphasize language and epistemology rather than phenomenology or ontology (or hayatology). Perhaps for some this is not merely an emphasis but an exclusion, that is, they do not intend to say anything about how things are, only about how they are conceived or known. But much Buddhist writing makes more sense to me when I understand it to say something about how things are and especially about how the self is. I identify this distinction because of its great importance in contemporary Christian theology and because I am curious whether it is felt as important for Buddhists and, if so, whether it is a source of contention among them.

I raise this question particularly with Pure Land Buddhists because the affirmation of other-power, or what Christians call grace, seems to place a greater emphasis on the metaphysical character of the world and human experience than is present in other Buddhist traditions. To me as a Christian the metaphysical reality of grace is of central importance, whereas many of my fellow theologians regard this as a social construction or a linguistic convention characteristic of certain communities. Is this division present in Pure Land Buddhism as well?

The issue is a complex one. Obviously there are a variety of ways of construing experience, and the notion of grace appears only in some of them. Can one say that those which include this notion are more complete, at least in this respect, than those that do not? My answer is affirmative. I do assert that experience is more accurately described when the aspects of givenness and call are included than when these are ignored or denied.

Nevertheless, I would not say that experience is a constant which is unaffected by the way it is thought of or described. On the contrary, when grace is highlighted this affects the whole of experience. An accurate description of experience in a context where grace is recognized leads to an increase in its role in the whole experience and to alteration of its other aspects. The relation between experience and the way it is understood is a dialectical one.

I believe that this way of thinking fits with what I read in Pure Land Buddhist writings. But I know that when I read them in this way I may be projecting my Christian process theology upon them. Hence I raise these questions in hopes of enlarging the community in which they are discussed. I am sure the nuances of the Buddhist discussion will be different and that I, as a Christian, will be able to learn from the contributions of Pure Land Buddhists.

Concluding Remarks

I appreciate the invitation to take part in this critical dialogue. In one sense, my remarks have not been particularly critical. The three chapters to which I have been asked to respond are richly informative and inspire confidence that they explain what Pure Land Buddhism is or can become. I find what I read here far more congenial than much of what is written by fellow Christians. Although I have no doubt about my own Christian identity, there are ways of distinguishing between groups of thinkers in which I would be classified with these Pure Land Buddhists and separated from many Christians.

It is obvious that there are some emphases, important to me as a Christian, that I have not found in Buddhism generally. These have played a large role in my comments. This is not because I want to establish the superiority of Christianity over Buddhism by showing what it has that Buddhism lacks. It is because I believe that while Christians are learning from Buddhists, Buddhists in general, and Pure Land Buddhists in particular can also be enriched as they respond to questions with which Christians may have been wrestling more intensively for a longer period of time. A Buddhism that grew in some of the ways I have suggested might gain some of Christianity's strengths without falling into the idolatries, superstitions, and distortions that clutter Christian history and contemporary reality.

What I do not know is whether the developments in Pure Land Buddhism that would please me would be seen as undesirable by Pure Land Buddhists. If so, then the differences between us are deeper than my comments would suggest. Goals that are of nearly ultimate importance to me would then appear as irrelevant or marginal for Pure Land Buddhists. If that is the case, we need to explore more deeply the sources of our contrasting sense of importance. I hope that responses to my comments can advance us toward greater clarity as to the nature of our agreements and disagreements.

PART THREE

Reconsiderations of
Buddhist Theological Reflection

6. Dialogic Engagement and Truth

Dennis Hirota

The medicine of the Tathagata's Vow destroys the poisons of our wisdom and foolishness.
> —*Shinran*, "Chapter on Shinjin," 51

One word of truth transforms evil karma into good.
> —*Tsung-hsiao*, quoted in "Chapter on Practice," 97

In chapter 1, I sought to illuminate the Shin Buddhist path by depicting the nature of engagement with Pure Land concepts and symbols in a manner intelligible in the contemporary situation and open to comparative consideration. This exposition was framed as a response to queries posed to Shin scholars in Japan by Gordon Kaufman, but one that would elucidate a conception of truth distinct from that embodied in his original questions. In particular, I focused not on the Pure Land teachings as objective propositions about the world to be assessed intellectually, but rather on the process by which the teachings are engaged and grasped as meaningful by practicers. I have argued that it is this latter issue of engagement that is Shinran's own central concern. I postulated two stages in engagement with the Shin teaching—initial, or provisional, and mature, or fulfilled—and showed that the understandings of the teachings as *true* differs between these two stages. Further, I asserted that it is precisely the shift from one sense of "true" to the other that constitutes the transformative awareness that Shinran terms "realization of shinjin."

163

It may be said that at the heart of Shinran's Pure Land path lies an existential Mahayanic awakening to nonduality, manifested in particular in the nonduality—without obliteration of the distinction—of falsity and truth, or samsaric existence and true reality, or blind passions and wisdom-compassion. Nonduality concretized in this way— and sustained in the awareness of persons who achieve no eradication of false conceptualization and self-attachment through meditative practices—is the characteristic quality of the Shin Buddhist path. In order to lay the groundwork for pursuing such issues raised by Kaufman and Cobb as the nature of the truth of personal (or impersonal) conceptions of reality and the basis of action for good in the world, it is necessary to probe more fully the shift itself from initial to fulfilled engagement and how it may occur. This will point toward a consideration of a different dimension of the teaching than that of narratives and symbols taken up directly in chapter 1, the dimension of language itself. Here, only a brief discussion of one aspect of the problem of language is possible, but I hope it will indicate how the issue of truth and falsity may be pursued in terms of a shift in religious awareness, and also demonstrate that in the Shin Buddhist path the liberative apprehension of truth is fused with self-awareness of false discrimination or evil (action arising from attachment to a delusional self). Before turning briefly to this topic in the latter part of this chapter, I will make some general observations regarding my understanding of the theological project in Shin Buddhism.

"Pragmatic," "Hermeneutic," and "Constructive" Theological Reflection

In chapter 4, Kaufman points out the "pragmatic" perspective of my approach to religious truth, and further characterizes it as "hermeneutic." Although the emphases and nuances with which I would use these terms may differ from Kaufman's, I find both terms appropriate. Moreover, I would assert that it is precisely an approach both "pragmatic" and "hermeneutical" that can best achieve a formulation of the Pure Land tradition that is at once true to its paramount aspirations as a Mahayana Buddhist path and disclosive of its significance for our contemporary situation.

Regarding the pragmatic emphasis in my view of Shinran's Pure Land path, I have sought to show that engagement with the teaching is not chiefly a matter of conviction or of ascertaining a conceptually coherent grasp of the world. It is not faith in the sense of adherence to propositions or claims about the world. Rather, the controlling image in the tradition is that of a "path," and in this context, the Pure Land teachings have a pragmatic or therapeutic function operative in ordinary life in society. At the core of a person's engagement with the teaching lies a transformation of human existence, an existence above all characterized by the apprehension of the world from a stance of self-attachment. This transformative quality of engagement reflects its illuminative and emancipatory nature as a Buddhist path.

Kaufman delineates an area of agreement of my approach with his own thinking, but is concerned to note, correctly I think, that a recognition of a therapeutic function does not dissolve the problem of truth-claims about the world. The concepts and narratives of the Pure Land teachings embody an analysis of the human situation and a vision of reality upon which engagement is founded. Although I have focused on a shift in engagement with the teaching, this does not mean that the teaching initially engaged comes itself to be considered false, for I have also asserted the enduring importance of these teachings—with both teleological and interpersonal modes of human apprehension—for providing a conceptual framework for the understanding of the self and the cosmos of the Shin Buddhist practicer, and in particular the one who has realized shinjin. In relation to the latter, I have spoken of fulfilled or mature engagement, in which conceptual understanding and its transcendence are held in nonresolving tension. The larger problem, therefore, is the nature of truth itself. Here, some clarification is possible through a consideration of Kaufman's second characterization of my approach as "hermeneutical," though again my understanding of the implications of this term holds different emphases from his.

Kaufman contrasts two modes of self-understanding in theological reflection, "hermeneutical" and "constructive." In a purely hermeneutical approach, one sees one's task chiefly as the reinterpretation of the tradition for the contemporary situation. While such an approach seeks to treat issues of immediate concern, it may tend to found itself finally on the authority of the tradition, that is, to assume the truth of the tradition and to take continuity with tradition as basic to its validity; hence, it may tend to be "internalist" in its argumentation, intended for those within the "circle of faith." Moreover, such reinterpretative work may be carried on at a level of sophistication or abstraction that makes it inherently elitist in attitude, far removed from the outlook of the ordinary faithful.

In contrast to a narrowly hermeneutical approach, Kaufman poses reflection that undertakes a "constructive reimagining" of the tradition. Here, one goes beyond simple reinterpretation to an assessment of various features of the tradition in the light of contemporary life, and to the work of recommending not merely adaptation, but conscious change of the tradition where necessary. Although Kaufman favors a "constructive" approach, it is important to consider whether his categories carry the same significance in Buddhist tradition, and whether there are not dimensions of continuity with tradition that present special concerns for Buddhists.

For Kaufman, the terms *hermeneutic* and *constructive* involve less the issue of the nature of truth than the attitude of the theologian in treating it. *Truth* itself signifies, above all, assertions about the cosmos and human existence, and the problem for the theologian is whether emphasis is placed on rephrasing the truth in a way acceptable to and meaningful for contemporary people or on selecting from among the truths of the tradition those that are pertinent and useful in the present and augmenting them with truths from other traditions or other fields of contemporary learning. In order to clarify my own approach, I will propose here a somewhat different view of the problem of truth and interpretation and a different configuration of contrasting approaches.

The Shin Buddhist path is rooted in the basic human activity of conceptually grasping and making sense of one's experience and the world. From this endeavor to find meaning arises the impetus for engagement with the path. This engagement is not simply an extension of such activity, however, but works to lead practicers to an awareness of the limitations and inevitable distortions of conceptual understanding. By doing so, it does not eradicate such activity, but leads from an objectifying, substantialist worldview centered in an absolutized or transcendent self to another mode of awareness. This new awareness arises within a matrix of cultural and historical interactions and interrelationships with other beings, but at the same time is self-aware of its conditioned nature and distortion.

Because the Shin path approaches the problem of defusing attachment to a falsely substantialized, constructed self not through eradicating conceptual thought, but through effecting a change in the mode of apprehending the self and the world, it is a hermeneutical approach—an approach treating the way the teaching and life in the world are interpreted—that best illuminates engagement with it. Such an approach reflects Shinran's own emphases and concerns in expounding the teaching; it thus probes the focal point of Shinran's own thought and methods, and in fact clarifies precisely why a conception of "faith" lies at the core of his path. In addition, this approach avoids the pitfalls of too quick and compromising an entry into comparative discussions on the level of abstract doctrine, an arena that tends to be framed by Western metaphysical and theistic presuppositions, with their concomitant conceptions of self. Thus, I use the term *hermeneutical* less to refer to the concerns of interpreting statements or assertions of the traditional teachings (Kaufman's usage), than to indicate what I regard as a prior concern: the problem of the mode of understanding itself.

Because of its functioning to guide the practicer to a new mode of awareness, and because of the nature of that new awareness, the Shin Buddhist tradition presents a model of truth, or of understanding, or of engagement with religious symbols, narratives, and conceptual structures that may be called, on different levels and in significant respects, "dialogic." This term also is currently used with a variety of meanings. The sense with which I adopt it for religious life as delineated in the Shin Buddhist path is not chiefly the notion of interreligious dialogue in which concepts and doctrinal statements are presented and compared. Such comparison of diverse pictures of the world may be one important aspect or extension of the dialogic engagement that characterizes the Shin Buddhist path as I see it, but rather than beginning with the isolation and abstracting out of propositions or truth-claims from the Shin Buddhist path, I have sought to identify an inner dynamic that characterizes engagement with it. This engagement is broader than one in which the teaching might be personified as a conversation partner, such as spoken of by Gadamer; nor am I concerned with various voices in the texts, such as treated by literary critics like Mikhail Bakhtin. The term *dialectical* might be more appropriate, except that, as seen in chapter 1, no final synthesis or resolution is to be reached. Nevertheless, it seems to me that it is a "dialogical" dynamic—an interaction between logics—that lies at the heart of the path, and further that this dynamic may be clarified in a way that allows for meaningful comparative treatment.

A Dialogic Model

Stated briefly, the crucial element in my notion of a dialogic engagement with truth is the movement toward relinquishing adherence to the stance of an absolutized, egocentric self or any absolutized conceptual perspective. In the notion of truth as dialogic in the sense I seek to employ it, truth emerges in, and manifests itself as, the movement toward the self-awareness of ignorance or evil in the Buddhist sense of attachment to a falsely reified self. It may be said that the teachings challenge our normal modes of understanding, and further that they provide a new model for understanding the self and the world. From a hermeneutical perspective concerned with the nature of understanding, the implications of theological reflection that is "constructive" also undergo a bit of a change.

I would pose my use of *dialogic* as contrastive with certain metaphors that are easily associated with the idea of *construction*. Although this may not be the intent of Kaufman's usage, to speak of a "constructive" theology might call up images of foundations and pillars, of closely fitted building blocks rising in a monolithic structure. Such metaphors might be suitable for the creation of a coherent system in which assertions about the world and truth-claims support each other and are held together by logical consistency and general empirical persuasiveness. Here, solidity and certainty are valued.

Shinran may be seen to present, instead of such an architectonic model, a dialogic model characterized by movement and counterpoint. Here, ideas are not welded into a consistent whole, but stand counterpoised, yielding to qualification, replacement, and readoption. My concerns in this volume, then, focus on the proposal of a model of truth and of engagement that might be called "hermeneutic" in that it concerns processes of understanding, and that might be called "dialogic" because it resists adherence to any absolutized perspective. There are three general features of the religious path as "dialogic."

The medium of language. The Shin Buddhist path and engagement with it are deeply wedded to language. They involve persons as listeners and speakers, hearers and sayers; as beings who grasp and order experience and build their world through concepts and narratives. In other words, they relate to persons as social beings, historically and culturally contextualized. There are two sides to the linguistic nature of engagement.

On the one hand, Shin Buddhist thought shares with Mahayana Buddhist thought in general a deep distrust of ordinary speech and conceptualization. Conventional or ordinary language use is characterized as delusional in that it gives expression to and reinforces a dualism of subject and object and a substantialist view of the self and the things of the world. The linguistic contextualization of human life in the Shin Buddhist tradition means, therefore, that human existence is characterized by ignorance, and by the pain and conflict arising from delusional attachments.

On the other hand, however, the Shin Buddhist path is also integrated with language. It is the "path of easy practice" (igyōdō) precisely because it provides a way to awakening—or contact with what is true and real—through and in the medium of language. When, borrowing a phrase from T'an-luan, Shinran states that in the Pure Land path, "nirvana is attained without severing blind passions,"[1] this may be understood to mean, in its intellectual aspect, that without reaching a point at which dichotomous thinking (language, conceptualization) has been eradicated or overcome, one attains suchness or true reality which is beyond words and concepts.[2]

The Process of Engagement.   Engagement with the path is characterized by a process that entails shifts in perspective or basic mode of understanding in relation to that which is true and real. In this sense, such engagement embodies a rejection of rigid conceptual attachments. Further, it is a decisive shift or conversion occurring in this process that is pivotal in the path, rather than adherence either to particular doctrinal formulations or to practices and moral precepts. This was my theme in chapter 1.

The Nature of Attainment.   The Shin Buddhist path presents a mode of awareness or of knowing in human life that is inherently pluralistic in that it nurtures an apprehension of reality through sustaining in tension disparate models of understanding. Further, this awareness, though pluralistic, is not merely relativistic in the sense of asserting the essential equality in falsity of all conceptual schemes. Rather, the Shin path shows what is required, in terms of self-awareness, of the functioning of human conceptuality for a nonegocentric apprehension of human existence to arise. The resistance to recognition of one's perspective on the world as finite, limited, and skewed by delusional attachments must fall away, though the perspectival nature of awareness, and much of the attachment, inevitably remain.

The arising of this complex awareness—awareness of the self and the other beings and things of the world together with the self-awareness of distortion and partiality—is inherently dialogic in that it holds together an inevitably egocentric view with awareness from beyond that center. In the Shin Buddhist path, the Name of the Buddha is the verbal embodiment of this awareness. Without apprehension from a stance beyond the delusional self and its world, there can be no thoroughgoing realization of the self's falsity. At the same time, no verbal formulation of that apprehension can be adequate.

What is of particular importance for our concerns here is that this engagement with the path harbors a dynamic by which one's views and judgments are repeatedly challenged as partial and as informed by self-interest and self-attachment. In this way, it provides a model for growth in the understanding of our lives in the world. Our engagement with the path calls us to see the self and the living world of beings and things with ever greater breadth, clarity, and compassion. As stated in chapter 1, this is the work of the Pure Land practicer, undertaken with the mind and power of Buddha.

In chapter 1 I sought to articulate, based on sources within the tradition, a new paradigm that might serve as a framework for reinterpreting the entire body of Pure Land concepts and symbols. I believe this paradigm, by illuminating the nonsubstantialist and dialogical character of conceptual structures within the Pure Land teaching, further suggests a Shin Buddhist perspective that may be developed to address issues of contemporary life and brought to conversations with persons of other religious traditions and of various fields of knowledge. It is this dialogic imperative that, finally, forms the impetus for theological reflection, and such conversations as represented in this volume.

Some Issues in Pure Land Buddhist Theological Reflection

Religious Practice and World-Construction

Before entering my discussion of the Shin Buddhist path and language, I will venture several general comments regarding the theological project in Shin. In the afterword to this volume, I attempt a general and reasonably objective comparative account of the approaches of Tachikawa, Yokota, and myself. Here, I will try to clarify the significance of my approach by critically assessing the approaches of my two colleagues.

Tachikawa's approach and my own may be considered complementary in that we both take a paradigm of practice as central to a Buddhist viewpoint, but while I seek to elucidate the distinctive nature and significance of Pure Land practice, Tachikawa seeks rather to demonstrate that the general contours of Pure Land practice conform to a larger Mahayana model. Tachikawa's project is a useful antidote to understandings of Pure Land Buddhism that attempt to expunge its foundations in Mahayana tradition.[3] Underlying this project is his attempt to fill what he sees as a major lacuna of the Japanese Pure Land tradition—a systematic picture of the world—through the adoption of the world-affirmation of esoteric realization. There is, however, a fundamental problem with his approach, for finally it obscures rather than elucidates issues surrounding the specific character of the Pure Land path and the nonegocentric vision of the world that it might develop, which is part of what I have termed "mature engagement."

Paradigms of meditative practice in Mahayana Buddhism turn on the attainment of awareness free of conceptual thought, judgment, and the subject-object dichotomy. Such realization is termed "wisdom," or "reality," or "emptiness." Here, Tachikawa's general exposition of emptiness and dependent origination in terms of practice is compatible with my own arguments. Japanese Pure Land Buddhists, however, grasp their incapacity to enter into meditative states and eradicate discriminative thinking and linguistic activity, even momentarily; hence, it is not taught that they attain emptiness. Nevertheless, they understand Mahayana conceptions of wisdom-compassion to imply a working or dynamic to lead all beings to awakening, and they view the Pure Land path as embodying this working of wisdom-compassion. Surely the theological task of Pure Land Buddhists includes at a high level of priority the need to clarify, and not merely assert, this seemingly paradoxical situation of Pure Land teachings (forms, concepts) as a Mahayana path (leading the unenlightened to emptiness). In order to accomplish this, I believe an approach like Tachikawa's, which delineates the theoretical structure of the path, must be supplemented with an approach like my own, which focuses reflectively on the awareness of the practicer.

To pursue this more concretely, part of Tachikawa's broad project is to establish a foundation for reflection on Buddhist tradition in general through an analysis of action as elemental to life, and through viewing religious practice as one kind of action. He discusses action as possessing three elements: assessment of present conditions, goal or purpose, and means. This analysis in itself, however, turns on the presupposition of an autonomous individual who possesses intentions and motives (subject-object dichotomy). In other words, it fails to allow for a treatment of a fundamental problem in classical Buddhist thought: confinement to the perspective of a single individual subject.[4]

Tachikawa, by seeking to incorporate a view of Pure Land Buddhism into a generalized Mahayana paradigm, overlooks the resources in the Pure Land tradition that offer a solution to the constricted focus on the individual subject in classical Buddhist thought, including Tantrism. As long as his esoteric model remains central, a mystical faith experience as a "leap" or "plunge" into emptiness (p. 111) will be seen as pivotal in making the Pure Land path genuinely Buddhist. (On this view, it is questionable, for example, whether Yokota's presentation can be viewed as Buddhist at all, although Yokota makes no response to Tachikawa on this point.)

In order to confront the problem of confinement to the perspective of a single individual subject, it is necessary to go beyond Tachikawa's analysis and to recognize the interpretive working of the subject, who is conditioned by social and historical contexts and by human existence itself, in the conceptualization of any action. That is, while Tachikawa analyzes action into three elements, including "present conditions," "end," and "means," he does not take the further step of consciously recognizing that the constituted "action" is therefore always a construct, the result of conceptualization and interpretation, and additionally in his case, always informed by instrumentality. In order to treat the problem of the subject, analysis of action must be done in a way that illuminates this interpretive functioning and its contextualization, and that does not merely assume the subject's existence as transcendent. In other words, instead of the view of religious practice as a single arc of action performed by a subject, specific points along the trajectory that Tachikawa sketches should be analyzed and the interpretive activity of the practicer at different moments of practice should be compared. When this is done, it becomes possible for the first time to treat the paradoxical situation of the self's movement toward no-self without simply lapsing into the invocation of entrance into emptiness. Moreover, concepts like the "sacralization of the world" also open to comparative treatment, for example, between esoteric and Pure Land realizations.

It is precisely such a treatment of interpretive activity in practice that I have sought to provide for Shinran's path through my discussion of modes of engagement with the teaching. Thus, a correlation exists between the modes of apprehension that I delineate and Tachikawa's elements of action. The interpersonal mode may be said to correspond to the synchronic dimension of the self's apprehension of its own existence in the world together with other beings, and the teleological to the diachronic dimension. The former corresponds in Tachikawa's analysis to the assessment of present conditions, and the latter to "ends" and "means."

My argument in chapter 1 is that a transformative shift occurs in the existence of the Pure Land practicer, and that this shift may be understood precisely as a movement from an interpretation of action in terms of an individual, substantial self and of objective means and goals to a new conception or interpretation of action, one in which attachment to such a self and such goals is constantly undercut by fresh awareness of the self's interrelation with the world of beings, the ocean of all life. Human existence remains informed by the processes of conceptualization and interpretation, and hence by "action." Nevertheless, on the one hand, the self has lost its absoluteness and the fixity of its perspective, and on the other hand, the goal has become present while remaining in the future. A reorientation of all action has been effected through shifts in the interpretive modes of apprehending Amida and the Pure Land. The story of Dharmakara-Amida may be viewed as a meta-narrative that frees us from, and for, our various contextual narratives of self by enabling us to see them whole, from beyond their individual confines and manipulative impulses.

Tachikawa has sought to find a basis for understanding religious practice as a natural extension of ordinary acts but undertaken in the awareness of death. Such a project may be difficult, however, if it takes as its starting point premises rooted in ordinary—in the Buddhist view, delusional—thinking. Rather, it is the activity of apprehending the self and the world—including through conceptions of actions encompassing judgments, means, and ends—that provides for continuity between endeavor in human existence and religious practice. This interpretive grasp of action, or action as possessing an interpretive, narrative dimension, also offers itself to comparative analysis that can elucidate the processes of practice. It is such analysis that underlies my discussion of the Pure Land path.

Truth in the World and Transcendent Truth

Yokota's approach raises a number of specific issues regarding the interpretation of Pure Land concepts, but the fundamental problem underlying differences with my approach—and also with Tachikawa's—may be sketched by considering his use of the Mahayana concept of the "two truths." This concept has been interpreted in various ways in the course of the history of Mahayana tradition, and different interpretations are seen in the scholarly literature today. The difficulty with Yokota's employment of this concept, however, lies not in a reliance on one or another of these traditions, but in a failure finally to recognize the need for the concept in the first place.

The concept of the "two truths" or "twofold truth"—supreme and worldly or, in Streng's rendering, "world-ensconced"[5]—concerns above all the problem of language or verbal teaching, and thus of interpretation. Supreme truth is synonymous with reality, nirvana, emptiness, wisdom; it is said to be formless and beyond conceptualization or linguistic expression. World-ensconced truth, in an understanding Yokota seems to accept, may be taken as supreme truth expressed in language by awakened beings to guide the unenlightened. The concept of world-ensconced truth thus allows for the possibility of the verbal teaching of inconceivable supreme truth. As Nagarjuna states: "The teaching by the Buddhas of the *dharma* has recourse to two truths."[6]

Yokota argues on the basis of the concept of twofold truth that "ultimate reality is always coming out of itself to reveal itself in the form of the second or worldly truth" (p. 207). Further: "Reality is one and this reality is ever coming out of itself to reveal itself. It is this reality we see and come to know partially and ever more comprehensively" (p. 215). Whether Mahayana traditions support Yokota's assertions that there is an "ultimate reality" that is "one," but that "comes out of itself" into our world, or whether such characterizations bespeak a monism alien to most Buddhist thinking, is open to question. From the perspective of our concern here with the twofold truth, however, Yokota's operative word seems to be *reveal*.

If Yokota's use of *reveal* is understood against a backdrop of Buddhas and bodhisattvas who, having attained supreme truth by eradicating discriminative thinking, thereby acquire the motive force and power to act compassionately in the realm of samsara by devising skillful means, then this seems an appropriate adoption of the notion of twofold truth. In this case, however, it is necessary to acknowledge that the opposite face of the activity of teaching as world-ensconced truth is the problem of reception of the teaching by the unenlightened. In fact, such reception is traditionally treated in such concepts as the "four reliances" (rely on dharma, not the teacher; rely on the meaning, not the words; and so on).[7]

If, however, *reveal* is taken to imply revelation as a rationally consistent system of objective propositions about reality, beginning with the existence of Amida, who is pervasive and compassionate, surely the tension in the Buddhist notion of twofold truth has vanished. If *reveal* has this sense, then in fact is there not simply the truth of revelation, with no need to insist on two distinct and contradictory dimensions? In other words, what need is there to speak of more than one truth?

Certainly, as Yokota states, the verbal teaching may be understood to guide the ignorant toward awakening at all moments of engagement by amending their grasp of the world. From the perspective of the ignorant, however, the decisive nexus with reality is traditionally understood to lie in practice. Moreover, for Shinran it is the figure of Ajatashatru (Ajātaśatru), profoundly despairing at having murdered his father in order to unsurp the throne and terrified of falling into hell, who is representative of the being existentially engaged with the Pure Land teaching. It is such a being "difficult to cure" who has entered upon the path. Where I have emphasized a qualitative shift in apprehension arising out of engagement, Yokota sees only knowing "more comprehensively" (p. 215). He is therefore willing to "construct" his theology by, in essence, elaborating upon, without direct reference, Shinran's statement that the Pure Land is light or wisdom (mentioned in chapter 1, p. 40). Insofar as he assumes this to be knowing or accepting revelation merely intellectually, he appears to depart from Mahayana tradition. The third of the four reliances instructs us to "rely on wisdom [in interpreting the teaching], not the ordinary working of the mind."

The centrality that Tachikawa and I give to practice is related to the rift between the world-ensconced truth and supreme truth. Yokota's lack of concern for practice—extending even to the nembutsu—is probably based on his notion of revelation. His criticisms of my use of "methodological approaches" and his claim that I assert an "unbridgeable break" between levels of "knowledge" (p. 215) indicate rather his own refusal to recognize more than one level of truth—the level of conceptual propositions about reality.

Yokota's project may thus be seen as assuming a coherence theory of truth in which the final terms of validation are provided by the issues and solutions developed in Whiteheadian process theology. In his brief criticism of my approach, Yokota expresses a rejection of what he labels a "special experience of the mind of entrusting to Amida," calling it "anathema to my own view of *the theological task*" (p. 215). He appears however, to waver between two meanings of *special*. If *special* applies accurately to shinjin (I do not apply either the word *special* or *experience*), it is surely because, to borrow Shinran's terms, shinjin is understood as the mind of Amida Buddha and not an attitude generated by our ordinary thought. Yokota conflates this meaning of *special* with the notion of uniqueness among religious traditions. However, it is precisely out of a comparative concern that I have sought to formulate the Shin Buddhist path in general terms of modes of engagement, which provides for a broader conception of religious truth than doctrinal assertions about reality.

The basic question is whether "the theological task" in Yokota's mind takes precedence over disclosing what it is that lies at the heart of a non-Western religious tradition. In Yokota's view, "the theological task" in its interreligious form is necessarily rationalist and empirical, and therefore the only comparativist stance is doctrinal. An approach like mine, which seeks to expand the comparative focus beyond bare metaphysical truth-claims to modes of engagement in different religious traditions, is automatically criticized as insisting on "uniqueness." It appears, however, that in the pursuit of a rationalist "universality" Yokota may be sacrificing significant elements of continuity with tradition merely to open a window onto another "circle of faith."

Although Yokota follows Cobb in taking such ideas as pratityasamutpada and nondualism to be metaphysical propositions, from a Buddhist perspective, a conceptual understanding of such teachings has never been considered adequate. The religious problem is not to ascertain intellectually that codependent origination as a statement about the world is true or to conduct one's life with the conviction that it is so, but to eradicate the false discrimination of reified things and of subject and object. When Nagarjuna states that codependent origination and emptiness are synonymous,[8] surely the implication is that codependent origination as well is authentically realized by the bodhisattva in contemplative practice. This does not mean that all Buddhist paths are meditational, or that realization is solely a matter of individual salvation. It does mean, however, that Buddhist statements about the world, including statements about grace, occur within contexts and require hermeneutical consideration.

Neither Meditation nor "Faith"

Both Kaufman and Cobb portray my approach by positioning it between those of Tachikawa and Yokota. In other words, they both situate our three perspectives along a linear continuum, though with different parameters. This is a useful observation, for it seems to me that it is just such a "middle" stance that may reflect, first, the distinctive position within Mahayana Buddhist tradition of the Pure Land Buddhist path as developed by Shinran, and second, an approach by which this path may be precisely formulated in contemporary terms and developed so that it casts light on human action in the contemporary situation.

The contrasting approaches of Tachikawa and Yokota should not be taken as forming poles of a simple continuum, such as one reflecting contrasting opinions resulting from differences in emphases within a well-defined field of discourse. Cobb suggests a contrast between meditation and faith, with Tachikawa giving emphasis to meditative awareness and Yokota to faith. But between Buddhist meditation as the transcendence of all conceptualization on the one hand and faith as conformity to the call of God or Amida on the other lies a fundamental discontinuity. A stance lying between these two positions must integrate, without dissolution of either pole, the transcendence of concepts with a medium of conceptuality. It is precisely this quality that allows Shinran's Pure Land path to remain Buddhist in fundamental outlook and yet claim accessibility to all in everyday life.

To stand on the side of "faith" as conviction, as Yokota does, leads to a daring insistence on augmenting Pure Land concepts with modern Western thought. But Yokota may have adopted too completely the framework of problems as they have arisen within Western religious traditions and therefore neglected to accommodate the perspective of the path, the concerns of which even such Christian theologians as Barth identify as distinguishing the Pure Land tradition from Christianity. Again, the problem of affirming particular propositions or truth-claims does not vanish; nevertheless, all truth-claims come to have a radically altered status. That is, two conditions concerning truth or the understanding of reality come to be seen as affirmed at entrance into fulfilled engagement with the teachings.

First, the realization of truth is inseparable from the realization of the final inadequacy of all human conceptuality or constructions of reality. This does not mean that one embraces the conviction of falsity or relativism as a further proposition within the field of conceptual life, nor is it a merely linguistic solution to metaphysical perplexities. It involves an existential reorientation grounded in self-awareness of evil. Moreover, the realization of the falsely substantializing and ego-centric nature of human conceptuality is itself an awakening to or manifestation of truth, and it moves one constantly toward "truer," decentered (and compassionate) perspectives and action. Second, the truth that is the opposite face of the self-realization of falsity can take on verbal expression, pervading the conceptual life of the Shin practicer; this is the role of the nembutsu. On the one hand, then, practicers do not transcend language and conceptuality (their engagement is not meditation). On the other hand, neither do they accept and affirm propositions about the world as finally adequate expressions of truth (their engagement is not faith in this sense).

Good and Evil

This book is intended as a general proposal for approaching Pure Land teachings, and it is impossible to articulate fully the implications regarding issues that have occupied an important place in Christian tradition and that require response from Buddhists today. Nevertheless, on the basis of the realization of truth as it pervades falsity, or the interpenetration of falsity and truth, we may consider briefly the kind of thinking—thinking characterized by a dynamism in perspective rather than by static and objective truth-claims—that we might expect Shin Buddhists to bring not only to metaphysical but also to ethical issues raised in the other chapters.

On a fundamental level, Shinran affirms the values of wisdom-compassion, of nonviolence and concern for the well-being of others. For Shin Buddhists, however, the problem of involvement in society, which Cobb raises, has its focus not in acting in accordance with Amida or the Vow as an object of faith or working to actualize the Pure Land in this world, but in Amida's action as itself the awareness of the practicer. In this, comparison may be possible with Cobb's concept of the "lure," which "calls us to trust" and "works in us always" (p. 153–54). As stated in chapter 1, Shinran speaks of the Vow's working in beings' existence as *jinen* ("spontaneous," "natural"), meaning that it is, for beings, freedom from calculative thinking. There is, however, a fundamental difference from Western conceptions of the working of an inner conscience to determine right and wrong and the moral decision of the self to perform good or eschew evil. This is because, for Shin Buddhists, the problem of moral action is located in a framework informed by the realization of falsity that is also the realization of truth mentioned above, and consequently not in the deliberations of an absolutized self or in the reification of good or evil. This is not an exclusive concern with cultivating inner states or achieving merely personal salvation, but precisely the overcoming of such egocentric concerns. The moral imperative of the nembutsu practicer is to see, to know as fully as possible the worlds of one's existence and the sources and effects of one's acts. It is the activity of such seeing that arises as the nembutsu, and it may harbor the human joy of love. At the same time, it is precisely through the self-awareness of the falsity of the reified self that one comes to perceive the inseparability of one's existence from that of all beings, or that personal salvation and the salvation of all life are one (see chapter 1, p. 64f.).

The question, then, is the nature of the moral functioning of awareness in which a substantializing grasp of the self, other beings, and good or evil is present together with its transcendence in the self-realization of falsity. The permeation of the judgmental self by its own emptiness results in a configuration of the basic moral question that is a mirror image of the common Western version. The question for those engaging in the Shin teaching has been not How does one act in accord with right? but rather How, being evil (acting from egocentric attachments), is any good and compassionate act—any act that would advance oneself and others along the path from painful existence to Buddhahood—possible at all? The total rejection of self-power based on the nature of human existence as possessed of delusional attachments may seem to imply that no positive action can be performed. Shinran, however, clearly rejects a view that only evil, and no good, can be performed as a merely conceptualized understanding.[9] The awareness of the Shin practicer constantly moves beyond the perspective of the constructed, egocentric self, opening the possibility for acts not self-consciously willed as compassionate but arising naturally and inevitably *(jinen)* from the broadened context. This is the moral dimension of the human subjectivity of daily life free of the reification of a transcendent self.

To draw on Shinran's words, there is no act of the delusional self that can lead other than to hell. We hardly know the evils of commission or omission we are capable of, given the conducive situation and the effects of all our past. Although Shin tradition has not developed this principle, the work of Shin Buddhists on both individual and corporate levels is to become aware of the nature of their existence—as members of family and community, as citizens of society and world, as human and sentient beings—and to discover and act from those contexts and perspectives in which one's existence individually and collectively ceases to be dominated in its depths by anger, jealousy, envy, and greed. This is Shinran's meaning when he speaks of experiencing revulsion at worldliness *(yo o itou)* and aspiration for the Pure Land. Though perhaps imperceptible in oneself, this quality may be visible in the lives of others. Shinran further states: "Since shinjin that aspires for attainment of birth arises through the encouragement of Shakyamuni and Amida, once the true and real mind is made to arise in us, how can we remain as we were, [wholly] possessed of blind passions?"[10]

To take a small example from Shinran's biography, he was once observed at a feast eating fish while wearing an outer surplice *(kesa)*, which monks normally removed before eating meat in view of their precepts against taking life. Asked why he neglected to observe priestly etiquette, he responded:

> Although I eat meat, I wish to bring those sentient beings to liberation. But though I am a disciple of Shakyamuni in name, my heart and mind are stained with the dust of worldly life, and I possess neither wisdom nor virtue. How could I save those beings? Because of all this, I eat the flesh while wearing my *kesa*. For the *kesa* is a sacred cloth that adorns the liberation of all the Buddhas of the past,

present, and future. I feel that if I eat while wearing it, through the virtuous power of the *kesa*, my wish to save living things and benefit beings may be fulfilled.[11]

This minor incident, though it may seem ineffectual and to concern merely the norms and symbolic meanings of clerical attire, is significant because it reveals not resignation to powerlessness and inaction, but the ability to perceive and reflect on the cost of one's own daily existence in the intricate ecology of life. This is also, necessarily, the ability to move without design beyond the common sense and dominant order of social convention. To learn to experience the pain at the other side of the self, which is but the opposite face of the self's porousness and its interdependence with the life of others, is perhaps the affective dimension of the realization of falsity that is also the realization of truth. If metaphysical statements are tempered in Shin, so are both the self-righteousness and practical cynicism that our strife-ridden world can ill afford.

The awareness from beyond worldly hierarchies and absolutist judgments illustrated above also manifested itself in Shinran's decision at the end of his exile to devote himself to propagating the teaching among people of the countryside. It may also be seen in his dedication to literary activity late in life, living in near anonymity in the capital, far from the following that had gathered around him. Shin Buddhists have traditionally acted in the locales in which they carried on their lives, for it is not conformity to an abstract norm, but concrete seeing that is their practice. Nevertheless, there is no question that today they must consciously pursue—and act from—the ever-broadening global perspectives now available, through scientific and other forms of knowledge, that draw out the implications of the ordinary acts of daily life. In this way, they aspire not in themselves to accomplish some formulation of Amida's Vow, but to see with something of the vision that originally informed it.

History and Historicity

The problem of historicity is similar in dynamic. In chapter 5 Cobb raises the question of whether historical grounding for the central "act of compassion" in the tradition—for example, the Vows and practice of Dharmakara Bodhisattva—is not necessary in Pure Land Buddhism

(p. 156). This is a question that arises from viewing the Pure Land tradition within a framework of faith in Western traditions, in which historical verifiability may be a crucial dimension of the object of faith. Without such grounding in a historical event, the narratives of the tradition appear to become merely "mythic" and arbitrary, incapable of supporting reasoned commitment. In response to Cobb's call for a transformation of Shin tradition through accepting the event of Christ as its historical grounding, Yokota asserts, from within the framework of Cobb's comments, that Shakyamuni as a historical figure provides firm basis for faith in the compassion of Amida.

If the narrative of Amida and the Primal Vow is a myth, however, so surely is the narrative of Shakyamuni's temptation to silence and his rising from the bodhi tree. It is difficult to understand how the fact of Shakyamuni's historical existence can ground faith when nothing the practicer would regard as decisively distinguishing him from many other religious teachers is similarly engraved in what Yokota calls "the objectivity of history" (p. 83). Yokota seeks to supply what he perceives to be deficient in the Pure Land tradition without recognizing that he is actually substituting a different paradigm of thought. He finds that the *Larger Sutra* discloses an underdeveloped sense of history, rather than a distinctive vision of the relationship between the historical and the transcendent. He states, for example, that "when the myth of Amida is viewed critically, the parallel with the life of Shakyamuni is obvious" (p. 83), as though the alert modern reader detects a hidden device employed by those who crafted the sutra. In fact, the sutra itself insists on the pattern. According to it, all the many bodhisattvas in Shakyamuni's company attain enlightenment by reenacting his biography; each one, for example, returns his white horse to the palace on renouncing princely life. What is central here is not the historical actuality and uniqueness of Shakyamuni but the vision of his life within the larger context of a dynamic of liberation. Yokota seems to assume that Shakyamuni's life gave rise to a number of "myths" that make sense only to the extent that they are historically founded. For the Shin tradition, the process is the reverse: the narrative of Amida Buddha provides a means for understanding the significance of Shakyamuni's life and the lives of others who have concretized the Pure Land path in history; it is not an objectified event, but the story of our own religious awakening.[12] It is not that the mythic as quasi-historical is sufficient to ground faith, but rather that the narrative of Amida Buddha enables us to say and apprehend that which decisively informs the quality of our own historical narratives.

The relationship between Amida and Shakyamuni is of course an ancient theme in Pure Land literature. As Yokota points out, Shinran views Shakyamuni as a manifestation of Amida. In following Cobb, however, Yokota adopts Western linear and eschatalogical views of history and an emphasis on the particularity of incarnation, while Shinran is in fact ringing a change on a traditional Pure Land notion. Honen states the earlier thinking in this form:

> Concerning the central purport [of the *Larger Sutra*]:
> Shakyamuni discarded the supreme Pure Land and appeared in this defiled world; this was to expound the teaching of the Pure Land and, by encouraging sentient beings, to bring them to birth in the Pure Land.
> Amida Tathagata discarded this defiled world and emerged in the Pure Land; this was to guide the sentient beings of this defiled world and bring them to birth in the Pure Land.
> This is none other than the fundamental intent with which all Buddhas go out to the Pure Land and emerge in the defiled world.[13]

Honen here views Shakyamuni and Amida as distinct and in reciprocal relationship. Typically, however (as with his concept of *jinen*), Shinran does not fix upon the personalities but seeks to grasp the underlying dynamic; hence, he sees the two Buddhas as essentially one. Shakyamuni is Amida historically manifest. What is important in the thinking here is not the factuality of the historical but rather the dynamic interfusion of the historical and the transcendent. Through the historical, the transcendent becomes present in history, and through the transcendent, the historical is enabled to touch that which is beyond temporality; it is this dialectical circularity that provides the motif by which historicity, including above all one's own realization of shinjin, may be understood. We find here not a framework of faith in which the factuality of an event grounds acceptance and the plane of linear time forms a totality, but rather the framework of transformed awareness in which present existence and the circumstances of awakening become the locus of the transcendent within history. For Shinran, his teacher Honen was the manifestation of a bodhisattva and of Amida. Surely no assertion of historical factuality could have held greater concreteness for him. For Yokota, however, it appears that while the relationship between the historical and the transcendent is tenable, multiple occurrence is not. It is difficult to understand why the modern mind-set that Yokota sees himself as speaking for should find it acceptable that an event of this nature should occur, but only once and in only one form, unless axioms of Christian eschatology are also assumed.

Ironically, it is insistence on historicity as a foundation of faith that prevents Yokota from following Cobb's suggestion that Shin Buddhists recognize Jesus as an historical embodiment of grace. Cobb goes on to ask, however: "If faith in the grace manifest in Jesus Christ had the same form and the same effect as faith in the compassion manifest in Gautama or the mythical Vow of Dharmakara, would this be *shinjin*, and would it be Buddhist?" (p. 157). When freed of insistence on a verifiable, objective historical event as the cornerstone of faith, this question seems to me to illuminate a context for comparative considerations and, at least with regard to shinjin, to be possible to answer from a Shin Buddhist perspective in the affirmative. In other words, where the issue is "salvific efficacy" (p. 155), it is my approach from outside the framework of faith grounded by a historical event, rather than Yokota's, that allows for an openness in reflecting on figures of other traditions. I believe that shinjin as a symbol of reality provides for a potentially nonmetaphysical, pluralistic conception of religious engagement, and further, that the practical aspects of its realization—the form and the effect—as the self-realization of falsity or evil and the interpenetration of falsity and truth or evil and enlightenment may indicate what is required for an authentically pluralistic, and not mere inclusivistic, stance.

Religious Awareness and Doctrinal Construction

Kaufman draws a different, but closely related, contrast between the approaches of Tachikawa and Yokota, with my own approach again occupying a middle ground. According to Kaufman, Tachikawa's approach (as well as my own) is basically hermeneutical; it seeks to understand the tradition and interpret it in contemporary terms. Yokota's method, however, is more explicitly constructive; it views the tradition critically and attempts to correct and augment those areas that, in the light of contemporary thought and of developments in other traditions, are seen to be inadequate. The relationship of

Kaufman's view with Cobb's contrast of meditation and faith may not be immediately apparent, but may be discerned in the following way. Tachikawa seeks to clarify the Pure Land tradition by identifying the meditative core that it shares with other forms of Mahayana Buddhism. In presenting the Pure Land path in this way, he may be said to adopt a *hermeneutical* approach. The difficulty with his treatment is that it does not illuminate the significance or account for the necessity of the specifically Pure Land elements; the Pure Land path, although one alternative among others, is in fact regarded as a peripheral development apart from the mainstream. Yokota, by contrast, is concerned with the conceptual consistency and comprehensiveness of the Pure Land teachings; in this sense his efforts are *constructive* and are directed to attaining cohesion with a modern worldview. No longer moored to the basic Mahayana conceptions of wisdom or reality that Tachikawa is concerned with, however, he finds few checks on the direction of conceptual development and runs the risk of random or arbitrary elaboration. Viewed in this light, we see that "hermeneutic" approaches to Buddhist tradition that are attentive to religious awareness involve far more than reconciliation—on the plane of the intellect—of scriptural truths and contemporary worldviews, and must function to balance any doctrinally constructivist efforts in a Buddhist theology.

In order to pursue our theological reflection further, and to prepare a basis for elucidating and treating comparatively such issues as the conception of falsity and truth and their nonduality or interpenetration, or the development of action for corporate good without reification of an absolute self, it will be useful to focus as precisely as possible on the nature and the dynamics of the pivotal shift in mode of apprehension that I have sketched in chapter 1. Shinran's employment and understanding of language provides an avenue for such an investigation. It suggests itself in part through a crucial element of the path, the nembutsu. The dimension of *practice* is often overlooked in the context of interreligious dialogue, where consideration of "faith" dominates; indeed, in Part One, neither Tachikawa nor Yokota makes any mention of the nembutsu at all. In the Chinese and Japanese Pure Land traditions, however, a popular expression states: "Attainment of Buddhahood through the nembutsu: this is the true essence [of the Pure Land way]."[14] When Karl Barth contrasts Pure Land Buddhism and Christianity, pointing out the "demand for an easier and simpler road to salvation" as the starting point of the Pure Land path but not of Reformed Christianity, he also is astutely taking note of the nembutsu and the centrality of its place in the tradition.

Since I have undertaken a treatment of Shinran's view of language elsewhere,[15] and since a full discussion is impossible here, I will attempt merely a sketch of one aspect of the problem.

Aspects of a Moment in Dialogic Engagement: A Passage from *Tannisho*

The importance of language in Shinran's thought may be seen in his characterizations of the central elements of the path, shinjin and practice. When he states that "the true cause of attaining nirvana is shinjin alone,"[16] it is easy to assume this to mean that when one "believes in" the teaching of Amida, who vowed to bring those who say his Name to his Pure Land, one will be saved. For Shinran, however, realization of shinjin is expressed in the *Larger Sutra* as to "hear the Name."[17] Further, practice, which indicates the nexus between our lives in the world and true reality, is "to say the Name of the Tathagata of unhindered light."[18] The religious path, then, is to hear and say Amida Buddha's Name.

Shinran's delineation of the path in linguistic terms raises a number of questions concerning the relationship between word and realization, and the nature both of the language that functions as the medium of such realization and of its apprehension and use. Briefly stated, the language of the path must be accessible to people who perform no meditative practices to break through ordinary, egocentric modes of thought, and at the same time, it must possess the power to transform their existence by severing the bonds of delusional thought. That is, language, which normally functions as the medium of false discrimination, also serves to lead people to break through the conceptual frameworks of the world and the self constructed through our cultural and social conditioning and our ordinary, egocentric use of language. How does the language of the path differ from ordinary language, and how does our engagement with it (hearing and saying the Name) differ from our usual, delusional linguistic activity, so that it becomes the cause of enlightenment? From the perspective of the path, how are its two dimensions—its linguistic medium and its transcendence of language—integrated?

Here, simply to indicate the nature of the dynamics that underlie engagement with the Shin Buddhist path, I will consider a passage from *Tannisho*, a record of the spoken words of Shinran.[19] For our purposes, *Tannisho* may be considered to comprise three main sections: a record of ten statements of Shinran of varying length; discussions of various misunderstandings of Shinran's teaching by Yuien, the compiler of *Tannisho* and a direct student of Shinran; and a postscript, also by Yuien. In the postscript, Yuien states:

> When you are confused by people who discuss among themselves such views as those noted above [in the second section of *Tannisho*], carefully read the sacred writings that accord with the late master's thought and that he himself used to read.
>
> In the sacred writings, the true and real is mixed with the accommodated and provisional. That we abandon the accommodated and take up the real, set aside the provisional and adopt the true is Shinran's fundamental meaning.
>
> You must under no circumstances misread the sacred writings. I have selected several important attestant passages and append them to this writing as a standard.[20]

There are several points to be noted in this passage. First, Yuien states that in the Pure Land scriptures, there are both "accommodated and provisional" teachings and "true and real" teachings. These two versions of the Pure Land path may be said to correspond to the understandings or modes of engagement with the teaching—initial and fulfilled—that I have delineated in chapter 1.

Second, according to Yuien, Shinran's "fundamental meaning" is that we "set aside the provisional and adopt the true." This corresponds to the shift in engagement I have emphasized.

Third, when one is confused in one's understanding, one should turn to the teachings. But it is important above all that one read the teachings correctly, in the way that Shinran did. This suggests the centrality of the hermeneutic problem in the Shin path. Provisional and true teachings must be distinguished, and one must move from a confused understanding in which these are not differentiated to an apprehension of the true.

Finally, in order to aid practicers to come to an authentic grasp of the teaching, Yuien provides attestant passages that will enable them to distinguish between the provisional and the true and guide them to a true understanding. It may be said, therefore, that Yuien's attestant passages should enable us to glimpse the shift from provisional to true engagement that is "Shinran's fundamental meaning."

Opinion is divided, however, on what passages are being singled out by Yuien as "important" and "attestant." Some scholars have asserted that they are the ten passages of Shinran's words in the first section of *Tannisho;* others, that they were originally appended to *Tannisho* but have since been lost. In view of the function the passages were to perform and the significance Yuien attached to them, however, I believe a third opinion the most reasonable. Immediately following his words in the postscript quoted above, Yuien records two quotations attributed to Shinran. They are, in fact, the most striking passages in the whole of *Tannisho.* It is entirely possible that these quotations are the attestant passages Yuien intended to guide our understanding of the teaching.[21] Here, I will take up the second passage, which I quote in full:

> I know nothing of what is good or evil. For if I could know thoroughly, as is known in the mind of Amida, that an act was good, then I would know the meaning of "good." If I could know thoroughly, as Amida knows, that an act was evil, then I would know "evil." But with a foolish being full of blind passions, in this fleeting world—this burning house—all matters without exception are lies and gibberish, totally without truth and sincerity. The nembutsu alone is true and real.[22]

As mentioned before, in Shinran's path, "nirvana is attained without severing blind passions." This means that one does not traverse the path by extricating oneself from the "lies and gibberish"—the language and thinking rooted in attachment to a delusional self—of ordinary life. Rather, it is an essential characteristic of the path that the verbal teaching be accessible to us just as we are, "possessed of blind passions" and bound to the linguistic universe of a particular locale in the history of a culture and society.

At the same time, the true language of the teaching—which arises from wisdom to manifest itself and lead beings to awakening—is not authentically apprehended if it is not distinct from the words of our ordinary life. If the words of the Buddha are grasped merely as confirming our delusional worldview or as teaching a means to improve our existence or enhance the egocentric self, we reduce them to language of ordinary life. It is here that we see the significance of Shinran's stark dichotomy of false and true language in the passage above.

It may be said, then, that unlike other paths, which lead out of the world of false language into awakening to true reality, Shinran's path leads from our customary thinking and consciousness into a world characterized by awareness of false and true language. Ordinarily, we carry on our lives using speech that may, judged by our relative standards of accuracy or veracity, be true or false or of various gradations between these poles. According to Shinran, however, to enter authentic engagement with the path is to move from such relative discrimination into a broader realm that includes at the same time an absolute dichotomy. It is here that we become aware, simultaneously, of the falsity of our ordinary thought and speech and of reality as true language. This awareness is realization of shinjin.

The Internal Dynamics of Shinran's Words

In considering Shinran's words above, we should first note two general points. To begin, we must recall that his words in fact represent only one half of a dialogue or conversation—only the reply to a statement or question that the compiler did not record. In the context of dialogue, Shinran was responding to a question of one engaged with the Pure Land teaching. It may be said that he was speaking to guide his interlocutor across the shift from provisional to fulfilled engagement, speaking from his stance within the realization of shinjin to one still uncertain of the path. Hence, it is possible to discern in Shinran's words a model for the shift from ordinary thought into fulfilled religious awareness.

The second general point to be noted is that concern with issues of good and evil and with false and true language occur together. This is because the problem of good and evil—making judgments, enacting good, and desisting from wrong—is the focal point of the action of the delusional self upon which the constructs of distorted understanding and false substantialization stand. Good and evil as determined from the stance of egocentric self-attachment, whatever their practical moral assessment, become objects of desire and aversion, that is, they reflect efforts to enhance the self and eradicate that which is threatening. This is true even of engagement with the Pure Land path when, as in initial engagement, it is embraced within ordinary modes of thought.

It is where adherence to the capacity to determine and perform absolute good is broken that recognition of the falsity in our egocentric conceptions of the self and the world can emerge. This awareness, being holistic, is experienced as arising from beyond the self, and since beings do not break the limitations of conceptual thought, it enters their linguistic universe as word, the Name of Amida. To grasp the thinking at work in Shinran's statements, let us consider the logical movements they manifest in closer detail. The basic elements are:

1. First is the context, which is informed by the basic question concerning the need to perform good acts and avoid evil in order to conform with Amida's Vow. It should be noted, therefore, that the teaching already constitutes the foundation for the question; engagement with the path, in the provisional mode, gives impetus and urgency to the question of practice, framed in terms of good and evil.

2. When asked, "Can I still be saved, though I have committed appalling evil, or though I perform little good?" Shinran rejects the premises of the question—not only that one can perform genuine good but, even prior to this, that one can determine what is good and what is evil in relation to the question of birth in the Pure Land—offering himself as example: "I know nothing of what is good or evil." A fundamental rift lies between the question and the mind-set from which it arises, on the one hand, and Shinran's response, on the other. In other words, Shinran's reply is not an attempt to lead the listener logically and discursively into the realm of shinjin, but rather an expression that manifests the difference between our ordinary thinking and the thinking that occurs as and through shinjin. Thus, the response begins with a presentation of a transformed vision of the issue raised and then proceeds to disclose the stance from which this perspective flows.

3. Shinran develops his refusal to take up the question presented into an absolute opposition between Buddha and self or good and evil: "If I could know thoroughly, as is known in the mind of Amida, that an act was good, then I would know good [but I cannot]."

4. Finally, there is a statement that manifests the coexistence of or interaction between the two sides of the dichotomy he has

drawn: "For a foolish being full of blind passions, in this fleeting world—this burning house—all matters without exception are *lies and gibberish,* totally without truth and sincerity. The nembutsu alone is *true and real."*

Taking these elements together, we see that Shinran's words embody two basic movements or changes in perspective within the shift from provisional to authentic engagement with the path:

I. In (1) to (3) above, we find a collapsing of ordinary presuppositions, together with a move from relative discrimination to absolute dichotomy or opposition.

II. In (4), we find expressed the practicer's interaction or interpenetration with reality that is simultaneous with opposition.

Let us consider these two aspects further.

Aspect I: From Relative Distinction to Absolute Opposition

A central aspect of our ordinary thought and speech is the tenacious effort, encapsulated in the discrimination of good and bad, to affirm the existence of the self as transcendent. In our daily lives, the ego-self asserts itself as true and real by judging its own acts and those of others, determining some to be good and others to be wrong or evil. This activity assumes the existence of a substantialized self standing apart from the world. In Shinran's view, such calculative thinking *(hakarai)* is the dominant element in the affirmation of and attachment to a delusional construction of the self and the world. The activity of this falsely reified subject ("mind") of calculative thinking is the focus in Shinran's definition of self-power:

> Self-power is the effort to attain birth, whether by invoking the names of Buddhas other than Amida and practicing good acts other than the nembutsu, in accordance with your particular circumstances and opportunities; or by endeavoring to make yourself worthy through mending the confusion in your acts, words, and thoughts, confident of your own powers and guided by your own calculation.[23]

We see here that the core of self-power lies in the will and effort to affirm one's own goodness, "guided by one's own calculation." "Calculation" signifies the judgment of the inner self that views and seeks to "mend one's acts, words, and thoughts." The phrase, "in accordance with your particular circumstances and opportunities," refers to our condition within the cultural and social contexts in which our images of the self and our standards of judgment are formed. This is, in other words, to assume the truth of one's own conceptions of the self and the world and to affirm the stance of the ego-self as transcendent and absolute.

The self standing behind and observing one's own thoughts, words, and acts implies a doubled structure. Shinran uses the term *double-mindedness (futagokoro)* as a synonym for doubt or the mind of self-power, and as an antonym for shinjin.[24] "Double-mindedness" expresses wavering and indecision, but at its core it indicates the hierarchical doubled self that is the subject of calculative thinking. For Shinran, all the acts of unenlightened beings manifest, to varying degrees, blind passions (desire and aversion) arising from self-attachment. Since, in the Pure Land path, beings attain the Buddha's mind through the entrusting of themselves to the working of the Vow and not through eradicating those passions, "you should not be anxious that the Tathagata will not receive you because you do wrong. A foolish being is by nature possessed of blind passions, so you must recognize yourself as a being of karmic evil."[25] In the Pure Land path, then, delusional acts of body, speech, and mind are not obstacles to attainment of enlightenment: "nirvana is attained without severing blind passions." The obstacle is the absolutized self within the self, which does not view itself "as a being of karmic evil," conditioned by the character of its existence in the world extending deep into the beginningless past, but instead, "confident of its own powers and guided by its own calculation," imagines that it stands apart from ignorance and attachment and its context in the history of the world with other beings, and further that it possesses the capacity and judgment to rectify its acts. It is this doubled, inner self that is "the mind of calculative thinking" or "the mind of self-power." Thus Shinran states:

> "To abandon the mind of self-power" admonishes the various and diverse kinds of people—masters of Hinayana or Mahayana, ignorant beings good or evil—to abandon the conviction that one is good, to cease relying on the self, to stop reflecting knowingly on one's evil heart, and further to abandon the judging of people as good and bad.[26]

The realization of shinjin is none other than the collapsing of this doubled self. It occurs as the shift from initial engagement with the path to fulfilled engagement.

As we have seen, in the words recorded in *Tannisho*, Shinran speaks across the gulf of the realization of shinjin to followers whose engagement with the path is still in the initial or provisional mode. Those who have come to Shinran, troubled by doubts regarding the efficacy of the nembutsu and concerned about the necessity of good conduct in order to attain birth in the Pure Land, have engaged the teaching by drawing it into their ordinary value judgments and frames of reference. They have grasped the Vow as an object or instrument within the universe of their own conceptions of cause and result and of good and evil, and seek to utilize it to affirm the self. In other words, it has become an element of their calculative thinking.

For Shinran, however, to "hear the Name" or Vow is to realize shinjin. This means that the horizons of our ordinary understanding and judgment have been fractured, and that the Vow stands free of egocentric appropriation. There are two phases in such hearing. The first is the collapse of the doubled self. When Shinran confronts the question of the necessity to do good and the fear of evil by exposing and undermining its assumptions—stating that he himself "knows nothing at all of the two, good and evil"—he is manifesting the absence of the doubled self or of calculative thinking, which has collapsed within him. This breakdown of the inner, judgmental self is the overturning or discarding of self-power, for the confidence that one can finally rectify one's thoughts and acts has vanished. When Shinran states that he "has no idea whether the nembutsu is truly the seed for being born in the Pure Land or whether it is the karmic act for which [he] must fall into hell,"[27] he is expressing this same absence of the determination of ultimate good and evil. The Name and the Vow have been extricated from the bounds of ordinary thought and have ceased to be means operating within the frames of reference of the delusional self.

The second phase is the emergence of opposition or polarity. Through the dissolution of egocentric calculation, so that one comes to "know nothing at all of good and evil," self-attachment as blind passions emerges as an actuality into a person's awareness. This does not mean that one ceases to make relative judgments of good and evil, or that one conceptually views all acts and events as "equally" evil. The discriminative categories of good and evil are not eliminated, but they come to be encompassed by a dichotomy in which our judgment of good and evil based on attachment to a substantialized self is seen to be pervaded by falsity and to be "evil" in that it binds us to further ignorance. Thus, rather than governing the means by which movement from ignorance to awakening is seen to be possible, the dichotomy of good and evil expands so that it comes into correspondence with that of Buddha and being. Here, all a person's means for movement along the path become inoperative.

In Shinran's words in *Tannisho*, this shift is expressed by a rejection of the questioners' assumptions of the need and the ability to judge and perform good. Further, the basis for this rejection of the questioners' presuppositions is that human existence is inherently characterized by egocentric passions: "With a foolish being full of blind passions, in this fleeting world—this burning house—all matters without exception are lies and gibberish, totally without truth and sincerity." With the rejection of any capability on the part of beings to determine and perform acts that might move them toward attainment of Buddhahood, the questions posed lose all significance. In the face of the correlated dichotomies of being/Buddha and evil/good, all relative discrimination embedded in attachment to a transcendent self is encompassed under the category of falsity and evil.

Aspect II: Interaction with Reality

It is here, where the nexus one had assumed between being and Buddha—one's means of access framed by a conception of practice and assessed by one's judgments of good and evil—has been dissolved through the shift described above, that a genuine apprehension of one's own existence and of true reality unfolds, informed in the awareness by the narratives of Vow and Pure Land. In Shinran's terms, the collapse of the doubled self is also Amida's giving the Buddha's pure mind to beings as the Name, which surfaces in their existence as the utterance of the nembutsu. It may be said that the nembutsu pervades our ordinary speech, rendering it, through its falsity, the vehicle of the true. That is, the awareness of that which is true and real—and the hearing and speaking of true language—is but the opposite face of the radical self-awareness of evil, and it arises spontaneously.

From the perspective of our ordinary thought, the first aspect—the movement into the larger framework of absolute dichotomy—may be described as an emerging awareness of the horizons of such thought. The relative intellection that functions at the core of the conception of the self becomes aware of itself as delusional blind passions and ignorance. This self-awareness of the limitations of one's ability to know and judge emerges because such judgment finds itself within a larger context of Buddha-wisdom. In other words, one's relative intellection (good and evil) comes to be seen as evil (rooted in false discrimination and tainted by self-attachment), and this in itself is for the self to become aware of itself from beyond its own horizons. It is also to experience—and give living voice to—the disclosive power that makes one aware of one's own existence. Shinran terms the arising of the horizon of our ordinary thought "being grasped, never to be abandoned," and such grasping or seeing is itself Amida.[28]

This is not a breaking through the horizons of ignorance from within; nevertheless, it is an unfolding of a new awareness. Apprehension of the horizons of one's own knowledge and conception arises only through awareness of the presence of a knowing (Buddha-wisdom) that transcends relative discrimination. For the limits of ordinary thought to rise to awareness means that the mind has come to stand beyond those limits and has been enabled, from that new perspective, to reflect on the horizon. For all that can be conceived to come to be seen as limited and in fact partially and falsely conceived means that there is at once an absolute dichotomy between ignorant thought and wisdom, and further that there is both an "interaction" and nonduality, in that ignorance has come to be aware of itself from beyond its own limits, and in that the work of Shin Buddhist life comes to include a fresh apprehension of the beings in the world from this new perspective.

A major contribution to contemporary religious thought found in the Shin Buddhist path of Shinran lies in his clear recognition of the implications of the linguistically bound, perspectival nature of human understanding. A thoroughgoing insight leads not to mere relativism or a logical lapse into self-refutation, but to an understanding of human existence in terms of evil in the Buddhist sense. It is where such a grasp of evil becomes comprehensive that the significance of human conceptual understanding and its limitations are genuinely plumbed. At the same time, according to Shinran, it is at this point that the apprehension of reality through self-awareness also arises. In a pluralistic world rife with human conflict and global crises, such engagement with religious symbols embodies a centripetal movement toward an authentically interrelated and interdependent self, which is a self that sees also from beyond the self.

Notes

1. "Hymn of True Shinjin and the Nembutsu" *(Shōshin nembutsu ge)*, in *The Collected Works of Shinran*, 1: 70.

2. This does not mean, of course, that one realizes nirvana while remaining fettered within samsaric existence. Rather, in Shinran's terms, it means that one attains or realizes the Buddha's mind as shinjin, so that the attainment of supreme nirvana at death comes about naturally and necessarily.

3. For example, *Understanding Shinran* (Fremont: Asian Humanities Press, 1995) by Hee-Sung Keel stands partly as a criticism of my *Shinran: An Introduction to His Thought* (Kyoto: Hongwanji International Center, 1989), written with Yoshifumi Ueda, in which the continuities between Pure Land tradition and Mahayana symbols, concepts, and modes of thought are delineated. For a detailed review of *Understanding Shinran*, see Gregory G. Gibbs, "*Understanding Shinran* and the Burden of Traditional Dogmatics," *Eastern Buddhist* 30, (1997): 267–86.

4. Tachikawa himself raises this issue; see pp. 230–31.

5. In Frederick J. Streng, *Emptiness: A Study in Religious Meaning* (Nashville: Abingdon Press, 1967), p. 213. I do not follow Streng's explanation of the two kinds of truth given in other parts of his book.

6. Ibid.

7. In Shinran, see *Teaching, Practice, and Realization*, "Chapter on Transformed Buddha-Bodies and Lands," 71, in *The Collected Works of Shinran*, 1: 241–242.

8. *Middle Stanzas*, 24: 18; see Streng, p. 213.

9. "It is indeed sorrowful to give way to impluses with the excuse that one is by nature possessed of blind passions—excusing acts that should not be committed, words that should not be said, and thoughts that should not be harbored—and to say that one may follow one's desires in any way whatever." *Lamp for the Latter Ages*, letter 20, in *The Collected Works of Shinran*, 1: 553.

Also: "Signs of long years of saying the nembutsu and aspiring for birth can be seen in the change in the heart that had been bad and in the deep warmth for friends and fellow-practicers; this is the sign of rejecting the world." *Lamp for the Latter Ages*, letter 19, in *The Collected Works of Shinran*, 1: 551.

10. Ibid., p. 554.

11. Kakunyo's *Kudenshō*, in *Shinshū Shōgyō Zensho* (Kyoto: Ōyagi Kōbundō, 1941), 3: 13–14.

12. Shinran states, "When I consider deeply the Vow of Amida, which arose from five kalpas of profound thought, I realize that it was entirely for the sake of myself alone!" *Tannishō: A Primer*, p. 43; *The Collected Works of Shinran*, 1: 679.

13. *Muryōjukyōshaku*, in *Hōnen Shōnin Zenshū* (Kyoto: Heirakuji Shoten, 1955), p. 67.

14. Quoted by Shinran in *Teaching, Practice, and Realization*, "Chapter on Practice," 72, in *The Collected Works of Shinran*, 1: 55.

15. See chapter 1, note 24, p. 70.

16. *Teaching, Practice, and Realization*, "Chapter on Shinjin," 19, in *The Collected Works of Shinran*, 1: 93–94.

17. *Teaching, Practice, and Realization*, "Chapter on Shinjin," 65, in *The Collected Works of Shinran*, 1: 112.

18. *The True Teaching, Practice, and Realization of the Pure Land Way*, "Chapter on Practice," 1, in *The Collected Works of Shinran*, 1: 13.

19. *Tannisho (Tannisho)* is one of the most popular religious classics of Japan; it has, however, come under critical scrutiny recently, partly in reaction to the burst of adulation from the Meiji period on, and some question has been raised regarding the accuracy of its representation of Shinran's thought (see, for example, Ishida Mizumaro, *Tannishō: Sono Hihan-teki Kōsatsu*, Shunjūsha, 1981). While *Tannisho* must be read with care, the results of the analysis that I undertake here can also be derived from Shinran's own writings, suggesting the continuing usefulness of the work.

20. *Tannishō: A Primer*, p. 43; also in *The Collected Works of Shinran*, 1: 679.

21. Taya Raishun sets forth this theory in *Tannishō Shinchū*, Kyoto: Hōzōkan, 1939. It has recently been supported by Yasuraoka Kōsaku in *Tannishō Zenkōdoku* (Tokyo: Daizō Shuppan, 1990), 457–459.

22. *Tannishō: A Primer*, "Postscript," p. 44; *The Collected Works of Shinran*, 1: 679.

23. *Lamp for the Latter Ages*, letter 2, in *The Collected Works of Shinran*, 1: 525.

24. See *Teaching, Practice, and Realization*, "Chapter on Shinjin," 65, in *The Collected Works of Shinran*, 1: 112.

25. *Lamp for the Latter Ages*, letter 2, in *The Collected Works of Shinran*, 1: 525.

26. *Notes on 'Essentials of Faith Alone'*, in *The Collected Works of Shinran*, 1: 459.

27. *Tannishō: A Primer*, section 2, p. 23; *The Collected Works of Shinran*, 1: 679.

28. See Shinran's verse in chapter 1, p. 61.

7. A Call to Compassion

John S. Yokota

Introductory Remarks

I will attempt to confront the problems indicated by professors Cobb and Kaufman in their comments and develop answers that will clarify and amplify my position. My position is understandably similar to Cobb's, since he has so intimately influenced my thinking. This presents one issue raised directly by my Buddhist colleagues. The incorporation of process thought in the reconsideration of certain Shin Buddhist doctrines needs to be addressed. In explaining why process categories of thought are congenial to an articulation of Shin Buddhist thought, other issues that need to be addressed naturally arise. It would be advantageous, therefore, to interweave discussion of these issues with the reasons for the incorporation of process modes of thought.

While a variety of issues have been introduced by our commentators, in focusing on Kaufman's comments, two central areas of contention are apparent—namely, issues concerning methodology and demythologization. It is in relation to this second area that I see the greatest difference between our premises. This point of contention, finally, is a matter concerned with the viability of metaphysics. Cobb addresses this issue in his last point when he discusses the matter of language and metaphysics. One fundamental reason I have found process thought helpful is its insistence on the metaphysical enterprise. While admittedly a philosophical rarity for the twentieth century, this insistence that our carefully thought out and articulated words about reality do indeed point to reality and tell us about that reality is the basic foundation for religious discussion.

The title of this response, "A Call to Compassion," is also the title of a recent article on process thought and the doctrine of Amida that summarizes my vision of the Shin Buddhist tradition's central preoccupation with compassion as a call to compassion.[1] It was this basic position that my earlier chapter in this volume attempted to articulate. My response will express this position anew. Finally, because of the nature of Kaufman's comments and concerns, which center on methodological questions almost to the exclusion of all others, the responses to the two areas of contention will necessarily overlap.

Methodology or Self-Conscious Reconstruction of the Tradition

I confess a lack of self-conscious methodological concern. Obviously, this lack of self-consciousness was impressed upon me by Kaufman's comments. To be honest, however, while recognizing the importance of these methodological concerns, I still harbor doubts about their final efficacy. I would venture to guess that it has a connection with the above noted issue of metaphysics. Voicing my mixed reaction to this point of methodological concern at the outset, I, however, do intend to confront this problem because of the many important issues it brings forth in thinking about the nature of constructive theology and of myth in one's own religious tradition.

Constructive Theology

The term *buddhology* may seem to be more appropriate, which while rarely used, on the whole, refers to general Buddhist Studies and its text-centered and sociological emphasis. This kind of approach is not what the theological enterprise primarily deals with. Of course, the term *theology* in its common usage almost exclusively refers to the Christian tradition. It can of course refer to any other monotheistic tradition as well, and if its original Greek usage is incorporated, it can refer to any polytheistic tradition also. The theological enterprise need not be confined to any one tradition, however. It is, indeed, a task that can be undertaken from the perspective of any religious commitment and always has, therefore, a dogmatic element that must be dealt with carefully. If carelessly emphasized, it can lead to a purely dogmatic tract defending the faith. The theological enterprise is simply thinking about one's tradition. We must follow through and ask, of course, How should we think about our tradition? Honesty, care, and consistency should be the norms. It is a task that professionals must endeavor in, obviously, but more importantly, it is a task that all thoughtful lay persons naturally engage in as well. Traditional sectarian dogmatics often fall into the trap of merely mouthing the traditional approach without a critical look at it. Contemporary Buddhist Studies opt for an alleged objectivity and noncommitment and often fall into the trap of talking about a tradition that exists only in their abstractions. In this sense of thinking about one's tradition, I have consciously been engaged in the theological enterprise for a number of years.

Again, a Buddhist theology may be a contradiction in terms. Even if the above meaning of theology as thinking about one's religious tradition with honesty, care, and consistency were willingly adopted, there is the problem of a theism that the theological enterprise assumes. The traditional vision of deity in Christianity cannot be the basis of this more inclusive sense of the theological enterprise. One reason I have found the process-articulated vision of God so congenial is that, as Cobb notes in his comments on Hirota's rearticulation of the problems with the traditional doctrine of God, process thought agrees, on the whole, with these criticisms. An absolute, unilaterally powerful, simply eternal, solitary force unto itself is not a deity worthy of worship from a process perspective or any other for that matter. The divine relativity (Charles Hartshorne), divine pathos (Abraham Heschel), and the lure of God (Lewis Ford), while needing fuller elaboration, indicate the process position and are motifs that have helped me think more carefully and fully about the reality of Amida.

All three of our chapters are theological endeavors in this inclusive sense. Moreover, as Kaufman notes, "all interpretive activity is in fact a matter of constructive reimagining." Thus, all three of our works are also involved in the task of imaginatively reconstructing our tradition. Here, I must plead not guilty to the charge of being unconscious of what I was doing. I see my task and that of any thoughtful person of faith as having this imaginative reconstruction as the core of one's religious responsibility. To reconstruct, that is, to reincorporate within oneself one's tradition anew in one's attempt to understand it has been an obvious fact to me for some time now. It is, I believe, the basic assumption of so-called Liberal Protestant efforts. The argument can be made clearer if the opposite position is critically examined. The problem with the claim of both traditional dogmatics and contemporary objective studies of religious phenomena is that both sides believe they can look at the tradition just as it was or is and somehow preserve it either for the purpose of worship or study. One of the basic lessons of at least the last century of academic study in all fields of research is the recognition of the intrusion of the subjective perspective in our research. Good researchers are hopefully more than the sum of their variegated social and academic backgrounds with concomitant unexamined premises and prejudices, but they are, to a larger extent than most would like to admit, precisely this sum of their backgrounds. It is a lesson hard to fully accept. The persistence of objective positions, both dogmatic and scientific, clearly shows that this lesson of recent history is indeed difficult to assimilate. That we are creatures of our times and positions in life with our own specific worldviews are facts Liberal Protestantism was painfully forced to confront from the severe criticisms early in this century. Yet responsible Liberal Protestantism has thrived and continued on by acknowledging this shortcoming and has continued its creative theological enterprise under the moderating force of this acknowledgment. Indeed, it is precisely because of this fact of conditionality and relativity that all interpretive efforts necessarily become efforts to think anew of one's tradition from the perspective of one's present situation. To look back to the past is to bring our present mind-set to bear on that past, and thus this look back always entails a reincorporation of that past and therefore a creative reconstruction of it.

If I correctly understand Kaufman here about the nature of the theological enterprise and its importance to the tradition, then I believe I am in essential agreement with him. Each generation of the faithful must engage in this effort to make their tradition their own. Our present situation, however, seems to warrant a special urgency. We, in this period marked as "postmodern" and faced with the relativity of all values, must confront this fact of our times and articulate our position as clearly and reasonably as possible. In that sense, our generation may actually face a unique challenge.

The Purpose of the Theological Enterprise

Two specific points need clarification. The first point is minor. Kaufman sees my work as being at the far end of the continuum that our three chapters make up in terms of use of outside sources. I believe my religious self-identity as a Shin Buddhist is strong enough to be engaged in explicit mutuality with Christianity and open dispute with my tradition, especially since I believe such mutuality and dispute benefit that tradition. Nevertheless, at the same time, I see my position as being, in many ways, the most traditional of the three. In my emphasis of compassion and the implications of such an emphasis on the doctrine of Amida, I believe I am being traditional. My position does go furthest afield. The reason for this, however, is to affirm in a conceptuality and language that make more fully consistent the central claims of the tradition. I find that the process conceptuality of God and its many nuances are particularly helpful in reconsidering how we can think of Amida Buddha and articulate this reality more convincingly. The claim of Mahayana Buddhism in general and Shin Buddhism in particular that reality is primordially and centrally characterized as compassionate is what I consciously set out to articulate. That is all. This I feel is the core of the tradition, and thus, a most traditional task.

It is precisely this central concern with compassion that may have caused a second misunderstanding. I must admit that after reading Kaufman's comments, the problem of myth did indeed look central to my argument. Moreover, I do admit that the problem has been a recurring theme throughout my work and thinking. However, the reason why this problem is brought up is that in focusing on the claim that reality is compassionate, the truth or actuality of that claim becomes an important issue. The tradition has used the myth of Amida (Dharmakara Bodhisattva) and its story of practice and fulfillment of practice to articulate this reality of compassion. This argument does not carry much weight. I did not want to get rid of myth so much as to find a more reliable form of actualization. That may be identical to the task of demythologization, but the focus has always been to secure the intuition that life and reality are compassionate on to a more concrete, historical foundation. To confront the problem of myth was only a consequence of my preoccupation with this central reality of compassion. This conscious task of seeking some form of affirmation of the claims of one's theological work changes the complexion of the demythologizing efforts and is an important distinction to keep in mind.

This is the excuse for not analyzing the concept of myth—in short, for not thinking explicitly about the problem of myth but just assuming it was problematic. I will try to rectify that lapse in the section on myth and demythologization. What will be discussed now is the methodological task of affirming the reality of compassion by means other than myth. Since the story that is myth does little to affirm the underlying reality of compassion, to my mind at least, then if I am serious about my claim as to the reality of compassion, I must look for some ways to help me reasonably hold to this conviction.

The Actualization of Compassion

While this aspect of the concretization of our theological claims is not directly broached in Kaufman's exposition of constructive theology, it is an essential part of any creative reconstructive attempt to make one's faith anew. One guiding principle of this creative endeavor would have to be to make its claims, especially its central claims, not only comprehensible but convincing. Two related emphases of process thought are helpful in this regard. While not used in their usual sense, they can best be expressed by the terms *incarnation* and *revelation*.

Incarnation.   The emphasis of the concrete rather than the abstract in process thought means that historical actualization is prized and seen as concretely securing notions of or intuitions into reality on to a firmer basis. This is the primary reason why Cobb and other process theologians emphasize the central place of the incarnation of Christ in the historical figure Jesus. It is this concrete actualization in history both in word and deed that gives credence to the intuition that reality is primordially characterized as loving and caring. In short, one finds God's loving reality definitively actualized in the historical figure Jesus of Nazareth. Admittedly, what can be confidently declared to be accurate, historical fact about Jesus is indefinite and ever-changing. Nevertheless, the fact of his mission and his eschatological emphasis of the ultimately saving power of God for the faithful seem to be undeniable central facts. It is in this mission and the teachings coming out of that mission that one can see an actualization of the love of God. This is one area where process theology is in agreement with mainline emphases on the incarnation. It obviously negates the quasi-magical nuances and absolutist religious superiority that accompanies most mainline conservative positions in regard to the incarnation.

The process position may be contrasted with John Hick's position of understanding the incarnation as metaphor. This position that caused quite a stir in Christian circles, especially in its earlier articulation not as metaphor but as myth, is Hick's attempt to transcend the absolutist tendencies of the tradition so that it can engage in constructive dialogue with other traditions. While Kaufman is not explicit in regard to his position on the incarnation in the present paper, I would assume that his position is close to if not similar to Hick's position. While Hick holds to a relatively orthodox notion of God and Kaufman to a more relativistic or practical image, they both seem to shy away from an affirmation of God's reality through the incarnation as Cobb does. No doubt, both Hick and Kaufman are probably more representative of present-day opinion in philosophical theology especially in the Anglo-American world in regard to affirmation of God's reality. I nevertheless am convinced by the process emphasis on this incarnating reality and the consequent affirming of God's reality and character therein. This is the reason why I discuss the relationship between Amida and Shakyamuni Buddhas in the second major section of my chapter. Again, it is not so much myth that I want to confront but the necessity and desirability to affirm the reality of Amida Buddha in a concrete and thereby hopefully convincing way.

As Cobb notes in his comments, I did try to respond to his earlier suggestion, especially as developed in *Beyond Dialogue*, about the need to secure the story of Amida on to firmer historical ground. As he also notes, in looking anew at Shakyamuni as the actualization of the compassionate reality of Amida Buddha through his act of going forth from the seat of enlightenment, I negate his proposal to look to Palestine and the figure Jesus for an expression of this compassionate reality. To repeat what I had hoped to convey in Part One, I see in the act of Shakyamuni as he goes forth from the seat of enlightenment the central act of historical actualization of the reality of compassion that Amida embodies. It is to this act that we Shin Buddhists can look back to and get confirmation of this reality of Amida Buddha. Finally, I must admit to an inclination in my more recent thinking to take more seriously Cobb's suggestion to look at Jesus and the Christ event as a significant historical actualization of Amida along with Shakyamuni. *Amida as the Christ* is a phrase that I have used and reflects this change in my thinking. The process emphasis on historical actualization and Cobb's elaboration makes a point that is important. This incarnation is specific and unique. The incarnation that is Jesus and the incarnation that is Shakyamuni are different, as is to be expected. They actualize different visions of reality. The similarities are striking but there are vital differences. To say "Amida as the Christ," then is not a simple equation of the two. It means to say that the notion of, indeed, the reality of Amida must grow and change as the differences that Christ encompasses come into contact with the reality of Amida. To say Amida as the Christ is both theoretically as well as emotionally quite difficult. Nevertheless, by so doing, it can help us look at Amida anew and extend the ground of actualizing its reality.

In expanding the geo-historical reference from Asia to include Palestine, there is a corresponding expansion of the confirmation of this vision of reality as compassionate. A similar but different intuition into reality is seen in a context both socio-historically and intellectually different. This adds in a different way to the confirmation of this intuition. We Shin Buddhists are not alone in how we see reality.

Revelation. The above notion of incarnation was not too different from its usual usage in that actualization as a specific historical figure—Jesus and Shakyamuni—was at its center. The usage of revelation here is a bit more removed from the traditional Christian one in that scripture as the revealed word of God/reality is not being claimed. If anything, the notion it is usually contrasted with—*natural theology*—may be more appropriate. My point in using the term is to emphasize the self-revealing, active character of reality. The ultimate is ever revealing itself in all aspects of reality both in the socio-historical and the physical world. Admittedly, there are problems with a crude notion of revelation as well as a crude notion of salvation history. A more inclusive notion of revelation as history in which hints of a compassionate and caring reality calling us toward that ideal in the story of humankind can be another source of actualizing the reality that is Amida. Our tradition, on the whole, has freely developed this notion of Amida coming into our personal or spiritual lives thus revealing itself and bringing about a transformation. It has on the other hand, on the whole, neglected the notion of Amida coming into the socio-historical realm, revealing itself and bringing about a transformation in this transsubjective arena. That we can see Amida active in our personal and collective lives, again, is an affirmation of the compassionate reality of Amida. It is therefore a worthwhile avenue to pursue if we hope to secure our notion of Amida's compassionate character on to firmer ground. This is an area that I hope to work on in the near future, and so will not pursue it any further here except to add a few general remarks that will hopefully indicate the direction of this future consideration.

In work on the doctrine of two truths,[2] one of two related conclusions of the analysis was that ultimate reality is always coming out of itself to reveal itself in the form of the second or worldly truth. In short, at the very core of the whole Buddhist tradition is the self-revealing activity of ultimate reality. This is, indeed, in itself the compassionate coming forth of reality. Because of this self-revelation in the form of the worldly truth, the second conclusion is that there are no two distinct realms but two intimately related and inseparable realms. Largely in work on Shin Buddhist social ethics,[3] the comment was oft-times made that while a hint of the compassionate intent of Amida could sometimes be faintly discerned in the passing of history, the opposite reality of evil and cruelty could be more often and more clearly discerned. This led to the paradoxical conclusion that it was precisely this discordant fact that called us to actualize the ideal of compassion that Amida embodies. I hope to develop this line of thought a bit more in the summarizing remarks that end this chapter. The evidence of this compassionate, self-revealing activity of reality in both our personal and larger socio-historical lives is anything but definite. This goes without saying. What is proposed here is not absolute affirmation of the compassionate reality but a hint of it, admittedly, coming out of this intuition of faith but nevertheless transcending the limits of faith to a more generally acceptable standard of judgment.

Finally, the physical world also provides another hint that our intuition of the compassionate nature of reality is indeed true. The basic Buddhist view of the world as an impermanent world of becoming where all entities are open to that which is around them is a vision of interdependent mutuality and sharing. It is only in such a world that the reality of compassion can truly exist. The largely Western vision of reality with a world of being and independent entities of reality not open to that which is around them is a world in which the notion of love and compassion is arbitrarily forced upon it. If, indeed, the world is something like what we Buddhists say it is, then the world is naturally and of a necessity a world where a compassionate caring must be at its center.

We have in the above, then, the seeds for a natural theology. We must be careful about having a crudely naive natural theology, yet if what we hold to be basic and essential to Amida Buddha is indeed true, then it seems to be imperative that we can see hints of this reality in the world around us. The Buddhist vision of reality in which all entities of existence are mutually related and open to all other entities of existence seems to be borne out not only by our common observations of reality but also by the recent developments in our scientific worldview, especially in physics. This affirmation in certain emphases in recent scientific inquiries into the nature of existence can only help to secure our own religious vision of reality on firmer ground. Again, nothing is definite. There is no great signature in the universe that says "Amida." We interpret what are the best speculations about the nature of existence through eyes and hearts colored by our convictions about the world garnered from the Buddhist worldview and Shin Buddhist insights into the reality of Amida Buddha. Again, the seeming correspondence between the contemporary scientific worldview and our own tradition's is reassuring. Think of the mental and emotional discomfort we would feel if this were not the case. The struggle and discomfort felt by thinking Christians as Darwin's view of the development of life came to the fore and the Newtonian worldview collapsed is something we Buddhists have not had to deal with. We have nevertheless not forced ourselves to look more deeply at these seeming parallels and have a little too heartily gloated to ourselves about our superiority vis-à-vis Christianity. Earnest and self-conscious dialogue with the scientific community must also take place as well as with other religious traditions. The goal is to see reality more clearly and as correctly as possible. To do this, we depend not only on our innertraditional resources but also on other religious and nonreligious traditions.

The Buddhist vision of reality based on the vision of the world as empty and dependently arising, with its varied development in the Buddhist traditions of India, China, and Japan, can and has been expressed in transpersonal language or, as Kaufman would have it, more fully demythologized language. This transpersonal vision of reality within the tradition cannot be denied nor do I propose to negate it as incorrect. Nevertheless, looking at the tradition as a whole apart from designations of transpersonal or personal, the self-revealing activity of reality along with this empty, dependent arising vision of reality primordially characterized as compassionate can be and is most fully expressed in the personal language of a compassionate figure of salvation. We will turn to the problem of myth and what I see as finally the metaphysical basis of this use of personal language to explain this position.

The Problem of Myth

Again, the point of my dismissal of the Amida story as the basis of the compassionate reality of Amida was to affirm my belief that the historical actualization of this compassionate intent in the person of Shakyamuni was much more firm and preferable ground on which to secure our tradition. It was not a consciously demythologizing effort. In other contexts, my efforts in dismissing the Amida story and looking anew at Shakyamuni (and later Jesus) as the ground to affirm our belief in the primordially compassionate character of the world has been taken to mean my disparagement of myth. In some ways this may be true. I am not a student of myth nor do I feel fully comfortable with it. Nevertheless, it is not bad in and of itself. What has struck me as wrongheaded is the refusal of many in the tradition to admit to the nonhistorical nature of the story and persist in using it as almost a magical confirmation of the compassionate reality of Amida. Yet, the myth of Amida cannot be simply negated. Indeed, it is to be vigorously affirmed.

I am not, again, a student of myth nor am I really all that interested in the phenomenon. That basic myths reach to the depths of human insight into the nature of existence is to be affirmed. These stories have a fundamental ability to grasp undeniable truths that our rational powers too often neglect. Myths arise from basic intuitions into the nature of reality that are rarely conscious or analytical in nature. The story comes forth as an attempt to articulate these intuitive insights more as poetic metaphor than as rationalistic explanation. It is precisely because of this basic insight into reality that it is imperative to affirm these truths apart from the myth. The truth or truths that myth articulates should be the focus of interest.

While it seems reasonable that the analysis from the history of religions perspective that the Amida figure has its roots in Persia is true and that even a cursory look at the story confirms the fact that aspects of the legend of Shakyamuni's life are mirrored in it, these facts, while of interest and importance, are beside the point. The intuition that reaches back to the very beginnings of the tradition, if not further, to a basic human intuition that reality is fundamentally compassionate is the ultimate genesis of the story, regardless of the specific historical conditions surrounding it. It is this basic myth and this basic intuition into reality that it reflects which are important.

This said, it would seem that the task before one is to affirm in ways unconnected with myth the truth of these insights and intuitions. If this is the task of demythologization, then I am consciously engaged in it. The point is that the demythologizing endeavor should take myth—or what myth expresses—seriously. I do take myth seriously and therefore want to affirm its insights. One problem with demythologization is its explicit connection with existentialist or subjectivistic approaches that hope to affirm the truth of the mythic insight through experiential insight. This is not what I have set out to do. This approach is not negated but, while rich in its suggestiveness and assuredly powerful in attracting the religiously faithful because of this centering on religious experience, is too fully within the circle of faith. I had hoped to transcend this circle to some extent in the above discussion of the actualization of compassion. My approach, while not fully outside this circle of faith, had hoped to expand the ground of affirmation and actualization.

The explicit and implicit point of the above is the conviction that reality, or at least a basic characteristic of reality, is articulated in myth. It is because of this conviction that I see it as imperative to affirm this image of compassionate reality beyond the confines of this myth and the faith from which it springs and for which it serves. This was the whole purpose of the discussion in Part Two. Something is being discussed whether in the form of story or philosophically religious language. The story and language are not tricks in an act of sleight of hand to fool us that something is there. They are different ways to point to this reality. Moreover, the personal figure that is the basis of the story as well as the language are the pivot both linguistically and metaphysically upon which this whole enterprise turns. To deny the personal character of this reality would rob it of its central characteristic.

The Personal Reality That Is Amida Buddha

This section will repeat much that has come before. It is both the simplest and most difficult yet the most central. It is the simplest, because it will just state my conviction about the metaphysical ground of Amida. It is the most difficult, because it cannot argue the truth of the claim. Finally, it is the most central, because it is the basis for the whole preceding discussion. The main thrust of my comments echo Cobb's section on language and metaphysics.

The whole point of the Buddhist analysis of reality with its emphasis on impermanence, becoming, openness/emptiness, and dependent arising is that it tells us that reality is like this so that we can act accordingly; that is, we should not behave as if this was a world made up of changeless, unconnected entities. The Buddhist insight into reality is just that—a recognition of that which is real. Since the world is one of openness/emptiness, we should act in mutual openness, freely giving to and receiving from the other; in short, we should act compassionately. We act compassionately because the makeup of the world demands it precisely because a world of openness and dependent arising is a compassionate world.

The specific Buddhist claim about the character of the world cannot be proven, nor can the underlying belief that there truly is a reality to be characterized. The relativism of the times leading to postmodern nihilistic or radically relativistic positions ultimately denying reality is a fact of the contemporary philosophical scene. The temper of the times cannot be denied. Indeed, Buddhism has sometimes been enlisted in declaring this postmodern message with an antimetaphysical understanding of emptiness at its center. That Buddhism has been characterized as antimetaphysical cannot be denied, but on closer examination, the point of contention is spurious speculation or prapañca and not the premise of ontological reality. Nevertheless, the reality of relativism or at least variegated views of reality is undeniable. There is, indeed, a richness of views. It is not a simple matter, but reality or at least a fuller understanding of reality can emerge from taking these views under consideration. This sense of relativism should not be taken as a denial of reality or the metaphysical enterprise. The point of Buddhism is that in coming to know reality, one is transformed by that knowledge. The point that Pure Land Buddhism adds to this formula is that we are made to come to know reality through that reality and are thereby transformed by it. Knowledge of reality is at the center of Buddhism and so a denial of reality is anathema to Buddhist practice.

The above statement about the activity of reality in revealing itself and bringing about transformation as well as the previously stated mutually open character of the Buddhist vision of reality all point to a compassionate center to existence, a compassionate, personal center to existence. If compassion is the primordial character of existence, then a personal center to existence is undeniable. Compassionate intent (the primal vow) is present and undeniable as well. This intent or will can and should be described as intentless. Obviously, we are talking metaphorically; there is no person Amida. Nevertheless, the personal quality of existence is at the core of this compassionate image of reality. One should not take this quality away. Our description of reality would be reduced if we did so.

Kaufman's criticism of not taking the demythologizing enterprise far enough in leaving the personal quality would be appropriate if it was not central to the description of reality. Again, if the metaphysical insights of Buddhism are true and we have a mutually open world of interdependence actively and continually coming out of itself to reveal itself so as to transform us and the world, then compassion is indeed central to the description. Compassion is a personal quality, and so it is with this language of the personal that reality is most fully described. Pure Land Buddhism should not go beyond the language of the personal.

Moreover, it is not only a problem of adequate language to describe reality. Reality is compassionate and therefore has this personal quality. No doubt, this does not resolve Kaufman's concerns. I must admit ignorance of his basic position on metaphysics and the efficacy of language to point beyond itself to reality. What little I know would suggest a complex position that tends toward a relativistic, pragmatic usage of language in which the preoccupation with methodological issues, at least for me, makes ambiguous the relationship between language and metaphysics.

Holding on to the efficacy of metaphysics is definitely not a mainstream position in contemporary thought. Kaufman's position is if anything a more mainstream one. Nevertheless, the religious endeavor in general and the Buddhist endeavor in particular would be for naught if not for the metaphysical premise.

The Innertraditional Dialogue

Being forced to reflect on the methodological approach to the study of our own tradition by Kaufman's comments and this entire endeavor among the five of us has reinforced my conviction of the benefits of a dialogical approach. To see the tradition not only from within the circle of faith but from varied perspectives outside this circle can stimulate us to consider aspects of our tradition that have been neglected. While this may lead to unwanted consequences in some instances, I would err in favor of that rather than remaining too comfortable among the familiar. At any rate, anyone who did venture too far (in fact or in evaluation) would soon be cautioned. To remain within the formally prescribed will not warrant a caution, yet that in and of itself is not a good. A bit of adventure is needed. Again, this is not without its dangers. I do see, however, the danger of the tradition, as it now stands, as being too comfortable in its institutional and doctrinal ways. It is nothing short of a crisis.

The way to break out of this crisis of habit is through dialogue with others. This dialogue must not be limited to only religious traditions but to other traditions that attempt to give us a picture of the world we live in. In this way, we may be able to fashion a more comprehensive image of reality. We need innertraditional dialogue as well. We must press each other to explain ourselves as precisely and consistently as possible as well as press each other to look at the premises of our positions and evaluate them in the presence of each other.

Tachikawa brings a depth and breadth of knowledge of the whole tradition to his discussion that I cannot match and an openness that our ecclesiastic ties and personal commitment to the Shin Buddhist tradition precludes, thus bringing a natural innertraditional dialogue that transcends all sectarian designations. This dialogue within the larger tradition is badly needed, yet rarely engaged in. One area where his implicit and often explicit assumptions clarify a totally different perspective from mine is the central place of practice, especially traditional Pure Land mandala contemplation, in his elaborations of his position. I have harbored a vague idea of reconsidering the traditional Shin Buddhist doctrinal negation of personal practice by looking at the tradition of practice in the wider Pure Land Buddhist context as one way to jerk us out of our sometimes too facile declaration of our inability to engage in any practice whatsoever. To be honest, I do not know where such a reconsideration will lead. We must look at this negation of practice and the whole issue of the self and other power opposition, however, so as to think again in a practical and concrete manner of the way of life of the Shin Buddhist devotee. This assumption of the place of contemplative practice in Tachikawa's approach is one catalyst that can force us to look again at this topic. The doctrinal problems this may cause are not negligible.

There are two other points in Tachikawa's work that will be commented on. The first is a seeming affirmation of one interpretation of reality that I have come to emphasize. The other is the explication of what I take to be the implicit premise of Tachikawa's position that he, however, fails to enunciate. His use of the sacred/profane dichotomy, as Kaufman points out, is not reflected in either Hirota's or my work. The subtlety of his treatment with its Mādhyamika and Tantric elaborations, in the end, rises above a simple dichotomy of the two in the sacralization of the profane. If this is the case, is this primarily an aspect of the meditational effects on the practitioner's view of the world or is this also the work of the sacred itself working in and transforming the profane? If the latter, this seems to be another example of the self-actualization of reality. I would hope that it could be interpreted that way.

The second point, again, deals with an omission rather than anything stated. It seems that the implicit premise of Tachikawa's position is that Buddhism takes the world seriously and therefore there is a metaphysical basis to the entire discussion. Granted, in considering the flow of the discussion, there is no explicit need to express this metaphysical premise. Yet it is obvious to me, at least, that there is this underlying premise. Is it really inappropriate for Buddhism explicitly to make this point? Obviously, I think not.

Hirota, too, brings a depth and breadth to the discussion that entails not only detailed knowledge of the Shin tradition but the wider Pure Land tradition and Japanese aesthetics as well. Of the three of us he brings the most indepth knowledge of the Shin Buddhist tradition in both its classical and more recent elaborations. Unlike Tachikawa, as Kaufman indicates, he engages in dialogue with certain strands of Christian thought. While he has engaged in dialogue and has thereby opened up the tradition to outside thought, it is limited to the incorporation of methodological approaches to the study of the tradition.

This is why there is resonance with Kaufman's position. However, the explicit incorporation of Kaufman's categories of thought is premised on a basic attitude that is anathema to Kaufman's own attitude toward religion. Hirota's insistence on the special experience of the mind of entrusting to Amida with its concomitant exclusive and unique knowledge of reality coming from a context of specifically Buddhist practice is, moreover, anathema to my own view of the theological task. To put the point rather broadly, he has taken a Barthianlike position that acknowledges other traditions while nonetheless claiming a uniqueness and incomparable quality to Shin Buddhist insights. These insights are like the revelatory knowledge of traditional Christian dogmatics shutting out all possibility or desirability of affirming these insights on a more general or universal level, in short, of seeing any real viability in the insights of any other tradition. I do acknowledge some truth in this insistence on uniqueness. The Buddhist worldview is unique and the context from which it has arisen is unique. However, these insights must also have general validity and be more generally affirmable. Moreover, his discussion of levels of knowledge, which is an aspect of this same perspective of the uniqueness of a special, higher level of knowledge, is understandable, but is there really a definite and unbridgeable break among these levels? I deny this and, again, my work on the doctrine of two truths is the reason for this. Reality is one and this reality is ever coming out of itself to reveal itself. It is this reality we see and come to know partially and ever more comprehensively, but there is no merely false knowing of this reality.

Summary

The Problem

In thinking about the conceptualization of the Pure Land in the context of our critical, modern mind-set, the initial and obvious problem is the lingering premodern mode of thinking of the Pure Land in the rather graphic and concrete terms of a realm to which one hopes to be reborn upon one's death. To think of the Pure Land literally as a land of blissful splendor, undefiled by our everyday world of pain and turmoil, is nothing but fanciful and supernatural wishful thinking. It is a sentiment that simply cannot and should not be believed by people in our modern age. Nevertheless, this does not mean that we must succumb completely to the contemporary bias against nonempirical or metaphysical reality. On the one hand, we cannot think of the Pure Land in the crude manner of an idealized realm physically existing somewhere. On the other hand, we cannot just deny the reality of the Pure Land as merely fanciful, wishful thinking. The problem, then, is to steer a course between the premodern literal sense of an other-worldly realm and the nearly all-pervasive denial of metaphysical reality of our contemporary way of thinking. How, then, can we conceptualize the Pure Land as an actual yet not literally existing realm?

A word should be made concerning two possible interpretations that consider these modern concerns but in my opinion do not fully avoid the two extremes of the premodern or the contemporary; one is relatively recent and the other presently in vogue. Both stem from an essentially subjectivistic orientation. The former can be seen as interpreting the Pure Land or birth in this land as a spiritual transformation marking one's full realization of Amida's compassionate reality. It is becoming one with the reality of Amida Buddha. The emphasis on spiritual transformation while answering many of the objections of our modern viewpoint, nevertheless blurs the issue. By emphasizing the subjective aspect of spiritual transformation, the transsubjective reality of the Pure Land is not addressed. The proponents of this and similarly existentialist positions seem, however, to presume the actuality of the Pure Land beyond their subjective state. This presumption or premise of the interpretation is not confronted and so the issue of the independent reality of the Pure Land is clouded.

The second, presently in vogue, trend is what is usually designated as a postmodern reinterpretation. While its many telling criticisms of modernity's worldview cannot be ignored—the general problem of dualism, the mind-body bifurcation and an almost religious faith in so-called scientific objectivity (scientism)—its radically relativistic, nihilistic outlook finally does not take the reality of the world seriously. I simply see it as affirming a quasi-premodern worldview simply because there is no longer a standard by which to dismiss it vis-à-vis others. It seems to be an abandonment of trying honestly to come to terms with reality by saying that any belief in reality is as valid as any other. Again, the problems with the modern worldview are real and should be constructively confronted. This does not mean, however, that all standards of judgment be abandoned and a position accepted—at least if it is not a modern one simply because it is possible and someone believes it.

This questioning of the postmodern enterprise asserts that one needs to go beyond modernity but not back to a premodern mind-set. The task is indeed to go beyond the literalness of the premodern and the confining restrictiveness of the modern. It is hopefully a constructive postmodern exercise. The process-thought-oriented premise I bring to this task has this critical yet constructive quality. Griffin in his series on "constructive postmodern thought" has attempted to do this in the Christian context. In a volume explicitly dealing with postmodern theology, he reviews the issues and clarifies the process stance.[4]

This postmodern position characterized above is no parody. In some recent Western sources, attitudes that mirror the above are evident. In the introductory comments to his English translation of the two Pure Land sutras from the original Sanskrit and their Chinese translations, Luis Gomez introduces notions of the Pure Land and birth in the Pure Land in a straightforward manner merely indicating that the faithful believe that they will be born into the Pure Land, leaving the impression that the existence of the Pure Land and rebirth is to be literally understood. There was no attempt to consider the meaning and implication of the conceptualizations.[5] While this may be an unfair criticism, since the task at hand is a general introduction to the ideas in the translated text, this all too oft-occurring attitude of many Western-trained Buddhologists to relate objectively the facts of the tradition without critically looking at them, while in many ways admirable, leaves the impression that anything can be accepted. Gomez is a well-studied, intelligent thinker and scholar and has, on occasion, voiced concern about taking the innertraditional beliefs just as is without critically taking them to task. My disappointment in his discussion for not trying to answer my concerns may be unfair, but I was hoping for a Western-educated outsider to at least make a point about this obviously problematic matter. Christians have been taken to task for their literal belief in a heaven; Buddhists should also be.

The above reference to Gomez may not fully illustrate my point about the postmodern trend. The following two references are a bit more to the point. Carl Becker in a discussion of the notions of afterlife in Buddhism, takes the general position of giving credence to paranormal phenomena and thereby takes the meaning of the Pure Land and birth in the Pure Land in a premodern sense as literal.[6] Becker is also a keen thinker with a wide range of knowledge and a subtlety of thought, but I simply cannot accept these, to me at least, fanciful notions of an afterlife. While this is clearly my prejudice, I do not know what can be gained by this premodern/postmodern indulgence. It does not seem to deal with the Pure Land in an earnest and creative manner. To just say that one will be reborn into a paranormal realm explains nothing.

The last reference is to some research/thought by Ian Reader and George Tanabe. While not directly concerned with the notion of Pure Land, it considers how Japanese scholars shy away from confronting certain embarrassing issues in their religious traditions through something like double-think or an explicitly postmodern attitude. The issue dealt with by these two scholars is *genze riyaku* ('concrete benefits now'), its central place in the everyday religious life of people in Japan, and its function as the moral glue that holds society together. Referring to survey work indicating the prevalence of belief in genze riyaku by Shin Buddhists whose official teaching condemns it, they note that "this has led to the movement to develop a 'post-modern Shin theology' that would be more sympathetic to genze riyaku, not because it is justifiable according to sectarian teachings but because the wide spread desire for benefits is too salient a fact to ignore."[7] This interesting observation reflects the tendency in Japanese sectarian circles to avoid thinking about embarrassing issues by seemingly confronting a situation but in reality slipping away in the murkiness of unclear, double-think agility. The thrust of some recent socio-historically oriented studies by a group of Western-trained specialists as reflected by the Reader/Tanabe work may be attempting to break out of this sectarian double-think. While quite in sympathy with this effort to force sectarian scholars to face certain problematic aspects of our doctrine and faith, to be content with recognizing the actuality of practice without looking at the norm of doctrine more fully also refuses to consider the full implications of the problem.

The task, again, is to see, as people engaged in the modern world, the problems in the literal understanding of the Pure Land as a concrete, real realm to which one is reborn upon one's death. It is also, however, to see the need for a viable and acceptable notion of the Pure Land, for to articulate the reality of the Pure Land convincingly in the midst of modernity's objections is finally the ultimate task.

A Proposal: The Pure Land as the Mind of Amida Buddha

The starting point for this conceptualization of the Pure Land is the spiritual transformation that is birth in the Pure Land brought about when one has come to realize the compassionate reality of Amida Buddha—that is, has become one with the reality of Amida Buddha. The point that is pertinent here is that this oneness with the reality of Amida is the basic description of the reality of the Pure Land. Whether in the preliminary engagement with this reality that is the awakening of the mind of entrusting oneself to Amida Buddha or the ultimate union in the reality of Amida in the full birth into the Pure Land upon one's death, the reality of the Pure Land is its basic synonymity with the reality of Amida Buddha. This reality is nothing but enlightenment itself, it is Amida's mind of enlightenment, the mind of Amida itself. It is from this basic definition or idea that a fuller and more meaningful and acceptable conceptualization of the Pure Land can be developed from the inner resources of the tradition itself with the catalyst of the process notion of objective immortality or the retentive nature of God/Amida.

The primordially compassionate Amida Buddha must be open to that which is around it. If compassion is the primordial characteristic of Amida Buddha, then Amida must be receptive to what is happening around it. It would be a strange kind of compassion if stoic apathy and unrelatedness characterized Amida Buddha. There must be a receptive quality in Amida, a feeling for the feelings of all existence. Moreover, if this receptivity is true, then this taking in of that which is around it would necessarily mean that Amida grows in experience as each new event is incorporated within it. It is therefore not an unresponsive receptivity but one in which Amida is affected by what happens. Amida reacts, as it were, to and receives into itself all events about it.

To put it in language more familiar to Buddhists, this openness and feeling the feelings of others can be explained in terms of the conceptuality of karma. All moments of existence affect later moments of existence and are thus felt by them. Amida Buddha as the storehouse of all karma naturally takes this activity in. Amida feels the existence of all moments of existence. Thinking of Amida Buddha as the ultimate storehouse of all karma is a fruitful beginning to think of what the Pure Land is. If the Pure Land is the land of Amida's enlightenment, the mind of Amida, we can say that the receiving and eternal recollection of our karma into the mind of Amida is birth in the Pure Land of Amida. Birth in Amida's Pure Land, then, is the gathering in, never-to-be-abandoned retention of our karma in the mind of Amida Buddha. In one sense, the notion of karma already provides for retention of the acts of the past in the accumulating passage of time. Yet this retention in the processes of karma is limited to the degree to which the vividness of the retention is maintained. Indeed all acts are forever, yet with the passage of time the influence of most acts fade, approaching insignificance. It is in the mind of Amida that timeless retention can occur, retaining the vividness of the act in all its fullness. This retention does not change that which we are, it only retains what we are, and it is this who we are at our deaths that is retained. For those who, through the call of Amida, have come to entrust themselves to Amida, this retention in the mind of Amida becomes an immersion into the enlightenment of Amida. For those who have not come to entrust themselves to Amida, this retention in the mind of Amida begins a process of enlightening through the power of Amida's vow by which this karma becomes the karma toward enlightenment.

Again, everything is posited on understanding Amida as having this receptive, retaining aspect. Moreover, we must understand that the enlightenment of Amida is not a mere static enlightenment unto itself but an enlightening power that through long processes eventually enlightens all existence. Thus, all existence coming into the mind of Amida eventually becomes one in the enlightenment that is Amida Buddha. This is how birth in the Pure Land can be understood without resorting to a literal belief in rebirth upon our deaths into an otherworldly realm. The existence of the Pure Land and the compassionate reality that is Amida Buddha upon which the former rests cannot be proven. The faith in the existence of the Pure Land may be mere human hope for something better. It is a hope, nevertheless, that makes all the difference in the world. The Pure Land exists for no other reason than that it must.

Notes

1. John S. Yokota, "A Call to Compassion: Process Thought and the Conceptualization of Amida Buddha," *Process Studies* 23, 2 (Summer 1994): 87–97.

2. John S. Ishihara, "Rethinking the Doctrine of Satya-dvaya," *Journal of Chikushi Jogakuen College* 1 (January 1989): 63–86.

3. John S. Ishihara, "A Shin Buddhist Social Ethics," *The Pure Land: Journal of Pure Land Buddhism* new series 4 (December 1987): 14–33; "Shin Buddhist Realism: An Essay on Shin Buddhist Social Ethics," *Journal of Chikushi Jogakuen College* 2 (January 1990): 63–89; John S. Yokota, "Compassion for the World: Buddhism and Ecological Concerns," *Journal of Chikushi Jogakuen College* 5 (January 1993): 53–69.

4. David Ray Griffin, *God and Religion in the Postmodern World: Essays in Postmodern Theology* (Albany: State University of New York Press, 1989). See especially the introduction and the chapter on God; I must admit some reservations with his giving credence to paranormal or parapsychological phenomena. I am very much a modern, Enlightenment-bound thinker in this regard.

5. Luis O. Gomez, *The Land of Bliss* (Honolulu: University of Hawaii Press, 1996), pp. 8–9, 13, 57–59, 306.

6. Carl B. Becker, *Breaking the Circle: Death and Afterlife in Buddhism* (Southern Illinois University Press, 1993), pp. 46–83.

7. Ian Reader and George Tanabe ("Genze Riyaku: The Common Religion of Benefits in Japan," Supplement to the February Issue of *The Japanese Religions Bulletin*, 1997), p. 6.

8.   The World and Amida Buddha

Musashi Tachikawa

Buddhist Theology and Provisional Exposition

In the world of Christianity, theology is an independent field among such other fields as Biblical studies, Biblical archeology, and church history. While founded upon the Bible, it has taken a path distinct from philological study, for it involves reflection on the particular problems of the times. In Buddhism, it is now necessary for a field corresponding to Christian theology to be established. It is not that such a field has been entirely lacking up to now. In some respects, the entire history of Buddhism may be viewed as a history of "Buddhist theology,"[1] and it might be said that Nagarjuna, Vasubandhu, and Tsong-kha-pa all established Buddhist theologies. In the modern period, however, self-conscious effort toward this kind of study has been inadequate.

This does not mean that Buddhists must attempt the same kind of work as figures like Nagarjuna and Tsong-kha pa. The problem lies in attitude and method. While it is unclear what kind of thought system built upon Buddhist tradition can be constructed at present, it is important for Buddhists to develop the methods to engage the problems of the period in which we are living. In Buddhist studies today, philological and textual research has established its own attitude and methods. Sectarian study has also, based on philological methods, functioned as a distinct field. It is time that, in addition to these established fields, a

Translated by Dennis Hirota

scholarly perspective that might be described as Buddhist theology be created. It should not be simply the interpretation of particular scriptures and should not belong to the traditional sectarian study of any school. While standing upon the results of textual research, it should attempt the theoretical formulation of personal Buddhist practice.

Buddhist theology will be extremely close to religious philosophy. These two differ, however, just as philosophy of religion and theology differ. In religious philosophy, the existence of the sacred is not necessarily recognized from the outset; its foundations must be investigated by the discipline itself. In a Buddhist theology, the existence of Buddha or the wisdom of enlightenment as the sacred is assumed. In the case of religious philosophy, whether the practitioner is Buddhist or not is not an issue, but in the case of a Buddhist theology, self-awareness as a Buddhist is necessary. While related to religious practice, however, Buddhist theology must possess a method communicable to others; in this sense, it differs from purely personal, unsystematic confession of faith.

In the Judeo-Christian tradition, language is regarded as trustworthy, while in Buddhism, this is not so. A theology constructed upon the reliability of language has not been nurtured in Buddhism, particularly Japanese Buddhism. The existence of God is known in the Judeo-Christian tradition through revelation, and that revelation is by language. In the New Testament, it is stated: "In the beginning was the word. The word was with God. The word was God." Thus, there is trust in words (logos), and this trust continued to be an important intellectual support in modern European philosophy as well. In the Old Testament, God created the world through language (dābār), and through language formed a covenant with human beings. Thus, in the Judeo-Christian tradition, trust in language has been a keynote down through history, even though it may be said to have been shaken in modern times.

In Buddhist traditions, however, language has been grasped as the "profane" that must be negated at least once. As I have noted in chapter 3, after negation there is rebirth, but fundamentally language is delusional and cannot transmit truth. As Hirota's chapters in this volume make clear, in Shinran, language is not merely negated. Reality becomes language, as the teaching or the Name, and transmits truth; at the same time, even such true language harbors negation within.

For Buddhists, enlightenment or nondichotomous wisdom transcends language. Amida Buddha and Vairochana (Vairocana, Dainichi Nyorai) are none other than personifications of such wisdom, which is also termed "emptiness." As Nagarjuna states, "In emptiness, all linguistic plurality ceases." From this stance, which takes that which brings all words to cessation to be ultimate existence, theological discourse is obviously extremely problematical. There is, however, a concept of provisional exposition (rebirth in language) as the working of emptiness. We find in this one point a basis upon which a Buddhist theology can stand. In chapter 3, I sought to lay the groundwork for Buddhist theological reflection by taking a largely historical perspective. Here, I will first outline an approach to various general problems in developing a Buddhist theology, then take up several issues raised by Kaufman and Cobb in their comments in chapters 4 and 5. I will conclude with a brief consideration of the stances of Hirota and Yokota.

The Worldview of a Buddhist Theology

In order for Buddhism to function now as a living religion, it must cast off its shell of ancient perspectives and be reborn as modern thought. In addition, it must further transcend the mind-set of modernity and learn to treat contemporary issues. In other words, Buddhism must quickly pass through two revolutions. In the process, it may be necessary to abandon what we have considered the core of Buddhist thought, and to adopt perspectives not present in the preceding tradition.

It is now nearly two thousand years since Nagarjuna wrote the *Middle Stanzas (Madhyamuka-kārikā)*. Even though the problems he took up remain meaningful in themselves, his discussion includes points that we find impossible to accept from our own perspective today. In studying Nagarjuna's thought, we must distinguish between what we can learn from and what must be discarded. To accomplish this, it is necessary for Buddhists not merely to consider contemporary problems from within the framework of Buddhist tradition, but to consider Buddhist tradition from the perspective of contemporary issues. We cannot expect that all the various social problems facing us today have been taken up in Buddhist texts. Such fields as nuclear arms and biological engineering were unknown to the ancients.

There are many who believe that neither the fundamental stance of Buddhism nor the nature of human existence has changed fundamentally, and that therefore ancient Buddhist thought remains effective with regard to today's problems. In part, this is true. If it were not so, seeking to learn from Buddhism today would be meaningless. Buddhists, however, have in their own periods always confronted the problems of their period. For Vasubandhu, who developed the Yogachara (*Yogācāra*) school in India, unifying the established worldview of his day with the traditional practice of yoga was at issue. For Chandrakirti (Candrakīrti) of the Madhyamika (*Mādhyamika*) school in the seventh century, unifying the worldview of his day with the conception of emptiness was at issue. Tantric Buddhists of the later period were deeply concerned about the opposition between sexual acts, which occupy a distinctive place in human activity, and the traditional attitude that such acts are impure. Examples of such reconsiderations of Shakyamuni's teachings by Buddhist masters within the contexts of their own periods may be found in China and Japan also.

Thus, Buddhism has freely engaged the various problems of different historical contexts. It may be said that precisely because of such engagement, the history of Buddhism appears as diverse and complex as it does. It is not easy, for example, to see why the teachings of Shakyamuni and those of the Tantric tradition focusing on the deity Heruka, depicted holding a blood-filled skull as chalice and embracing his consort, are both Buddhism. It is difficult to explain why the southern tradition practiced in Thailand and the Amidist tradition of Japan are both to be called Buddhism. Herein lies Buddhism's strength. In various locales, through interaction with diverse conditions, disparate forms of Buddhism have been born. This is how it has been in the past, and how it must be in the future.

The Buddhist masters who emerged in Japan nearly a thousand years ago, including Honen, Shinran, and many others, were eminent. So great were they, it is probably useless to hope that persons of comparable stature will appear. The age and the society in which they lived, however, differs from our own. The conditions of today were unknown to them. That human beings, as biological life systems, are born, grow, and die, remains unchanged. Buddhism, however, and all religious traditions, do not involve human beings as biological life systems, but rather as existences within social conditions. As long as this is true, we ourselves must consider our own conditions while learning from the paths taken by our forebears.

Four central topics may be enumerated as issues to be treated in a Buddhist theology: (1) the world; (2) human life; (3) Buddha; and (4) action. Through these topics, our present historical and social situation may be considered. I will discuss how these concepts have been treated in Buddhist history and the attitude we should take toward them now.

1. The World

The concept of "world" does not exist in early Buddhism. To such metaphysical questions as whether or not the world is finite, Shakyamuni did not answer. His attitude and methods were not founded on the acquisition of a metaphysical awareness of the world.

The "five aggregates" (skandha), frequently understood as the component elements of the world, are strictly speaking the component elements of the body and mind of an individual. The first aggregate is matter, and the remaining four (sensation, thought, feeling, consciousness) may be understood to indicate the mind and its functions. This method of analysis is not, however, a division of the world into matter and mind. Rather, the concept of the five aggregates indicates the totality of that which appears, through the sense organs, as the object of an individual's cognitive activity, together with the mental functions responding to that object. The world is not thought of as the environment in which many individuals coexist; rather, it is the assemblage surrounding a single individual that emerges through the functioning of that person's consciousness.

In this way of thought, nature is not viewed as alive, but instead is analyzed in terms of the various inanimate categories of form, sound, smell, taste, and touch—the objects of the sense organs of eye, ear, nose, tongue, and body. This apprehension of the world as the sense object of a single individual is not limited to early Buddhism, but may be seen as common to the Mahayana that emerged later, and to Indian philosophy in general. It is not, of course, that "nature" is unknown in India. Indian court poetry speaks of nature as a living, unified, dynamic body. In Buddhism and mainstream Indian philosophy, however, the world has been grasped by a different method.

As long as the world is conceived in terms of an individual human being, it is grasped as the locus of the individual's experience. Even if the world is perceived through our sense organs, however, it is necessary for us today to recognize that the various objects are a unified totality that transcends the cognition of the individual, for even if the individual perishes, the world continues to exist. This is not to debate such questions as whether or not the world is eternal or exists objectively. I am simply pointing out that Buddhist tradition has not sought to establish the theoretical foundation for adopting into its own system, or to problematize, the "laws of nature." It is neither possible nor necessary for Buddhism to include the systems of all natural sciences. With the conception of the five aggregates alone, however, we cannot understand the dynamic configuration of nature illuminated by the natural sciences. It may be said that what the natural sciences seek to illuminate and what Buddhism is concerned with are of different dimensions. But by allowing consideration to end there, Buddhism has increasingly been seen as outdated.

The world where we live and of which we are parts clearly moves according to laws that transcend the activity of individuals. Let us consider, as an example, the world as earth, which as a dynamic body should not be analyzed merely as the object of the senses. No one knows toward what the earth is moving, but we know that it is alive, as though the entire universe were a single biologically living body. Previously, it was believed that the earth was an inexhaustible store of nurture for living things. Now, however, it is clear that it is not inexhaustible. We know that nature on earth may die. In such conditions, we must consider anew how Buddhism is to grasp the world.

Early Buddhist tradition teaches that the five aggregates are empty. How are we to understand today the meaning of the assertion that the world is empty? The esoteric tradition has taught that the world is the manifestation of the Buddha Vairochana. Here, the problem is the same. We must reconsider all the various conceptions relating to the world. We now hesitate to grasp the universe or the world in personal terms. Modern scientific culture resists envisioning the universe in the form of a giant human figure, as occurs in ancient myths. We cannot today impart human personality to the world or the universe as was done in ancient India. This does not necessarily mean, however, that the universe cannot emerge for us as a living, sacred totality. To grasp the world as a dynamic totality is not to see it as eternal and substantial. It is not fully consummated and unchanging, but constantly undergoes a process of formation and disintegration. Or rather, it is itself this process. This is the meaning of the assertion that all things are empty.

2. Human Life

In Hinduism, three aims of human life were identified: social rectitude and duties *(dharma)*, acquisition of wealth, and fulfillment of desires. Later a fourth—emancipation from the world of transmigration—was added. The first concerned social norms to be observed in obtaining possessions and pursuing desires. The Hindu tradition thus comprises a rule for living, and there are scriptures for pursuing each of the four ends of human existence. Of course, those pursuing the first three and those pursuing the last had different attitudes toward life. The former followed the path of prosperity, the path of affirmation of human life, while the latter followed the path of extinction, the path of the negation of human life. The fourth end is not realized in the midst of society, but is pursued by individuals who have separated themselves from society to face the universe or the sacred. Regarding this goal, Hindu religious tradition focuses on the relationship between the individual and the universe, and little attention has been paid to the nature of the community in which practicers seeking to experience the oneness of the universe and the self may live.

Buddhism existed in a world surrounded by Brahmanism and Hinduism and adopted much from these traditions, even though it arose in opposition to Brahmanism and, after a history of incessant conflict with Hinduism, was finally driven from the Indian subcontinent. The Buddhist community was supported by people who pursued the goals of social rectitude, wealth, and fulfillment of desires. In the lives of people involved in Hindu society, the Buddhist community was recognized as a group devoted solely to the fourth goal. Originally, Buddhism asserted the necessity of leaving household life. Until the time of the esoteric tradition, the Buddhist teaching was chiefly formulated in monasteries. Even in the period of esoteric teachings, the active lay practicers were people who had separated themselves from the secular world, and monks also studied esoteric teachings and engaged in their systematization. This monastically centered Buddhism vanished from the Indian subcontinent early in the thirteenth century.

While contributing greatly to the achievements of Indian culture in the course of its development, particularly in such areas as systematization of knowledge and rituals, Buddhism functioned within the Hindu world as a focal point of opposition and was never in a position to offer a model for the three goals of social norms and the pursuit of wealth and desires—that is, for human society apart from the monastery. This situation has been the same with the Buddhism transmitted outside of India. In China and Korea, Buddhism found itself in opposition to the Confucian society. In Japan, Buddhism divided the religious sphere with native religious practices, later formulated as Shinto, and with Confucianism, and was also in conflict with these two. Tibetan Buddhism, based on late Indian Mahayana, affords an unusual example of Buddhism possessing within itself two ideological levels, holding together in itself both world affirmation and world negation. At the same time, however, it also found itself in opposition to the native culture and religion. Thus, throughout its history Buddhism has always been an opponent. Those who sought the fourth of the aims of Hindu life, emancipation, stood in opposition to the secular world that pursued the other goals of wealth and fulfillment of desires.

Buddhists have been concerned chiefly with the problem of how an individual can attain emancipation or awakening, and the strategy is roughly the same as with the fourth aim of Hinduism. The relations among practicers or between the individual and the group were not considered important. Even precepts were restricted to the special group. Within the Indian religious vision of the individual practicer and the universal Self (or awakening), the concept of the bodhisattva is unique. The thinking expressed in the bodhisattva's vow, "Until all people attain awakening or salvation, I will not attain awakening," clearly indicates an involvement with others and is one reason for Buddhism's widespread transmission. But for us today, the ancient conception of the bodhisattva alone is inadequate.

The basic schema of the bodhisattva ideal involves a single, elite religious practicer who attains enlightenment and saves others. Others are seen as beings to be saved. When a religious genius emerges historically to lead people to salvation, perhaps such a vision is valid. At present, however, we view an individual as a person. Each is grasped not as an indistinguishable collection of the five aggregates, but as a unified, irreplaceable individual possessing his or her own history. This conception of a person is not very old in the West either. That each human being must be treated as a single totality has been clarified by Freud, and today, it is impossible for us, in our understanding of the person, to ignore the methods that he, Jung, and others have developed.

Buddhism is correctly understood as that which breaks through personhood or self. The problem, however, is the nature of the person or self. It is not formed from within itself, but through a variety of causes and conditions, just as taught in the principle of dependent origination. A single person is formed within history and society by numerous persons. This was not made clear in ancient Buddhist thought. Vasubandhu's *Thirty Verses (Triṃśikā)*, a basic text of the Yogachara school, treats the question of the structure of a single individual (though awareness as an individual is absent), but the interaction of an individual possessing the eight modes of consciousness with other such individuals is not taken up. This is perhaps not surprising, but precisely here lies the problem. The question is whether Buddhism has been able to undergo philosophical self-reformation in its various periods.

At present, a human being is grasped as an irreplaceable individual, and it is only through relations among individuals that the formation of the individual can be understood. Buddhism, standing in opposition to such a conception of the individual, leads the individual to extinction and to authentic rebirth. It is when a relevant understanding of the person has been achieved that the concept of the bodhisattva will take on meaning for our own age.

3. Buddha

Buddhist theology begins where individuals in their own circumstances come to apprehend the working of Buddha. Buddha is not understood through logical reflection on the world or human existence. Even when apprehension results from long practice or meditation, Buddhist theology begins with this result.

Buddhism has its origins in the enlightenment of Shakyamuni. This is commonly accepted as a historical event, but its religious significance tends to be forgotten. The fact that Buddha emerged in history is not a start, but a closing or completion, for the difficult journey from the world of delusion to arrival at enlightenment has already been accomplished by Shakyamuni. As long as we are followers of Shakyamuni, we take our beginning from this end. It is the same with Amidist faith. That Amida's working can be apprehended means that Dharmakara Bodhisattva's Vow has been fulfilled. It also means that we are already saved. In other words, we begin from having already reached the end.

This idea of beginning at the end is clear in the esoteric tradition, in which this phenomenal world is none other than the form of Buddha. The world unfolding before our eyes is itself the sacred. The issue of the world, which was on the whole disregarded as a problem in Amidist faith, received direct consideration in the esoteric tradition, in which the mandala depicts the sacralized world. To practicers sitting before the mandala, the world emerges as that which has already been sacralized. Seeing before them the sacred world—or the form of Vairochana Buddha—they enter that sacred world.

A personal relationship exists between Buddha and ourselves. At times Buddha stands before one, at times behind, and at times completely fills one. Recording the dynamics of this relationship with Buddha is one of the central roles of Buddhist theology. Whether we call the Buddha Amida or Vairochana or some other name is not the issue here. We probably must learn of the personal relationship with Buddha from Amidist faith, and of the sacralization of the world, or the Buddha as the foundation of that sacralization, from the esoteric tradition. Thus, the most important theological problem facing us today is the demonstration of the "fulfilled body" Buddha (Buddha who possesses a body as the result of fulfilling practices in the past, such as Amida) not as merely a mythical sublimation of Shakyamuni but as a living, active Buddha. The mandala must not be simply a symbolic depiction; rather, the present, actual world must become the sacred mandala, and we must confront the issue of how this world of ignorance can be the sacralized world. This is to face the problem of history and time. The question of how Amida Buddha or Vairochana act is the question of how Dharma manifests itself in time and how, in the history of Dharma, Buddha has functioned.

Fulfilled-body Buddha is the form with which that transcending time emerges in time. To transcend time is to arrive at the end. We must manifest in ourselves the condition of starting from this end, and as beings in the world, we must continue to inquire into the meaning of this condition.

4. Action

In Buddhist history, there have been two attitudes taken toward action. First, human action has been considered an obstruction to attainment of enlightenment; hence, the cessation of action has been sought. Second, action has been considered originally sacred; hence, purification or sacralization has been sought. These two attitudes are not unrelated. Since action is always a function of time, cessation holds the significance of transcendence of time. Through the cessation of action, action is sacralized.

For us today, action means work. As with the conception of the world, we must take a broad view of action in contemporary society. Fundamentally, however, the traditional Buddhist method of the sacralization of action through cessation remains valid. Although we seek to realize our desires to the widest possible extent and ignore the effects of our actions on later generations, Buddhism offers a critical stance. It must, however, be reborn in the present to be effective.

Theological Issues in Pure Land Buddhism

Below, I will consider several questions that arise in theological reflection on Pure Land Buddhism. Although, as an individual, I have deep interest in Amidist faith, I am not a Buddhist of the Pure Land (*Jōdoshū*) or Shin (*Jōdo Shinshū*) traditions. Neither am I a member of any other Buddhist institution. It might be asked how one who is not a member of the Pure Land communities can discuss Amidist faith.

I respond to this question in two ways. First, I wish to consider the history of Amidist faith, or the nembutsu, from a stance separate from the founders Honen and Shinran. We have now reached a point at which we must reconsider Shinran's position in the entire history of Buddhism beginning in India. Japanese Buddhism occupies a peripheral position within the history of Buddhism as a whole, and within the history of Japanese Buddhism, the Pure Land schools are no more than one important pillar. Moreover, in recent years the understanding of the position of Pure Land Buddhism in the history of Japanese Buddhism has been undergoing revision in relation to Nara Buddhism, which was more deeply influenced by Indian Buddhist traditions, and also in relation to Heian Buddhism, in which the theory and practice of esoteric Buddhism and Tendai teachings were significant elements. This does not mean that the status of Pure Land Buddhism is being questioned. It does mean, however, that the historical significance of the teachings of Honen and Shinran is being reduced. To view Japanese Amidist faith or the nembutsu against this background, we must ask where in the history of Buddhism Shinran and Honen should be placed, and not assume a stance within the thought of either.

Second, there is no necessity for us to follow what has historically been the orthodoxy. Of course, we should regard with great respect and care the results of philological research into what Honen or Shinran sought to transmit. Such questions, however, and how Amida or the nembutsu should be considered at the present point in history are different. This second point is of course connected with the first. It is precisely when the historical significance of Pure Land Buddhism is questioned anew that we are in position to consider its contemporary meaning.

Emptiness and Amida Buddha

The concept of emptiness set forth in chapter 3 may be viewed as possessing two, apparently contradictory, aspects. One is a self-negating aspect, which expresses the vector of religious practice by which a person seeks to attain the sacred (emptiness) that negates the profane (karma, blind passions). The second is an affirmative aspect. The vector of religious practice that has extinguished the profane and attained emptiness, in the next instant, allows for the establishment of karma or blind passions—the phenomenal world—as the profane.

Thus, the concept of emptiness includes three elements: the vector of seeking to attain emptiness as the negation of karma or blind passions; emptiness itself, which cannot be grasped objectively; and the vector of the sacralization of the world through the working of emptiness. These three elements may be depicted as in figure 8.1. In this illustration, the vector of self-negation is temporally continuous and directed upward from the profane to the sacred. By contrast, the vector representing the affirmative aspect drops perpendicularly from emptiness to the world, indicating that the rebirth of the world through the working of emptiness comes about instantaneously. Amida Buddha's Primal Vow possesses the same structure as these three elements of emptiness.

The structure of the vector of practice seen in this illustration is the same as that of dependent origination indicated in chapter 3 (p. 108). There, dependent origination in Nagarjuna's *Middle Stanzas* is used with three meanings: (1) the phenomenal world expressed by words and language; (2) emptiness as true reality that transcends language; and (3) language reborn after being negated and the world referred to by it. Thus, emptiness and dependent origination possess

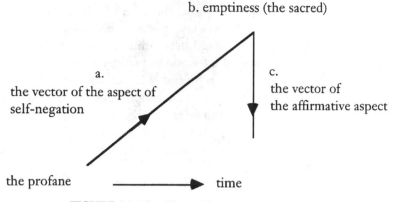

FIGURE 8.1 The Three Elements of Emptiness

the same structure. In its narrow sense, however, emptiness corresponds to the second meaning of dependent origination. The third meaning of dependent origination refers to the aspect of the working of emptiness upon others, and this working may be understood as the fulfilled or recompense Buddha-body (*hōjin butsu*). In general, Amida Buddha is understood to be a fulfilled Buddha-body and a personification of the working of emptiness.

Dependent origination fundamentally means that "through something (x), something else (y) comes into existence." It relates to the structure of the world and asserts that this world has not arisen from a permanent fundamental reality (cosmic truth) such as Brahman, but rather from various causal relationships. The world of "dependently originated things" that entered the field of vision of early Buddhism differs from what we now understand as the "world." For the early Buddhists, the human environment experienced by an individual person (the world as mind and body) was taken to issue, not the entire cosmos that encompassed all humankind. Thus, the world was not at all the universe as a single great system that included rivers, the earth, the sun, and so on. This is true not only of early Buddhism, but throughout the later history of Buddhism.

In the time of Tantrism in its latest developments, a concept of the world in a sense broader than that which existed in the preceding Buddhism emerged, and the cosmos as a whole came to be conceived in relation to religious practice. In Buddhist Tantrism, which inherited the spiritual tradition of ancient India, the aspect of the self in mutual identity with the cosmos (homology) came to be emphasized. The Tantric Buddhists, following Buddhist tradition, did not forget that self and universe arise dependently and are empty, but they believed that the universe, while empty, manifested its form to human beings.

What is important for our considerations here is that in later Buddhism, Tantric as well as non-Tantric, the world that manifests itself is that which is sacralized through emptiness or dependent origination. That is to say, the world is sacralized ultimately because Amida Buddha's Vow has been fulfilled.

Amida Buddha and the World

Not only the path of nembutsu, but almost all traditional schools of Japanese Buddhism have been aloof from social problems. The history of Buddhist engagement with global issues has been extremely brief. Today, when all human beings and even the earth on a global scale is facing profound crisis, we must consider how Buddhist faith can deal with such issues. If Amidism is to remain a viable possibility, it must indicate concretely what powers it possesses to treat such problems.

Let us consider briefly the world as conceived in Japanese Pure Land Buddhism. In the traditions established by Honen and Shinran in the Kamakura period, the effort to attain systematic knowledge regarding the structure of the world was completely abandoned. In the schools of Indian Buddhism, great importance had been given to systematic knowledge about the structure of the world, and even in the Nara and Heian period Buddhism that emphasized Indian tradition, this issue remained important. In Kamakura period Pure Land Buddhism, however, the structure of the world was not a matter of concern. What was of concern was each person's karmic hindrances and attainment of birth. These questions, however, were not developed into issues of how "karmic hindrance" was created within the world or society, or how people living in the world—in involvement with others—should seek birth in the Pure Land.

Today, consideration must be given within the Pure Land tradition also to the structure of the world. The relationship between Amida Buddha and the world (universe) appears to have been almost completely neglected in Pure Land school and Shin thought. It is no longer possible to regard the world or the universe merely as a collection of objects grasped through the various senses. It is clear, for example, that the earth is an autonomous, active system apart from the sense perceptions of a single human being. This perspective arose in modern times, and was of course unknown to traditional Pure Land thought and Amidist faith. Today, however, we must recognize that we live in conditions that differ from the environment of traditional Pure Land thinking.

Teleological and Interpersonal Aspects

In this section, I will touch on the articles of Hirota and Yokota. In chapter 1, Hirota takes the teleological and the interpersonal as central concepts, adopting them from Kaufman but differing somewhat in his usage. These two aspects may be seen as in a parallel relationship with concepts that I have discussed: (1) the polar relationship of the sacred and the profane, and (2) the paradigm regarding emptiness or dependent origination. By considering the teleological and interpersonal aspects within the paradigms of (1) and (2) above, the similarities and differences between the ways of thinking of Hirota and myself will be highlighted.

In chapter 2, Yokota asserts that Shakyamuni is "the concrete actualization of Amida's compassion" (p. 86). He adds that this may appear to contradict the historicity of our modern thinking, but in Shin Buddhist theology, how this historicity is to be incorporated is a pressing current issue. The relationship between Amida and Shakyamuni may be seen in fact as a crucial moment in the teleological aspect and the interpersonal aspect that cannot be overlooked. In this section, I will also discuss the problem of historicity that Yokota raises, viewing it in relation to the two aspects developed by Hirota. In addition, I will position the relationship between Amida and Shakyamuni within the conceptual frameworks of (1) and (2) above.

The structure of teleology follows that of an act. All acts possess the three moments of (a) recognition of present conditions, (b) aim or goal, and (c) means, and similarly, teleology also assumes the existence of acts in which one seeks to go from present conditions to an intended destination. For example, in the case of persons in the world of ignorance seeking to reach the realm of enlightenment, there is an assumption that one should perform acts in order to move from one place to another that is sought. In Buddhism, this has been called moving from "the condition of cause" (world of ignorance) to "realm of result" (enlightenment). In this way, teleology takes as its fundamental content acts to move from condition A to another, better realm (or existence) B, which is deemed worthy of being sought. Here, we can recognize three aspects: A, B, and the one moving between these two. Let us call these the three factors of teleology.

If it is asked, however, how it is possible for there to be a process of movement by which one seeks to go from A to B, then we must pursue a different way of thought. For here, we must take up the question of why a person seeks enlightenment. It is doubtful that it can be asserted today as a universal truth that one must go out from the world of ignorance and attain enlightenment. It is impossible to impose on all people the thinking that "one should seek enlightenment" or that "one should aspire to be in accord with the mind of God." This is not because the traditional truth of Buddhism or Christianity is losing its meaning, but rather because there is no clear answer to the fundamental question Why should we seek enlightenment? Why does one seek to hear the voice of Amida? Such questions threaten the very foundations of teleology. Teleology has the function, however, of thrusting that fundamental question before us. That is, teleology possesses a negative aspect of bringing into question the basis of religious action.

We should note the parallel relationship between the paradigm of the sacred and the profane that I proposed and Hirota's teleological aspect. The course from the profane to the sacred corresponds to Hirota's teleological aspect. In this case, two of the three factors of teleology, A and B, form a polarity, and whether the practicer is transformed into the same nature as the pole B that is sought or merely approaches it depends on the type of religious system to which the teleology belongs.

As Hirota emphasizes in his chapter, for Shinran, the practicer does not give rise to a transformation of self into the same nature as B. In Shinran's thought, the person of nembutsu does not become Amida. On the other hand, another person of nembutsu, Ippen, though he does not say that one becomes Amida, does state, "When one says the Name, there is neither person nor Buddha." Here, there is less distance between practicer and B than seen in Shinran. As stated in chapter 3, esoteric practicers, though they may be at a point in contemplative practice, believe that they have become Buddha.

Why does religion urge people to move from A to B? In other words, why does religion assert the attainment of or closeness to the sacred to be good? Is "the sacred" in actuality the good for human beings? Though it is good, in what sense is it good? Such questions lead to the issue of whether Amida is good, or whether Amida is necessary. These questions arise because factor B possesses some power with regard to factor A (or the practicer that takes factor A as his or her fundamental nature). The difference between factor A and factor B is expressed as the power of factor B with regard to factor A. Of course, this does not answer why the sacred is necessary. However, this power becomes an important clue in considering the second interpersonal aspect.

Whether or not a persona is recognized in factor B differs according to religious tradition and thought. When there is a persona, the interpersonal aspect becomes clearly apparent, and at the same time, the persona is used as the basis of the teleological process. For example, the shift or process from factor A to factor B may depend on the power of factor B as possessing a persona. In short, it is because of Amida's guidance that a person is able to seek salvation. This way of thinking is perhaps one explanation of the basis of teleology itself. It is no more than one possibility, however. This is because for those who do not demand an answer to the question of why Amida has that kind of power, the explanation may be a final answer, but for those who seek an answer to this question, it cannot be a final explanation.

The questions I posed earlier—Why should a person seek the sacred? How is it possible for Amida to have a persona?—are not clarified. Hirota states that "the realization of shinjin is the unfolding in one of Buddha-nature." I do not intend to take issue with this matter in itself. Why, however, is the realization of shinjin necessary? How is it possible for Buddha-nature to unfold? How can such questions be answered?

Does the historicity that Yokota speaks of offer an answer? Putting such historicity on firm footing, however, is extremely difficult from a stance of Buddhist theory. Suppose that Shinran asserted that in the depths—or as the basis—of Shakyamuni's historical existence (transformed body) there was Amida, in whom historicity is thinner, as that which possesses greater universality. Even so, it is extremely difficult as theology. As a Buddhist, I believe that rather than Amida as actual existence, it is Amida as emptiness that is more certain within the theological operation.

To repeat, it is necessary for Buddhism and Christianity today to answer such questions as Why seek the sacred? and Why is salvation necessary? To do this, we must have axes of thought greater than the frameworks of the teleological and interpersonal aspects and the sacred and the profane.

Note

1. In the original Japanese, Tachikawa has coined the term *butsugaku*, used to distinguish the approach from what is commonly termed "Buddhist Studies" or "Buddhology" (*bukkyōgaku*). [Translator's note.]

Afterword

Dennis Hirota

The three Buddhists presenting new interpretations of Pure Land Buddhism in this volume agree on the need to develop contemporary perspectives for the tradition, and in their attempts to do so, adopt methods and concepts from the broader Buddhist tradition and from Western religious study. They differ, however, in their understandings of the nature of Pure Land Buddhism and in their choices of the appropriate modern resources with which to interact. Clearly, no general synthesis or resolution of divergences has been reached in the process of this book, and no conclusion is possible in this sense. The clarification of general points of difference may, however, cast light on the general theological enterprise undertaken here and its possible course in the future.

   In their chapters both Kaufman and Cobb suggest that our three approaches might be grasped as distinct points on a continuum. Certainly we each assume distinct but related stances. Here, however, I will suggest a different triadic configuration of our approaches, formed of contrasting positions regarding three fundamental issues. This may illuminate the underlying differences in assumptions among us, and also our interrelationships. Concerning how our approaches develop from these assumptions, readers should return to the chapters themselves, but perhaps the delineation of groupings here will suggest directions for development, specific areas in need of further consideration from our various stances, and even the outlines of new approaches.

Instead of locating the three authors along linear continuums as suggested by Kaufman and Cobb, I propose a triangular relationship, formed of a triad of polarities. This may have the advantage of illuminating both the perspectives held in common with the others and those deemphasized by each of the authors. The three polarities are religious tradition, religious life, and religious worldview.

Religious Tradition: Stance Within versus View from Outside

Among our three approaches, there is a contrast between a tendency to view the Buddhist path through the conceptual structures of the Pure Land tradition and an effort to understand those structures in broader Buddhist terms. Here, Yokota and Hirota may be seen to stand together in opposition to Tachikawa.

This does not mean that Yokota and Hirota attempt to speak for or from within the developed Shin tradition as formulated historically in Japan, nor does it mean that Tachikawa's concern with Pure Land Buddhism has no roots at all in personal encounter with the living Japanese Pure Land tradition stemming from Honen and Shinran. There tends to be, however, a difference of emphasis in attitude toward the Pure Land teaching. Although Yokota and Hirota both seek to bring about new developments in the tradition, at a fundamental level they begin with an initial, if provisional, acceptance of the authority of the historical roots of the tradition. For Yokota, the figure of Shakyamuni and the biographical details of his life hold the power to validate the Pure Land teaching, and for Hirota, the religious awareness of Shinran as manifested in his writings is taken to inform what is crucial in the later tradition.

Tachikawa's approach differs in that the Pure Land tradition as a whole is validated from outside, because of its structural similarities with basic patterns of Buddhist practice and realization. It may be noted that something of Tachikawa's approach is seen concretely in propagation efforts by Shin temples in the United States, particularly in the eastern part of the country, that adopt pan-Buddhist elements such as forms of meditational practice, generalized worship rituals, and distinctive monk-like attire for ministers. Such efforts, however, have yet to develop understandings of doctrine and practice that integrate these elements with a fully formulated Pure Land stance. More broadly, it may be said that Tachikawa seeks to treat Buddhist tradition within a framework of human religious experience articulated in terms of the polarity of the sacred and the profane. For him, the final terms of explanation may lie, therefore, in a kind of religious anthropology.

Each of the three authors seeks to deal with the problem of the authority of the tradition, and all three recognize the need to ground acceptance of the tradition in terms broader than institutional authority. This issue leads to another, differently configured divergence among the three authors. While assuming a stance within the tradition and seeking to develop it from within, Yokota focuses on the teaching and on its possible evolution through confronting the intellectual challenges of the present, while Hirota seeks instead to articulate the religious transformation he sees at the heart of the tradition. Here, Hirota stands closer to Tachikawa, who would also affirm the dimension of religious awakening and transformed awareness as fundamental to Buddhist tradition. This divergence forms our second polarity.

Religious Life: Practice versus Faith

There appears to be a contrast of approaches between an emphasis on religious practice or awareness as primary, on the one hand, and emphasis on a persuasive picture of the world and conceptual consistency, on the other. In Pure Land Buddhist terms, and even more general religious terms, this may be a contrast between praxis and doctrine, or between action and faith. It may also hint at a contrast of general emphasis or fundamental categories between Buddhist and Christian traditions themselves.

It may be said that Tachikawa and Hirota base their articulations of the tradition in significant ways on a conception of a process of practice and a transformative attainment or realization, while Yokota is most concerned to find consistency in the statements about human existence, the world, and reality that he finds in the Pure Land teachings. From a broader perspective, on the one hand, Yokota is concerned to bring Pure Land teachings into the framework of contemporary intellectual life and to subject it to questions that face all thinking people educated in the assumptions of modern scientific and technological civilization. On the other hand, Tachikawa and Hirota seek to develop contemporary understandings of the practical dimension of the Buddhist teachings. Tachikawa and Hirota might question the character of Yokota's assertions *as Buddhist,* and argue that as long as he pursues only a system of coherent beliefs about the world, he is missing the point of the Buddhist path. Yokota might argue that Tachikawa and Hirota, with their emphasis on the aspect of religious realization, in essence take an elitist stance removed from the actual reality of the Pure Land tradition as it has been lived by ordinary practicers down through history, and as in fact it has portrayed itself, as "the easy path."

The question raised here is the very nature of religious life. As Hirota has pointed out in the introduction, the polarization of faith and practice appeared as a concrete issue early in the Japanese Pure Land tradition flowing from Honen and gave rise to social conflict caused by antinomian tendencies among some nembutsu practicers. The underlying distinction between a fundamental conversion and deepening conviction is, of course, familiar from the work of William James on religious experience. Here again, however, the three authors tend to form a new grouping. Though sharing a view of transformative awakening as primary, Tachikawa is concerned to develop a comprehensive system of Buddhist thought, while Hirota is cautious about taking any formulation as more than provisional. Here, Tachikawa stands close to Yokota, who, as we have seen, values the coherence of a systematic view of the cosmos. This leads to the third polarity.

Religious Worldview: Metaphysical Concerns versus Awareness of Historical, Cultural, and Human Contextualizations

All three authors recognize that the Pure Land teachings as seen in the basic sutras are couched in terms of broader Indian secular and religious worldviews of the period, and that the narratives and descriptions of the cosmos, including Amida Buddha and sentient beings, the Pure Land and this world, have been discussed and passed down in the commentarial tradition in China, Korea, and Japan continuously to the modern period. Tachikawa and Yokota point out that the picture of the universe presented in the Indian sutras and transmitted in the tradition is no longer intelligible either in Japan or the contemporary West. Yokota is therefore concerned to conduct, with regard to the Pure Land teaching, the project that has been termed "demythologization" in Christian theology, while Tachikawa suggests that the contemplative experience and cosmological vision of Tantric traditions may indicate possibilities for a Buddhist worldview. Their aim is to construct, using broad frameworks intelligible to contemporary people, coherent and systematic understandings of the universe that perhaps may, in providing intellectually or experientially persuasive pictures of human life and the world, fulfill the function of earlier mythic worldviews. It should be noted, however, that the structure of Tachikawa's sacralized world may, in the end, hold more in common with the seeing of the practicer of fulfilled engagement that Hirota emphasizes than with Yokota's process-oriented construction.

Hirota also accepts that the worldview of the Pure Land sutras was formed in a cultural and historical context far removed from contemporary life, and that it is difficult for Pure Land practicers to adopt into their pictures of the world such elements as the existence of Amida's Pure Land countless worlds away in the western direction. For Hirota, however, the intellectual acceptance of such descriptions as ultimate depictions of the world is not the fundamental issue. Rather, the Pure Land tradition, particularly as formulated by Shinran, takes basic assumptions in the mode of our ordinary understanding as problematic, and functions to lead practicers to a radical change in awareness. Thus, for Hirota, the formulation of a "demythologized" Pure Land teaching is not unimportant, but it must be accomplished in full realization that the new, contemporary formulation will be itself culturally, historically, and humanly conditioned, and not a final, objective, comprehensive, and "correct" statement of ontological truth.

The attitude regarding metaphysical concerns is reflected in the area of ethics as well. Tachikawa points out that consideration of a human being as an individual in society has not been developed yet in Buddhist tradition, and calls for the establishment of a relevant conception of the person. Yokota seeks to delineate a vision of compassionate reality forming a basis for an imperative to compassionate action. Again, Hirota, while recognizing the necessity of articulating social and corporate values, points out that the fundamental collapse of calculative thinking rooted in self-attachment must be the keystone of such thought, and further argues that it is precisely the recognition of the conditioned nature and the deep-seated egocentricity of human values that is necessary in confronting the urgent problems that face all life on the globe.

Perhaps the polarities regarding the three issues stated above may be diagrammed as in figure A. On the basis of this configuration, the

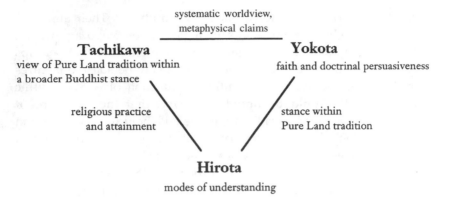

FIGURE A

stance of each of the three authors, and also the concerns that have been deemphasized in their various approaches, may be briefly characterized. Tachikawa's dual interest in the metaphysical outlook of the Pure Land teachings and in religious practice results in a highly experiential attempt to understand Pure Land faith within a generalized paradigm of Buddhist practice. In his particular formulation, he consciously stands outside any specific Pure Land tradition in order to gain a broad perspective that has resonances with all human religious experience. The question becomes, however, what status Tachikawa's Pure Land formulation has. If it is a "new" path, why is it, in addition to mandala practice, necessary, and how does one know that it actually "works"; if it is his own reformulation of what has worked in the past, how does it relate to past formulations?

As stated before, Yokota's concern is to bring Pure Land teachings under contemporary scrutiny. In order to articulate answers to perplexing questions regarding conceptions of Amida Buddha and the Pure Land, he finds it useful to adopt ideas developed in Whiteheadian process theology. Perhaps the chief question facing Yokota's attempts to "modernize" Shin thought is whether he has formulated it in a way that allows for the elucidation and development of the tradition, or whether instead continuity with the tradition has not yet fully or genuinely appeared within the framework he has selected. Although he may resolve certain metaphysically formulated difficulties, it may be necessary to explain why his proposal is not merely one possible contemporary conceptual construct but also a Buddhist *path*.

Hirota's stance of reinterpreting the tradition and his concern with its practical dimension has led him to focus on Shinran's view of language and human understanding. This has the advantage of highlighting both the roots of Shinran's thought in general Mahayana Buddhist views and also the specific aspects of the path that characterize Shinran's Pure Land Buddhism and that make it potentially vital and effective in the present. Yokota affirms a view of language as legitimately propositional and referential, and Tachikawa, while recognizing a fundamental difference between Christian acceptance of the "trustworthiness" of language and Buddhist suspicion, seems inclined to draw on an affirmation or rebirth of language as disclosive of a sacralized cosmos such as achieved in esoteric Buddhist practice. Hirota has sketched an integrative paradigm in which everyday modes of thought (falsity) and self-awareness (truth) are interfused in our ordinary language through the functioning of the nembutsu. The problem for Hirota may be that he has not yet adequately identified his own ontological presuppositions (at least in this volume) or the resources in current philosophical thought and cognitive science that might support his approach, and therefore has not yet brought Pure Land symbols into a frame of reference with sufficient resonance in the present. It should be noted, however, that his approach seeks to open up a doorway to our contemporary situation from the heart of the tradition and in no way denies either the accomplishments of modern science or the possibility of elaborating a cosmological understanding that is consonant with various forms of Mahayana or process thought.

In the view of all three authors, the Pure Land Buddhist tradition, in spite of the richness and relevance it possessed in the past, lies dormant at present. In Japan, it survives largely in fossilized form, in the huge institutional infrastructure of local, hereditary temples, many of which have ceased to fulfill more than a ritual function in the lives of members and in society at large. In the United States, after one hundred years of existence, Shin Buddhism is no more than an example of an ill-adapted and moribund immigrant Buddhism, while the communities that built nearly one hundred temples on the mainland and in Hawaii are vanishing. And yet, we wonder, might not the reinvigoration of this Buddhist path contribute significantly to the global religious culture in these times of crisis?

Bibliography of Related Works
by the Contributors

The English books on Buddhism published in Japan are available from The Buddhist Bookstore, 1710 Octavia Street, San Francisco, CA 94109. Telephone (415) 776-7887; fax (415) 771-6293.

Cobb, John B., Jr. "Can a Christian Be a Buddhist, Too?" *Japanese Religions* 10, 3 (December 1978): 1–20.

_____. *Beyond Dialogue: Toward a Mutual Transformation of Christianity and Buddhism*. Philadelphia: Fortress Press, 1982.

Hirota, Dennis. *Tannishō: A Primer*. Kyoto: Ryukoku University, 1982.

_____. *No Abode: The Record of Ippen*. Kyoto: Ryukoku University, 1986; rev. ed. Honolulu: University of Hawaii Press, 1997. Japanese Pure Land Buddhist thought influenced by esoteric and native religious practices.

_____. "Religious Transformation in Shinran and Shōku," *Pure Land*, 3 (December 1987): 57–69.

_____. *Plain Words on the Pure Land Way: Sayings of the Wandering Monks of Medieval Japan. A Translation of Ichigon Hōdan*. Kyoto: Ryukoku University, 1989. Gives a picture of other forms of Pure Land practice in Shinran's time.

_____. "Breaking the Darkness: Images of Reality in the Shin Buddhist Path," *Japanese Religions* 16, 3 (January 1991): 17–45.

_____. "Shinran's View of Language: A Buddhist Hermeneutics of Faith," *Eastern Buddhist* 30, 1 (Spring 1993): 50–93, and 26, 2 (Autumn 1993): 91–130.

_____. *Wind in the Pines: Classic Writings of the Way of Tea as a Buddhist Path*. Asian Humanities Press, 1995. Includes a section on the aesthetic implications of Japanese Pure Land Buddhist thought.

250 Bibliography

_____. "Shinran," in Ian McGreal, ed., *Great Thinkers of the Eastern World*. New York: HarperCollins, 1995, pp. 315–21.

_____. "Nishida's Gutoku Shinran," *Eastern Buddhist*, 28, 2 (Autumn 1995): 231–44. Comments on Shinran's concept of religious life as "neither monk nor worldly."

_____. "Shinran no Gengo-kan [Shinran's View of Language]," *Shisō* (Iwanami Shoten) 871 (January 1997): 54–80.

_____. "Shinran Shisō to Kaishaku [Shinran's Thought and Interpretation]," *Nihon Kenkyū* (Kokusai Nihon Bunka Kenkyū Sentā/Kadokawa Shoten) 17 (February 1998): 47–86.

_____. "Chūsei Jōdo Shisō to Waka: Ippen, Shinran no Ikkōsatsu [Medieval Pure Land Thought and Waka Poetry: On Ippen and Shinran]." *Nihon Shisōshi*, 52 (February 1998): 19–43. Includes a consideration of Shinran's self-awareness as author and teacher of dharma.

_____. *Shinran: Shūkyō Gengo no Kakumeisha* [Shinran: Revolutionist of Religious Language]. Kyoto: Hōzōkan, 1998.

_____, and Ueda Yoshifumi. *Shinran: An Introduction to His Thought*. Kyoto: Hongwanji International Center, 1989.

_____ et al., trans., *The Collected Works of Shinran*. Vol. 1: The Writings. Vol. 2: Introductions, Glossaries, and Reading Aids. Kyoto: Jōdo Shinshū Hongwanji-ha, 1997.

Kaufman, Gordon D. *God the Problem*. Cambridge: Harvard University Press, 1972.

_____. *Essay on Theological Method*. Atlanta: Scholars Press, 1975; rev. ed. 1979.

_____. *The Theological Imagination: Constructing the Concept of God*. Philadelphia: Westminster Press, 1981.

_____. *In Face of Mystery: A Constructive Theology*. Cambridge: Harvard University Press, 1993.

_____. *God—Mystery—Diversity: Christian Theology in a Pluralistic World*. Minneapolis: Fortress Press, 1996.

Tachikawa Musashi. *Nihon Bukkyō no Shisō* [Japanese Buddhist Thought]. Tokyo: Kōdansha Gendai Shinsho, 1995.

_____. *An Introduction to the Philosophy of Nāgārjuna*. Trans. Rolf W. Giebel. Delhi: Motilal Banarsidass, 1997.

_____. *Budda no Tetsugaku: Gendai Shisō to shite no Bukkyō* [The Philosophy of Buddha: Buddhism as Contemporary Thought]. Kyoto: Hōzōkan, 1998.

Yokota [Ishihara], John S. "Śākyamuni within the Jōdo Shinshū Tradition," *Pacific World* 2 (1986): 31–41.

_____. "Luther and Shinran: *Simul Iustus Et Peccator and Nishu Jinshin*," *Japanese Religions* 14: 4 (July 1987): 31–54.

_____. "A Shin Buddhist Social Ethics," *Pure Land* 4 (1987): 14–33.

_____. "Rethinking the Doctrine of Satya-dvaya," *Journal of Chikushi Jogakuen College* 1 (January 1989): 63–86.

_____. "Continuity and Novelty: A Contribution to the Dialogue between Buddhism and Process Thought," in Santiago Sia, ed., *Charles Hartshorne's Concept of God.* Dordrecht, the Netherlands: Kluwer Academic Publishers, 1990.

_____. "A Call to Compassion: Process Thought and the Conceptualization of Amida Buddha," *Process Studies* 23, 2 (Summer 1994): 87–97.

Contributors

JOHN B. COBB, JR., is Avery Professor of Theology Emeritus, Claremont Graduate School, and former Director of the Center for Process Studies at Claremont.

DENNIS HIROTA (Ph.D. Nagoya University) is Professor of Asian Studies, Chikushi Jogakuen University, Dazaifu, and former Head Translator of the Shin Buddhism Translation Series, Kyoto.

GORDON D. KAUFMAN is Edward Mallinckrodt, Jr., Professor of Divinity Emeritus, Harvard Divinity School.

MUSASHI TACHIKAWA (Ph.D. Harvard University) is Professor, National Museum of Ethnology, Osaka, and former Professor of Indian Philosophy, Nagoya University.

JOHN S. YOKOTA (Ph.D. Claremont) is Professor of Japanese Studies, Chikushi Jogakuen University, Dazaifu, and formerly a minister of the Buddhist Churches of America.

Index